Henley Royal Regatta

*H*ENLEY ROYAL REGATTA

Christopher Dodd

Stanley Paul
London Melbourne Sydney Auckland Johannesburg

Stanley Paul & Co. Ltd

An imprint of the Hutchinson Publishing Group

3 Fitzroy Square, London W1P 6JD

Hutchinson Group (Australia) Pty Ltd
30–32 Cremorne Street, Richmond South, Victoria 3121
PO Box 151, Broadway, New South Wales 2007

Hutchinson Group (NZ) Ltd
32–34 View Road, PO Box 40–086, Glenfield, Auckland 10

Hutchinson Group (SA) Pty Ltd
PO Box 337, Bergvlei 2012, South Africa

First published 1981

Set in Sabon by D. P. Media Limited, Hitchin, Hertfordshire

Printed in Great Britain by The Anchor Press Ltd
and bound by Wm Brendon & Son Ltd,
both of Tiptree, Essex

British Library Cataloguing in Publication Data

Dodd, Christopher
  Henley Royal Regatta.
  I. Title
  797.1′4   GV798

ISBN 0 09 145160 4

Contents

Acknowledgements

I am deeply grateful to the Stewards of Henley Royal Regatta and their staff for allowing me to consult their records and their collection of books and documents, including the Brittain library. In particular, thanks go to the Chairman, Peter Coni, and the President, John Garton, who have taken immense trouble to assist with information. They also read and corrected the manuscript with alacrity, and any errors which remain are not their doing. Opinions expressed in the book are those of the characters or the author; the Regatta authorities have allowed freedom of research and have not sought to influence the interpretation of events.

Dozens of people have assisted in the preparation of this book, some knowingly and others unwittingly, and to them, both writers and keepers of manuscripts and oarsmen of several generations, I owe thanks. I will have to be unfair in singling out some of those who have given freely of their time in talking or writing of their memories of days at Henley. Here are a few of them, with acknowledgements to the unsung: Ernie Arlett, Lou Barry, Raymond Blake, Alan Browne, Philip 'Farne' Carpmael, Dick Cashin, Penny Chuter, Sean Colgan, Alistair Cooke, Lord Cottesloe, Thérèse Fisher, Maurice Horan, Michael Johnstone, John B. Kelly, John McKeown, Tom Mendenhall, Hart Perry Jr, Dick Phelps, Bobby Steen, and Thomas 'Tote' Walker. Librarians have also been of great assistance, notably those at the British Museum Newspaper Library, the *Guardian*, the *Observer*, the *Field*, the Universities of British Columbia, Columbia (NY), Cornell, Dublin, Harvard, Pennsylvania, Westminster School, the Harvard Athletic Association, Trinity College Cambridge, and St John's College Cambridge.

Thanks also to John Betjeman and John Murray (Publishers) Ltd for permission to quote a stanza of 'Henley-on-Thames' from Betjeman's *Collected Poems* and to A. D. Peters and Co. Ltd for permission to quote from Edmund Blunden's 'Cricket Country'.

I would also like to thank colleagues at the *Guardian* and among the rowing press for their encouragement and cooperation, particularly the Sports Editor of the page, John Samuel, and the Editor, Peter Preston, who take a view of the world broad enough to admit rowing as part of a man's work. They and the indefatigable reporter, John Rodda, encourage writers and fan enthusiasm for obscure corners of life such as this. Sue Hogg, Managing Editor at Hutchinson, has taken immense trouble and edited the manuscript with sympathy; thanks to Roddy Bloomfield, Stanley Paul's Editorial Director, for his enthusiasm. Lastly, thanks also go to friends and relatives who have had to put up with the creation of the book, particularly Heather Cupit who read it as it went along, my parents John and Dora Dodd who helped with the index, and my aunt, Elizabeth Cook, who was a great inspiration.

Photographic acknowledgements

For permission to use photographs reproduced in this book the author and publisher would like to thank Geo. Bushell and Son, the *Daily Mail*, Fox Photos, the *Guardian*, Peter Johns, Keystone, Robin Laurance, Frank Martin, Eamonn McCabe, Planet News, Press Association, John Shore, Sport and General.

Selected Chronology

1829 First Boat Race between Oxford and Cambridge at Henley

1839 First regatta. Grand Challenge Cup for eights, Town Challenge Cup for fours, special race for watermen

1840 District Challenge Cup for fours introduced (until 1847)

1841 Stewards' Challenge Cup for fours introduced

1843 Oxford won the Grand with seven-man crew

1844 Diamond Challenge Sculls introduced

1845 Ladies' Challenge Plate for eights and Silver Wherries for pairs introduced. Outriggers used at Henley for first time by J. W. Conant in Diamonds

1846 Silver Wherry for Henley amateur scullers introduced (until 1857)

1847 Wyfold Challenge Cup for winners of Grand heats and Visitors' Challenge Cup for fours introduced

1850 Silver Wherries became Silver Goblets

1851 Prince Albert became patron and regatta granted Royal title. New laws of racing adopted, drawn up by Oxford, Cambridge and Metropolitan clubs

1855 Wyfold Cup became a fours event. Royal Chester won in keelless boat

1856 Royal Chester RC used keelless eight built by Matt Taylor of Newcastle upon Tyne

1857 Draw replaced toss for stations. GWR reached Henley

1858 District Goblets for pairs introduced (until 1867)

1868 Thames Challenge Cup for eights introduced. Minimum weights for coxswains introduced. Brasenose disqualified from Stewards' after cox jumped overboard

1869 Presentation Cup for fours without coxswains introduced for one year only

1872 London RC and Pembroke College, Oxford, first used sliding seats at the regatta. E. Smith of New York entered the Diamonds, the first foreigner

1873 Stewards' became coxless

1874 Visitors' and Wyfolds became coxless

1878 First American crews came, Shoe-wae-cae-mette BC and Columbia University

1879 Definition of amateur excepting manual workers adopted. Public Schools' Challenge Cup started (until 1884)

1880 First foreign entry for Grand, Germania RC, Frankfurt

1886 Course changed to finish at Poplar Point with staggered start below Temple Island. Heats reduced to two crews instead of three by introduction of third day's racing

1894 Amateur definition brought into line with ARA's amended version. Swans removed for first time

1895 Tom Nickalls presented Nickalls' Challenge Cup to go with Goblets

1897 Minor adjustments to course to tackle Bushes Wind

1899 Preliminary heats used for first time

1902 Professional coaching banned

1906 Club Nautique de Gand (Belgium) became first foreign crew to win Grand. Overseas entries must conform with Henley's amateur definition. First four-day regatta

1908 Olympic regatta held at Henley

1911 Remenham Club built. Finals moved to Saturday

1912 First visit of a reigning sovereign, George V

1919 Peace regatta for special trophies. Stewards' Enclosure opened

1923 Experimental shortened straight course used

1924 Full-length straight course introduced

1938 'Manual labour' bar lifted

1939 Centenary Double Sculling Race held, resulting in dead heat. Became Challenge Cup in 1946

1945 One-day peace regatta over shortened course for special events

1946 Princess Elizabeth Challenge Cup introduced for school eights over shortened course. Full course used from 1947

1948 Olympic regatta held at Henley

1954 First visit of Soviet crews

1963 Prince Philip Challenge Cup for coxed fours introduced

1964 Harvard's 1914 crew returned for their anniversary

1967 New starting arrangements so that all bows covered 1 mile 550 yards

1968 Henley Prize for coxed fours introduced, becoming Britannia Challenge Cup in 1969

1969 Selection used for first time in draw. Bell introduced for false starts

1970 Composite crews allowed in Grand, Stewards', Prince Philip

1971 Composite rule extended to Ladies' and Visitors'

1973 Disqualification for two false starts introduced. Rules preventing use of dope came into force. Crews allowed to finish with fewer oarsmen than at the start, but coxswains must stay on board

1974 Sunday finals introduced. Special Race for Schools introduced over shortened course

1975 Women permitted as coxswains

1978 Membership of Stewards' Enclosure tops 4000. Record attendance of 13,500 on the Saturday

1981 Quadruple sculls event introduced. Invitation events for women's coxed fours and double sculls introduced over shortened course

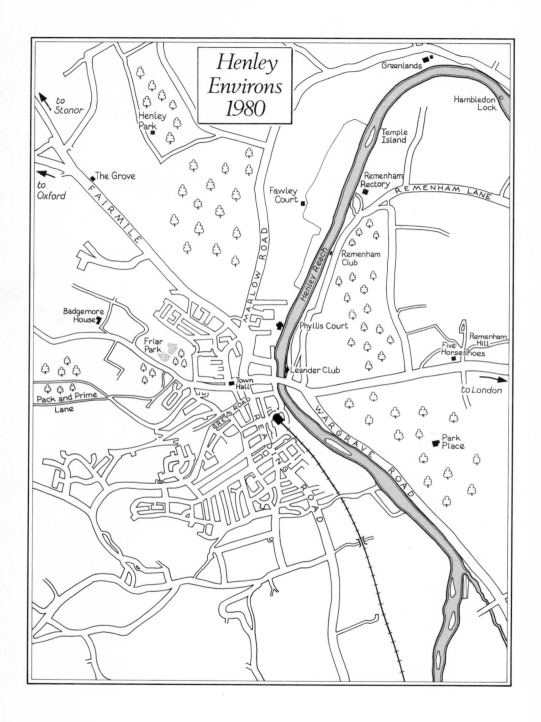

Henley
Environs
1980

to Stonor

Greenlands

Hambledon
Lock

Henley
Park

Temple
Island

The Grove

Remenham
Rectory

to Oxford

FAIRMILE

MARLOW ROAD

Fawley
Court

REMENHAM LANE

Henley Reach

Remenham
Club

Badgemore
House

Phyllis Court

Remenham
Hill

Friar
Park

Five
Horseshoes

Town
Hall

Leander Club

to London

Pack and Prime
Lane

GREY'S ROAD

Park
Place

WARGRAVE ROAD

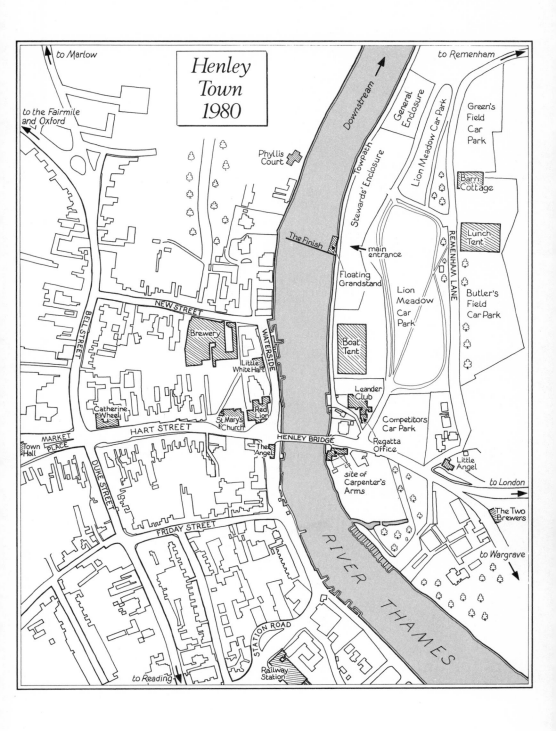

1

W. W. *Smyth opens the Panthermanticon*
1839: Voyage of discovery

Warington Wilkinson Smyth rowed into town on the evening of
Tuesday, 11 June 1839. The *Black Prince* carried him and his eight
companions to the bank at Mr Cooper's garden and they were loudly
saluted by the natives from the bridge and shores. At Cooper's invitation they lifted their ship onto his lawn, covered her and strode over
the bridge at Henley-on-Thames. Smyth and Gough, Taylor and
Lonsdale, Penrose and Strickland, Cross, Massey and coxswain Barclay were on a quest for silver, and their first sight of the waters which
they were to explore was from the Red Lion, close by the river
Thames on the town side of the bridge. 'On looking about us,' Smyth
recalled in his log, 'we found that the fine reach on which we were to
pull is from the bridge extending a mile and a half downwards, where a
little temple on an island marks the starting point.'

The flurry on the bridge in the streets and inns which greeted these
Cambridge men in the *Black Prince* met other arrivals that week. The
Grand Challenge Cup was being contested also by three Oxford clubs
– Brasenose, Wadham and the Oxford Etonians. The punters were
expectant, for those with long memories recalled the excitement of the
first Oxford versus Cambridge Boat Race which had taken place at
Henley ten years previously, and of an encounter in 1831 between
Oxford and the Leander Club of London. And then in 1837, after
Oxford had declined a challenge from Cambridge, the head of the
river colleges at the respective universities had met, Queen's College,
Oxford, defeating St John's College, Cambridge. The opportunities
for a little entertainment were not lost on the townsfolk, and the idea
of a regatta being good for trade had been received with enthusiasm at

the public meeting in the town hall on 26 March 1839. The landed
gentry and principal townspeople had been well represented there.

As the posse of Trinity men entered the Red Lion where they were to
stay they noticed that the town was already very full, though racing
was not to take place until Friday. Stands were being erected along the
whole river frontage of the little place. Those who had been made
perpetual stewards for the regulation of the regatta at the meeting in
March were busying themselves near the water, pleased that their
plans to attract new faces and craft more exciting than the barges
carrying loads of up to 100 tons which were trundled past by six or
eight horses were coming to fruition. These men – Thomas Stonor Esq.,
William P. Williams-Freeman Esq., William Fuller-Maitland Esq.,
Charles Lane Esq., Edmund Gardiner Esq., and the Mayor of Henley –
were fired to their task by the optimistic cannon from the town hall.
Captain Gardiner had proposed

> that from the lively interest which had been manifested at the various boat
> races which have taken place on the Henley reach during the last few years,
> and the great influx of visitors on such occasions, this meeting is of the
> opinion that the establishing of an annual regatta, under judicious and
> respectable management, would not only be productive of the most benefi-
> cial results to the town of Henley, but from its peculiar attractions would
> also be a source of amusement and gratification to the neighbourhood, and
> the public in general.

Bell's Life in London for Sunday, 2 June, came more down to earth
and recognized, too, the interests of the rowing men. The weekly paper
reported:

> The reproach that the beautiful reach of water at Henley has so long
> remained a blank as regards a regatta is happily at an end, and the treat of
> Friday the 14th inst promises to be of the most interesting description. . . .
> No amusement is more harmless or more conducive to health than aquatic
> exercises, and all who witnessed the grand match between Oxford and
> Cambridge in 1829 will agree with us that a more beautifully picturesque
> and animated scene cannot be conceived than the river presented on that
> occasion.

If Smyth and his friends had read *Bell's* they would have been
pleased to hear that 'the innkeepers are all on the alert; their houses
have been renovated and every attention manifested for storing their

larders with suitable delicacies to meet the great demand which is expected to be made on them.'

Smyth himself left Henley almost as soon as he arrived. After checking in at the inn he was lucky to get a place on the *Paul Pry*, the 10.30 p.m. stage to Oxford, for he had to take breakfast there with his parents the following morning on the occasion of the conferment of an honorary degree on his father. Of the appearance of the country he could say very little as he slept for the whole way. This was not surprising as he had helped row the *Black Prince* on the two-day voyage from Oxford to Henley and was expected back on the Thames for practice on the following afternoon. Smyth Sr was an admiral who had moved from Westminster to Bedford, where he set up an observatory. In his naval days he spent much time surveying the Italian, Greek, Sicilian and African coasts, and he was greatly interested in antiquarian matters. Captain William married Annaretta, daughter of Thomas Warington, British Consul at Naples, and W.W. was their first-born.

The young Smyth was inspired by his father's exploits as a sailor, antiquarian and astronomer. The summer of 1839 was a final fling after his undergraduate days at Trinity, Cambridge. After attending Westminster School as a small boy and Bedford later, he had now got his bachelor of arts from the university and had been awarded a travelling bachelorship from the Worts foundation which would soon enable him to pursue his interest in mineralogy in Germany and Austria. On the voyage from Oxford, though, he may well have reflected on his outstanding exploits in oar-powered ships, craft very different from those that his father knew.

The years of Smyth's boyhood had seen more and more young gentlemen taking to the rivers for recreation. He heard many stories from Eton and his old school, Westminster, about outings, pranks and contests on the Thames, many of them frowned upon by the school authorities. A young journalist, Charles Dickens, compared the Westminster schoolboys unfavourably in matters of rowdiness with the waiters of an inn in a hugely successful monthly serial called *The Posthumous Papers of the Pickwick Club* in 1836 and 1837. The boys were not unknown to enter great arguments with bargees, even boarding their barges and pelting them with their own coal.

A series of meetings between Westminster and Eton had started in 1829, when the Eton boys, dressed in broad blue-striped guernsey frocks and dark straw hats with blue ribbons, brought the *Britannia* to Putney and beat the Westminster scholars from there to Hammersmith. The Westminsters arrived in an open barouche drawn by four greys, wore white shirts with straw hats, and raced in a boat which was built by Searle for Cambridge for their race at Henley with Oxford that year. Forty or fifty gentlemen followed the event on horseback.

In 1837 the contest took place at Windsor over two and a half miles, and the boys were very excited because King William IV himself expressed a desire to witness the contest. He was seriously ill at the time and his doctors, who were Old Westminsters, advised him to stay indoors. However, he arrived in a closed carriage on the afternoon of the match and was cheered by both crews, and Rogers, who rowed in Eton's number five seat, jotted down his impressions.

> I remember well his figure, seated in a closed carriage, wrapped in a great white coat, about a hundred and fifty yards from the bridge. As soon as he saw that the Westminsters were ahead he pulled down the blinds and drove back to the Castle, which I do not think he afterwards left.

This was on 4 May; Westminster were first and the King died on 20 June. Many Etonians that Smyth had met still believed that the King's illness was at least partially due to their defeat by the pinks that day. For his part the King thought the light blues of Eton were defeated because Dr Hawtrey, their Master, was looking on. The headmasters did not always look kindly upon their charges' activities on the Thames, and in 1838 the Westminster authorities stopped the race when the Etonians were already prepared in their boat at Westminster Bridge.

Many good oars came out of Eton. The Oxford Etonians were one of the crews opposing First Trinity for this new challenge at Henley, and at Smyth's own college was the Third Trinity club, exclusive to Etonians and Westminsters. It was said that two of the masters were encouraging Dr Hawtrey to allow freedom for boating which meant that no boy could take part until he had a pass in swimming. The sudden interest of the school authorities was caused by a boy called Montague, who was drowned just above Windsor Bridge when a barge rope swept him out of his boat.

The Westminsters, too, were active, and they told Smyth of great expeditions. That of 1825 had passed into the school's folklore. A crew took the opportunity of time off on St George's Day to row to

Windsor and back. They left Horseferry at 3 a.m. and stopped for breakfast at Sunbury four and a quarter hours later, reaching Windsor Bridge after a further stop for lunch at two in the afternoon. After seeing over Eton they had a hellish journey back in heavy rain. The stroke and number seven man both collapsed and had to give up, but the remaining six arrived back at the steps at Horseferry by midnight, having covered 112 miles in twenty-one hours including seven hours' worth of stoppages.

When Smyth went up to Trinity the college was thriving at aquatics and was enjoying a renaissance of intellectual activity under Christopher Wordsworth, whose brother was the Lakeland poet, and who had become Master in 1820 when Smyth was but three years old. In Wordworth's time there had been a succession of fellows and students who had become noted scholastic names. Discussion of the Master usually concluded that Wordsworth was not a strong man or one judicious. But he was anxious and resourceful in matters relating to the good of the college. There was still much talk of the scandal of 1834 when C. Thirlwall, the assistant tutor, boldly suggested that it would be better if attendance at chapel were made voluntary and not enforced as an act of discipline. Wordsworth argued that the alternatives were compulsory religion or no religion. Thirlwall replied that he regretted he had to confess that the distinction between them was too subtle to grasp. The Master removed him from office, and the courts and commonrooms were awash with condemnation of his high-handed action. Wordsworth stuck to his decision.

There was plenty of stimulation for the minds of the young gentlemen who visited one another in their rooms about the quadrangle or dined round the great brazier under the open lantern of the hall. The fire filled the place with charcoal fumes, roasting those unlucky enough to sit near it while undercooking those unlucky enough to eat at a distance from it. For recreation and fresh air they naturally took to the nearby Cam. Nor were the Trinity clubs averse to venturing farther afield. Somebody in the college had a cutting from a newspaper published in Lincoln and Boston which told of a college voyage in *King Edward II* to Lincoln. It reported:

The vessel in which this very spirited expedition was conducted was an open boat, very long and narrow, being about forty-two feet by three or four, evidently well adapted for speed, but more to be trusted upon the smooth waters of the Bedford level than upon the inconsistent main; in this wherry, however, having descended the Cam and the Ouse to Lynn, the gallant crew crossed the estuary of the Wash on Friday last, ever to the mouth of the Witham, with the assistance of a Lynn pilot engaged for the purpose. Passing through Boston, they arrived at Tattershall the same evening, the castle at which place belongs to Lord Fortescue, the father of one of the adventurers, and on the following day reached Lincoln, about eighteen miles further. The subordination of the boat's crew to their commander, with their seamanlike movements, afforded great gratification and augurs much for Cambridge discipline, against certain cavillers of our day.

Smyth had furthered the tradition set by his college forebears when he took part in a similar expedition on the Ouse in 1836, but by this time racing had long usurped pure recreation as the object of putting boats on the river. The University Boat Club had been in existence since 1827, the year in which regular bumping races had begun. Before that, competition had been less formal. Boats would go off on picnics, and according to the Rev. Dr Merrivale, who was up at John's and who sat in Cambridge's first boat to race Oxford in 1829, there were only two eight-oars on the river in 1826. They were a Trinity boat and a Johnian, and each went casually downstream and laid in wait, one of them sounding a bugle to intimate its whereabouts, when the other, coming up, would give chase. In 1827 Trinity procured a ten-oar, and soon several colleges had got hold of six-oars and eight-oars. Picnicking was well catered for, also. The Rev. Gwatkin presented a tin panthermanticon to the Johnians which contained two kettles, nine cups and saucers, teaspoons and plates, four dishes and four basins, a mustard pot, a box and a salt box, two grates and nine eggholders and eggspoons. A separate box contained a dozen knives and forks, a phosphorus box with blowpipe, a charcoal bag, a canvas table marked 'Lady Margaret' with iron screws and legs, two tablecloths and six napkins.

Smyth had only joined First Trinity Boat Club in his last year as an undergraduate. Previously he belonged to Second Trinity which had been started in 1831 chiefly for combining reading with rowing, but this year the club had taken its boats off the water. In the second of the Lent races on the Cam, First Trinity with Smyth on board bumped John's and regained the headship of the river, and kept their place in the third and fourth races. Smyth then represented his university in the Boat Race with Oxford on 3 April, and rowed from Westminster to Putney. They moved ahead of Oxford at Lambeth church and won by one minute forty seconds. There were great celebrations at Mrs Avis's public house in Putney, where the Cambridge men put up.

Back on the Cam for the May series of bumps, Smyth and First Trinity kept their headship in the first race over their college rivals Third Trinity, the club exclusively for Old Etonians and Old Westminsters, and they kept it up for the remaining six races. While things were going so well the meeting of the club on Sunday, 20 May, decided to send *Black Prince* to contend the Challenge Cup at Henley, a pot worth one hundred guineas, and a new regatta which they thought was worth looking into. It might be fun to venture towards Oxford territory in June. And on the Monday after the final May race ninety-six men sat down to dine at the Sun with W. Massey, the captain and stroke of the winning boat, in the chair. The tally came to 70 bottles of champagne, 38 of Moselle, 12 of claret, 17 of sherry, 57 quarts of ale, and £6 7s 6d worth of punch. This year the party was not broken up at an early hour as it had been the year before by the unexpected appearance of a junior proctor.

At a further meeting on 26 May the combined post of secretary and treasurer changed hands. 'Here endeth my secretaryship,' wrote Charles Penrose in the minute book, and he passed it to the newly elected man, John Gylby Lonsdale. 'Here beginneth my secretaryship,' wrote Lonsdale.

Thus the men of Trinity had much enjoyment, but some of them had to work hard for it. To gain the headship of the river this year First Trinity had taken part in four races in the Lent term and seven in the Easter term. The expedition to Henley meant a lot of time and preparation, not least in getting the *Black Prince* transported to Oxford and rowing her down river. The ship may not have possessed her own tin panthermanticon but she had some comforts to help the body endure physical discomfort. She was built of best English oak, painted black outside and green inside, with gilt beadings and lines inside and out. She had a lion and crowns on the bows and was fitted with green cushions. She cost about £60.

In the winter, the club saw to it that their boats were blackleaded, the mixture being composed of two quarts of small beer, a pound of black lead and six eggs. Attention was paid also to the appearance of the crews, and Smyth benefited from the decision made in 1835 by

First Trinity to have a new die for the club buttons, 'and to abuse Creek for the present one, which is so vile'.

These, then, were the influences on Smyth's aquatic life until June of 1839. After the May races finished on the 26th he went home to Bedford. The crew were to assemble in Oxford, and after waiting in vain for news from Lonsdale, who did not excel in his first duties as secretary, Smyth thought it high time to be started. Mr Fletcher, the coachman, assisted by taking one more passenger than he was licensed to carry, although one gent was obliged to descend from the outside to the inside of the coach, which soured his temper for the whole of the way.

Smyth himself was thrilled with the journey. 'Though the land on this road is generally uninteresting,' he wrote in his log on that night of 8 June, 'the slopes were so green, and the foliage of the trees so rich, that I could not find any part to be dissatisfied with.' On such a fine day at a beautiful time of the year he journeyed by way of Leighton Buzzard and Thame to Oxford, and he was not sorry to see the tower of Magdalen and the domes and spires. The fine appearance of the High Street made him feel that Cambridge must give up all idea of rivalry as a town or as a whole when considering the university buildings, but, he wrote, she may very safely pit single buildings and colleges against any at Oxford.

And so to find the crew. Smyth went down to the river, where he found 'nautical particulars' of interest. First he had to run the gauntlet of men and boys operating a ferry service in their punts to the opposite meadows. He saw that the dressing rooms were in large covered barges and the boats were hauled out upon floating rafts and covered with painted canvas. He thought the boats most beautifully built as far as neatness and lightness went, but too pinched in the bows 'so that they have not bearings enough forward'. He found *Black Prince* and fell in with some of his crew. They told him that they had been in Oxford for several days, during which time, he noted tetchily later, 'the hospitality of the Oxford men had acted in a manner nowise favourable to training for a race.' He was a little annoyed as he filled in his diary that he had missed the opportunity of being thus corrupted.

Not for long, however. On Sunday morning he went with the rest to breakfast with Gregson of Brasenose, at whose rooms there was a large party and a conversation hinging largely on sporting matters. Smyth had a look round Christ Church during the day and spent the evening at the rooms of various friends, where myths were laid and, no doubt, a few started. There was a rumour at large that half the members of the Queen's crew who had beaten the Johnians two years earlier had died from 'over exertions', etc. In the course of the social round that evening, however, Smyth met the bow and the stroke of the crew who assured him that all the others were alive and kicking. Thus was refuted one of the lies which some 'brainless persons' were circulating from Oxford to the detriment of rowing; and Smyth found another falsehood answered when he met a boat builder called King.

King had steered six officers from the Third Guards when they attempted to row from Oxford to London in under sixteen hours back in 1824. Elaborate preparations were made for this, a wager of £200 having been laid between Captain Standen and Sir John Burgoyne. A boat was built by Sullivan of Millbank for captains Standen, Short, Hon. J. Westenra, Douglas, Blane and Hudson, the time was kept by watches previously wound in Oxford and London, and the Commissioners for Locks agreed to assist in clearing the locks for the crew and ensuring a plentiful supply of water as they passed through. The wager arose from a bet seventeen months before made by Lord Newry that he and five of his servants would do Oxford to London in eighteen hours.

There was some controversy over Newry's expedition. The lord and his servants, 'men not accustomed to the work' as one account put it, left the bridge at Oxford as Great Tom struck three and arrived at Godrey and Searle's wharf in a state of great exhaustion at one and a half minutes before nine, winning by ninety seconds, although the margin was reduced to a minute when the chronometer was sent down to Oxford.

The Guards assembled at a quarter to three on the morning of 12 May 1824, wearing blue-striped shirts, crimson neckcloths and white hats. They took a little *aqua vitae* and sandwiches, and at a minute past three Isaac King gave the word 'All's ready.' The rowers removed their oars from the perpendicular to the horizontal and amidst the cheers of great numbers of persons the wherry 'cleft the liquid stream', according to a contemporary account, and bore away at the rate of above eight miles per hour. At Boulter's Lock, Maidenhead, King vacated his seat for the second coxswain, James Carnnon.

Windsor Bridge was passed at one o'clock and at 5.30 p.m. they took refreshment in Teddington Lock, supplied by the Talbot Inn, and Thomas Hill, the third coxswain, was taken on board. The last part of the Guards' wager was spectacular. From Teddington to Westminster two eight-oared guard boats cleared the way for the wherry, and 'but for the cheering of the spectators which excited the liveliest emulation among the rowers it is thought they would have sunk under the excessive exertion.' At Battersea the rowers were 'completely knocked up', but now they had the tide in their favour and took a little brandy. The river was covered by members of London's aquatic clubs, and the umpire, Colonel Meyrick, was on Westminster Bridge. Several members of the Bow Street patrol guarded Whitehall stairs, the place of disembarkation, and spectators lined everything which had a view of the place. The exhausted crew arrived at the bridge at a quarter to seven, thus winning their wager by getting fifteen minutes inside sixteen hours for the 118 miles from Oxford. Fifteen thousand pounds changed ownership as a result. Amidst the acclamations of thousands of spectators Mr Sullivan, the boatbuilder, towed the boat to Whitehall stairs.

What Smyth and his contemporaries had heard since was that the whole crew had died within five or six years of their voyage. Isaac King recalled the event with relish, refuting the tale of doom. He frequently saw some of the officers, he said, and heard that the rest enjoyed a state of health and strength that would 'quite distress these propagators of untruths', as he put it to Smyth.

On the Monday morning the Trinity crew took breakfast and went down to the river to practise. They found out what Oxford's social life had done for them. They went over the 'ground' which Smyth found longer than that at Cambridge but less tortured with sudden meanderings. Smyth soon confessed to himself that he had had sufficient work and noticed that the pace and style of the crew was a long way from what it had been, and would have to be again if they were to have a chance of the Henley cup. He could not believe that two or three weeks' interval would have made so great a difference.

In the evening they set off for Henley, passing the Oxford procession as they went downstream to Iffley lock. They tossed their oars and cheered for the head boats of the divisions as they passed, obtaining hearty responses. The divisions were the eights, the Torpids or second boats, and the fours, but fewer and fewer fours were being entered for races at Oxford at this time, and among the larger boats there were several without a centre gangboard. Smyth had seen much of interest in the way of boat design at Oxford. Organized racing had begun there before it had at his *alma mater*. The boats rowed down to Sandford and then raced back from Iffley lock, a fitting end to a good jaunt and a picnic. Several boats would enter the lock together. When the gates opened the stroke of the head boat, who was standing in the bows with a boathook, would run down the centre of his boat along the gangplank while pushing the boat out of the lock. He would take his rowing seat as his crew dropped their oars from the perpendicular. The next boat would follow as swiftly as possible, and so on. But now, by 1839, the races started from above the lock.

Clearing Iffley lock, the *Black Prince* found more breathing space after a passage through the hundreds of small boats witnessing Oxford's processional end to the racing season. The Trinity crew passed several boats returning from picnic parties at Sandford and Nuneham. Slipping by the Harcourts' seat at Nuneham, they rowed through the woods and along a tortuous piece of water towards Abingdon, a place, if they did but know it, rich in ecclesiastical legend and heritage. Centuries before, the monks had diverted the Thames to a channel which almost washed the walls of their abbey, and they controlled everything else in the town and enjoyed the fruits of their vineyard besides, until this enterprise was stopped by the Angevin kings. The chronicles of the Abbey also harboured facts of interest to rowing men. In the eleventh century the citizens of Oxford were suffering from lack of trade because rowers had much difficulty with the bed of the river near Abingdon. 'The land below, being steeper than that above, often made the said channel slack of water.' The Oxfordians petitioned that the course of the river be diverted through Barton church's meadow, farther south, and after that each vessel had to pay a toll to the cellarer of the monastery.

The Trinity men were little concerned about the legendary links of Abingdon with Diocletian and Constantine, with the hospitality which the mitred abbots gave to William the Conqueror or the education they gave to Henry I, or with Essex's exploits there in the Civil War. They were tired and hungry, and they deposited their boat under the bridge thoughtfully provided by the guild of the Brotherhood of Christ more than four hundred years beforehand, which links the island of Andersey to the town. They took a walk round, passing the county hall after a design by Inigo Jones, and the churches of St Nicholas and St Helen, to the inn, where they 'committed great havoc on the mutton chops'. The party enjoyed an undergraduate evening of ale by the quart while ragging a rubicund and drunken bagman in the bar.

The next morning, Smyth recalled, 'we started, considering all things, in tolerable time, after a breakfast where ale, tea, milk, and beef were extensively patronized by their several votaries.' They passed the Tudor almshouses and had a marvellous view of St Helen's spire as they progressed towards Culham. At the lock they admired the manner in which a terrier dodged and slew a rat whilst the water was running through. The country began to improve on them, two fine hills appearing on their left, each with a circular crown of trees on its head. Their name must be Coronation Hills, Wythe said. He was a substitute in the boat, engaged for the voyage to Henley, and on this morning he kept the company amused with an undertow of joking which soothed sore heads.

> Throughout the voyage down [wrote Smyth] we found our bow possessed of so intimate a knowledge of localities as to be able to give the name of every spot, but which, though very appropriate and generally causing great amusement, we unfortunately could not find in any map, a circumstance showing that the maps of the river ought not to have been published till approved of by Cantabs. Soon after, the remarks of bow caused much laughter and very little work to be performed by 2 and 3, somewhat to the annoyance of the after-end of the boat, who heard the peals and felt the quivering of the timbers without joining in the amusement.

Smyth himself was in the number two seat.

The crew passed Clifton Hampden on their right and Little Wittenham on their left and Dorchester, a sleepy little town just off the river from where St Birinus once converted heathen Wessex to Christianity as St Augustine did for Kent from Canterbury. They passed the ancient ramparts of Dyke Hills and the Wittenham Clumps – Wythe's Coronation Hills – and Shillingford, until coxswain Barclay had a fine view of St Peter's church and the bridge at Wallingford. Here refreshment was taken for an hour and the bow section continued their tactics of delaying physical exertion, but the *Black Prince* eventually set sail once more, the crew finding themselves in wider and more beautiful water. They passed the wooden spire of St John the Baptist at Moulsford and the embattled belfry of St Andrew's at South Stoke, and passed Goring and Streatley, running southwards into the cleft between the Chilterns on their right and the Berkshire Downs on their left, carried by the Thames on its escape route to the sea.

They pulled under a bridge being built to carry a railway across the water near Streatley, and Smyth was carried away by the wonders he saw around him.

On the left rose a hill of considerable height, covered from the water's edge to the top with magnificent trees, and now and then some beautiful villa appearing amongst them; the river, too, is of noble width, and from the calmness of the day and strong sunshine reflected all objects with a very pretty effect. This continued for miles almost without interruption.

At a lock here Wythe speared an enormous perch with the boat hook, hoisting it into the *Black Prince* amid cheers and congratulations of the lock-keeper and his wife.

The reach to Pangbourne was spoilt, Smyth thought, by the railroad running along on its embankment. The great heat of the day made the crew unanimous in wishing to remain an hour or two at Pangbourne, where they found the lashers near the lock refreshing in both sight and sound. They enjoyed the scenery around the village and behind Whitchurch on the opposite bank and they glimpsed trout as they rested.

Setting off once more, the *Black Prince* passed the ancient house of Hardwicke, seat of the Lybbes and a favourite bowling spot for Charles I, the Tudor manor house at Mapledurham, and Purley Hall where Warren Hastings, an oarsman when at school at Westminster, had stayed awaiting his trial on charges of corruption and cruelty as Governor of Bengal forty odd years before. He had been acquitted after 145 days of wrangling spread over seven years. And so to Caversham, where they sighted the housetops and steeples of Reading, and passed Sonning and Shiplake to Wargrave, where the secluded churchyard gave rest to one Thomas Day, author of a humourless and austere volume called *The History of Sandford and Merton*. It expounds the virtue of virtue and was a volume unwelcome to those of Smyth's contemporaries who had been unfortunate enough to have it placed before them.

Tired and perspiring, the nine men neared the end of their voyage into the unknown of England's back garden, through green and watered hills and pasture that had harboured warriors both Roundhead and Cavalier, where the wealthy looked out on their parks and the labourers toiled on the land, where the abbots prayed and traded to good effect, and where the generals skirmished and the Empire's governors retired.

The boat passed Park Place, where George IV sometimes stayed long before he was king.

We arrived at the splendid bank about two miles above Henley [wrote Smyth in his log] and we did not know what to admire most, the hill wooded to its summit, the fine water, or the tasteful positions of a large seat near the top of the hill and a Swiss cottage and boathouse near the water's edge, adjoining which a large arch between the trees gives a view of a verdant lawn beyond a lower part of the hill.

When the men of Trinity unloaded their boat at the foot of Mr Cooper's lawn and crossed the bridge to enter the Red Lion, they had rowed forty-seven miles – and dropped 78 feet 7 inches nearer to sea level – with two days in hand before taking up the challenge to chase a silver cup.

2

The Black Prince *pulls for silver off Squire Freeman's Island*
1839: The first Henley

Warington Smyth had a strenuous time after rowing to Henley. He had returned to Oxford that evening for his father's degree ceremony. He saw the poet William Wordsworth there, brother of the Master of Trinity, who was another recipient. He then had difficulty getting back to Henley after the ceremony because in this age of fast stages there was no such thing as a seat on a coach to be obtained anywhere in Oxford. He had to take a gig for twelve miles and walk the remaining twelve to Henley, bringing with him Wythe's coat which had been left accidentally in Oxford.

Smyth admired the fine countryside, particularly the last five miles into town, the road running through a fir wood and descending to the broad Fairmile with its noble line of elms, maturing now after the eighty years since Sir William Stapleton saw fit to plant them there. Along one side was an eight-foot brick and flint wall, boundary of the Fawley Court estate. King Charles had once ridden this way in unhappier circumstances than Smyth's, carrying a cloak bag behind him on his horse like a serving man and assuming the name of Harry, Master Ashburnam's man. The king had probably left the main road near Assendon or Grove House and slipped into town by Pack and Prime Lane, but Smyth swung his legs along the Fairmile, passing hilly banks pink with clover, cheered by the merry peal of Henley church heard long before he could see the flintstone Gothic tower. The bells were the call to *Black Prince*'s evening outing. He arrived just in time to stop Wythe substituting for him. They pulled down to Temple Island and returned at racing speed, very much to their satisfaction in point of time and style. They considered that the cup was theirs already, and determined to take it with them to London by boat when they got delivery.

On the following day Smyth went to the Swiss boat house he had so admired on the way into Henley by water, learning that it belonged to one of the stewards of the regatta, Fuller-Maitland, and that he was an old Trinity man. Smyth stayed there a long time sketching, and then met some of the others and bathed in the river. They went practising at noon and in the evening, in between sketching and popjoying for gudgeon up river. They dined before the evening outing and saw some of their antagonists, but without drawing conclusions. Most thought the Etonians looked the best and the Wadham crew much the worst. Smyth thought it odd at first that they were cheered wherever they went by the town's *profanum vulgus*. Later he realized that they seemed to cheer for Oxford or Cambridge according to whence they thought the men came.

It was obvious, though, that the town was taking the event seriously. An Oxford paper reported that between fifteen and twenty thousand people were awaited by the organizers and that 'mine hosts with smiling faces were expecting a regular squeeze'. The meadows were thronged nightly with townspeople who went out to watch the evening practice of the Henley clubs, who had got up fours to compete for the Town Challenge Cup. London watermen were also expected to race, and the day would be concluded by a firework display on the river.

So there was excitement in the air on regatta eve. The men from Trinity retired to roost early, on this night wishing for the peace which Shenstone had found when in 1750 he used a diamond to scratch his famous poem on a pane of glass at the Red Lion.

> To thee, fair Freedom! I retire
> From flattery, cards, and dice, and din;
> Nor are thou found in mansions higher
> Than the low cot or humble inn.

The inn, which within living memory had entertained General Blücher and the Duke of Wellington, Mr Boswell and Dr Johnson, George III and Queen Charlotte, was not a humble place when full of oarsmen hankering for quiet before their storm and supporters bent on a storm before the night's quiet.

Smyth could not sleep after the bells in the nearby church tower rang

out at 5 a.m. While he lay dozing there were early stirrings in many of
the houses of the vicinity, large and small. Workmen still had tasks to
do and committee men had to see that they did them. Stewards and
corporation made eager and early departures from their solid piles of
bricks and mortar. Apart from the grain, poultry and vegetable market
on a Thursday, there had been little action in the town since their
forefathers were engaged in civil war. Between them, though, their
houses had witnessed many strands of social history among the well-
to-do. Thomas Stonor's family seat at Stonor stretched back to before
the Norman Conquest and had provided shelter for those of the old
faith since the Reformation. Fuller-Maitland's Park Place was one of
the loveliest parks in the land and contained a potpourri of eccen-
tricities collected by General Conway. William Peere Williams-
Freeman, holder of manorial rights, lived at Fawley Court, a house
designed by Sir Christopher Wren. The old manor house had run into
trouble when Royalist troops billeted there had emulated the Vandals,
according to Sir Bulstrode Whitelocke, the owner at the time. They
had used his books to light their tobacco and killed most of his deer, as
well as smashing up the furniture. Sir Bulstrode also owned a house at
Phyllis Court, also downstream from the bridge but much nearer the
town, and it was fortified by Major General Skipton in 1643 and
garrisoned by several hundred foot soldiers and a troop of horse.
Henley was a frontier town in those troubled times between King at
Oxford and Parliament in London, and it was seized by the Earl of
Essex in 1643. Sir Arthur Aston's Royalists from Reading tried to take
the town by entering Duke Street under cover of darkness, but were
dispersed by an enormous cannon. The Battle of Henley lasted fifteen
minutes and cost ten Royalist lives and three Parliamentary ones,
apart from Sir Bulstrode's anguish at the fate of his property while he
wore an uneasy Cromwellian mantle.

He probably preferred his days away in France or his ambassadorial
tasks at the Swedish court more than Henley's war. But among his
prolific writing and memoirs he left a eulogy to the little town he lived
in, for his children:

> These hills are richly adorned with pleasant woods and groves, consisting
> for the most part of beech, which crown the toppes of the hills, and at the
> foot of them gently glides the river Thames, offering to carry their burdens
> (which are not small) of wood and corne, to their chiefe citty, London,
> which he doth, and returns money and other necessary commodities in

exchange for them. Indeed he is a good neighbour, enriching this countrey by his navigableness, and allowing them sufficient meadow for their hay and store of salmons, trouts, pikes, perches, eels, and other good fish for their provisions, he hastens not by a quick though clear and smarte streame, through this countrey, butt gravely keeps on his way, delighted with his flowing bankes, and bending groves saluting him.

Park Place lay almost hidden at the top of a thickly wooded slope on the Berkshire bank. William Fuller-Maitland's house had seen eminent people and curious fads. Frederick Prince of Wales had lived there from 1738, and then General Conway bought it in 1752. He built a rugged arched bridge across Happy Valley near the Thames and imported the remains of a Druid temple from St Helier when he left Jersey after being Governor there. He also planted the first Lombardy poplar to reach England. Fuller-Maitland had continued the general's quirkiness only recently, when, to celebrate the accession to the throne of the young Queen, he erected the top section of the spire of St Bride's church, Fleet Street, on the highest point of the estate. Wren's original spire at St Bride's had been struck by lightning and shortened many years before. Victoria as monarch was something to celebrate. By June of 1839 she was only twenty and had not yet reigned for two years. She was virtually unknown to her subjects but already she had blown away the disreputable and selfish age of her ridiculous uncles. Inexperienced in politics, she doted on her Prime Minister, Lord Melbourne, and his Whig policies which were gathering unpopularity elsewhere. But she also turned her attention to manners, eroding the upper-class male habit of getting pickled after dinner by cutting down the ladies' retirement time at court to five minutes.

Fuller-Maitland may not have known this but, in company with the new Victorians, he could sense the change of climate at the end of a depressing decade. There was continuous trouble over the Corn Laws and around Henley it was not hard to find real hardship among the disinherited farm workers. Cobbett was always rabbiting on about it in Parliament and papers, and brewers were complaining about cottagers who opened up as alehouses outside the jurisdiction of the justices. William Brakspear had had considerable difficulty since he took over the brewery in 1830 with rival alehouses and customers who had been thrown out of work by threshing machines. And there was unrest in the cities. In May troops had to be sent from Woolwich to

Bristol because of Chartist disturbances, and reinforcements to Nottingham also.

Among the things which had come to Fuller-Maitland with his country seat were fifty acres of lavender beds carefully developed by the enterprising general, the fragrance of which greeted Smyth and his friends when they rested their heads on the pillows of the Red Lion.

Smyth's restlessness got him out of bed and he set out for a walk before breakfast along the riverside meadows, disappointed to find a dull, overcast morning. There were few other pedestrians about, and some out riding, although he had heard that horses were to be banned from the meadow when the racing started. They had caused danger and confusion during the Oxford versus Cambridge match ten years beforehand. While he admired the large blue flowers of the meadow cranesbill and the yellow bladder worts along the river bank the peace of the valley, albeit dulled by cloud, dispelled some of his worries about the forthcoming event.

Williams-Freeman left his colonnaded mansion at Fawley with its interior hangings by Cuyp, Rembrandt, and Titian; Charles Lane came down through the market place from Badgemore, a farmhouse enlarged by bricks from the site of St Paul's by the late Richard Jennings, master-builder of the cathedral; Stonor descended the Fairmile from Stonor; Fuller-Maitland emerged from the spire and poplars of Park Place; and they set about the finishing touches to the various erections along Waterside, adding a different flurry to the normal sleepier dawn chorus of a small town in southern England.

There were those of much lesser estate who were glad of the chance of a little carpentering and labouring, dung-sweeping and pot-clearing which the influx of visitors caused. The well-paved streets and the handsome buildings gave an air of prosperity, but times were uneasy if one didn't have a trade and wasn't secure in the nation's largest industry, domestic service. A few pence might stave off the appeal to the benevolent society for relief for the wife while lying in.

Brakspear's brewery was waking up to another day of a rather satisfactory week, the stable lads mucking out the dray horses in their stable close to the churchyard; upstream Mr Elsee's paper mill was stirring and so was a recently established silk mill. The only other mills in these parts were for flour. Flour and wood were shipped in considerable quantities to the metropolis, and on this morning Casey and

Thompson's were preparing for the arrival of their Original Fly Wag-
gon from London, and their rival Morgan was awaiting his.

At about eight o'clock the day darkened, lightning rent the sky over
the church tower, and a clap of thunder sent Smyth scuttling back over
the five-arch bridge to the Red Lion. During breakfast the storm
intensified to such a pitch that the crew thought the inn had been
struck, but it was Mr Cooper's house in Bell Street which was smitten
by the electric fluid. The chimney crashed to the ground, several
windows were broken, and a workman was knocked over but, hap-
pily, not injured seriously. The torrent soaked the stands and the
booths and caused little floods here and there, and throughout visitors
poured in as thickly as the raindrops fell, choking up the inn yard with
gigs and other carriages and filling the rooms with their persons and
baggage, cursing and soaked whether arriving by land or water. James
Dixon, landlord, was having another busy day in a succession of them,
and the keepers at the Catherine Wheel and the White Hart were also
coping with the sodden influx as the London and Oxford and Chel-
tenham coaches plashed their way in and out of town.

After breakfast the Trinity men sallied up the wet street to the town
hall for the draw, looking like so many bundles of peacoats, though
some of them sported the very latest cloth and rubber waterproofs of
Charles Mackintosh. The piazza underneath the hall was crowded
with refugees from the inclement weather, while upstairs in the handsome pillared hall under the portraits of George I and the Earl of
Macclesfield, ancestor of the present earl who was patron of the
regatta, were assembled the captains of boats, many of the stewards,
Messrs Nash and Towsey, the secretaries of the regatta, busying
themselves with paperwork and coordinating errand-runners, and Mr
P. B. Cooper, the treasurer, who had the pleasant task of collecting the
subscriptions which afforded the one hundred guinea Grand Challenge Cup and other goodies besides. He also collected the entry fees of
five guineas per crew, which paid for the winners' medals. These were
the men who had fixed the course of about a mile and a half from the
island to the bridge, who had fixed the rules and set themselves as
arbiters of disputes over entries. They made their challenge open to
college crews from the universities of Oxford, Cambridge and London, the schools of Eton and Westminster, officers of either brigade of
the Household Troops, or members of a club established for at least a
year prior to entry. And they required all the eight-oared boats to be

steered by an amateur member of the club or clubs. They also provided a Town Challenge Cup, value thirty guineas, for four-oared boats. The cast of the townsmen's vision, first seen in this same hall in March, was now present for the names of the contestants to be written on pieces of paper and placed in the hat, and butterflies were active in stomachs.

Both University College and Exeter College had withdrawn their challenges for the Grand, and the result of the draw was the Etonian Club of Oxford against Brasenose in the first heat and the Trinity men of Cambridge against Wadham of Oxford in the second.

The silverware was then put on display. Smyth found the dead-frosted silver of the Grand Cup impressive: it was unfinished but of remarkably handsome design, he thought. Father Thames was represented in bold relief on one side, whilst the opposite was occupied with an inscription; around him flourished water lilies, bulrushes and all the plants to which he was partial. The handles rested on bases which were imitations of the keystones of Henley bridge, bearing the heads of Thames and Isis as sculpted by the Hon. Mrs Damier, daughter of General Conway. The cup was in the form of the celebrated Warwick vase, beautifully designed and chiselled, Father Thames's recumbent figure supported by a stem of aquatic plants growing from a rich and boldly chased foot. The Town Cup was scarcely less magnificent, with Thames holding a garland in each hand, the flowers intersecting the lower part of the cup, while swans' necks formed the handles. The silversmiths, Makepiece and Co. of Lincoln's Inn, had done the regatta proud. The medals, too, were handsome: so much so that they infused fresh spirit into Smyth, and he knew he was going to need it.

While the public and the rowers admired the silverware in the town hall the heavens gave the four thousand inhabitants and the folks who lived on the hills a real soaking. The Leander men who had rowed up from London arrived at about eleven, and carried their drenched things to the Catherine Wheel. Boxall's *Reading Sociable* arrived at about the same time, and considerable traffic built up from all directions as conveyances brought passengers from Wycombe and Marlow, and further afield, and from Mr Brunel's Great Western Railway station at Maidenhead. The rain fell on the grave of Richard Jennings, master-builder of St Paul's, watched by old inhabitants who lived in the almshouses on the east and west sides of the churchyard. It poured on the schools and the malthouses and the cottages and neat houses. It

soaked the terrace and the bowling green and topped up the fish pond
at Phyllis Court, the only features left of the magnificent house which
stood in Civil War days on the site of the modern residence now rising
on the site. Only part of the kitchen was still standing from the old
building.

Some took refuge in shops and inns and business premises
round the Market Place and in Hart Street and Duke Street and up
Grey's Road, like Hickman and Kinch's, the printers, booksellers,
stationers, dispensing chemists and agents for Twining's Genuine
Teas. Others made for the reading rooms where the paint was scarcely
dry, there to scan the newspapers and learn a little of the world beyond
the Fairmile. Here they could read accounts of Chartist disruption in
faraway places, of the opening of railway lines which were causing great
anxiety to the proprietors of canals and which were already having an
effect on the trade of Henley's waggoners, Morgan's and Casey and
Thompson's. They could get scant notice of goings-on at the court,
where the young and blossoming queen was beginning to upset the
staid political life of several factions, but particularly the Tories. They
could keep their minds off the dismal day with an account of a cricket
match or bloodstock prices or horse races, of challenge matches on the
Thames or the Tyne, of pedestrian wagers at Belle Vue, Manchester.
They could follow the goings-on in the ring on some hillside conveniently positioned on a county boundary to avoid the close attention
of the law. They could read the latest speech of the crusty old Duke of
Wellington who had lived at the fountainhead of Waterloo ever since
that day of glory back in '15; or the latest instalment of Mr Dickens's
Nicholas Nickleby, or the aquatic notes of sailing and rowing, or the
answers to readers' mysterious queries.

The most interesting intelligence for some was the small print of a
review in 1 June's *Jackson's Oxford Journal*. It was of a book telling of
the southern shores of South America and the circumnavigation of the
globe by HMS *Beagle*. Charles Darwin's work, said the paper, adds
considerably to our knowledge of hydrography, geography and
natural history, and of the habits of aborigines. Darwin's novel ideas
about coral islands and geology are admirably illustrated by Mr
Landseer and others, and a more important work 'has rarely been our
lot to notice'.

To dream the rain away was to read of faraway places, or dip into
the intriguing advertisements in the London Sunday paper, *Bell's Life*

and Sporting Chronicle. The Golden Perch at 52 The Strand offered an enormous range of fishing rods and riding whips and silk or fast-coloured gingham umbrellas from two shillings each upwards. Dubourg's Splendid Mechanical Museum in Windmill Street was advertising 500 automaton figures on display, including the state procession of the Queen, the Coronation, the Battle of Navarino, etc. Prints of winning race horses, telescopes, acoustic cornets, patent medicines and patent toothbrushes, masquerades, shooting galleries, public houses with scenic gardens or concerts – there was much in bustling Westminster and Southwark and London itself to keep one's mind off the puddled streets and squelching meadows and dripping stands of Henley on the day of a fair.

The toll-keeper on the Berkshire side of the bridge could not remember such a day as this. Past noon the traffic grew as more and more coaches came down the London road. Some took up positions on the bridge ready for the afternoon's events. Visitors took advantage of cold collations laid out at the houses of Brakspear, Nash, Hickman and Stubbs, and other members of the committee. An eight manned by Cambridge men arrived from the Cambridge Subscription Rooms at Lambeth, and at the Red Lion the Trinity men were easily outnumbered by Oxonians, who had made the inn their unofficial headquarters. The Brasenose men had come by water also, but wisely on the day before. Those who braved the weather rode in from Wargrave, from Marlow, or down the Fairmile from Assendon on the Oxford road, walked in through the woods and across the fields from Medmenham and Hambledon and Shiplake. They rowed in, downstream from the Upper Thames and upstream from the Lower – gentlemen of the universities, the shires and town, watermen of London and Oxford. From whichever direction, by land or water, the travellers first saw the noble flint tower of the little town's church and were spurred on by frequent peals of bells. The London and Oxford steamer arrived with a moderate party and moored close to Phyllis Court, her stern paddles quiet now, leaving the disturbance of the water to rowers' blades. Ladies in much finery began to take their seats in the stands along Waterside and on the Remenham bank. The stall-holders and vendors and hawkers renewed their entreaties for the purchase of ribbons, lollipops, cakes and the like, and spectators took to the barges and craft along the banks. Cannon were fired and bands on the barges played popular airs. And so Henley prepared for boat racing, guard boats appointed by the stewards keeping a clear channel for the competitors, and the starters, Messrs Higgins and Gibson of Leander Club, taking up their positions down near Temple Island. The umpire was another Leander man, Mr Bishop. The sun broke through the rainclouds to beckon people into the meadows.

At four o'clock Smyth and Gough and Taylor and Lonsdale, Penrose, Strickland, Cross and Massey were led through the crowded streets by little coxswain Barclay. They embarked wearing their blue-striped guernseys with rosettes of french blue and pulled slowly down to Squire Freeman's Island, where they and their opponents, Wadham, disembarked to watch the first heat, between Brasenose and the Oxford Etonians. Smyth found that the little temple on the island contained on its first floor a good semicircular room which faced the river, adorned neatly with paintings in the style of decoration on Etruscan vases. On the roof above was a little colonnade where he took his stand, giving him a fine view of the race from the starter's gun on the island to within a quarter of a mile from the bridge, after which point the action became indistinct. The Brasenose at starting took the lead but their time was disgraceful, and in half a mile the Etonians passed them, beating them easily by about six boats' lengths.

Trinity now embarked, most of them in a very nervous state. They were as suspicious of each other as they were of the Wadham sitting alongside them, neat in their white guernseys with narrow blue stripes, dark blue caps, light blue velvet bands and scarves. One mile and about 600 yards away was the finish at the bridge; behind them was the man with the starting pistol. 'Are you ready?' was followed by a report. Trinity were inclined to hold their adversaries too cheaply, as Smyth put it afterwards, and they consequently drew ahead nearly a boat's length. This much alarmed some of them and they began rather to increase their pace. It was stroke for stroke for much of the way until the Cambridge men edged ahead, amongst great excitement from the stands, coming in at the bridge little more than a length in front of the Wadham. Both crews looked distressed, but Smyth had the satisfaction of hearing that several of his crew had been saving themselves throughout for the final heat, which explained away for him both why they had beaten the poorly rated Wadham by so little and why an extra share of the work had fallen on the shoulders of a few.

They were congratulated by troops of old Cambridge men and Mr Cooper kindly hung out refreshments for them in his garden, while times for the two heats were compared and the voices of salvation met the voices of doom. Smyth paid little attention to the speculators, simply making up his mind that the final was to be a very close race.

The regatta continued with a £12 wager race between the three pairs of London watermen from the bridge round the island and back again. Williams and Pyner took an early lead, were overhauled by W. Campbell and Barrow, Williams having broken his thole; but on the return leg it was Phelps and H. Campbell who cleverly mastered the others to win. There followed the four-oared race between three Henley crews – *The Wave* (Capt. Mr Z. Allnutt), *The Dreadnought* (Capt. Mr James Forrest), and *The Albion* (Capt. Mr Robert Webb). There was bad temper and furious activity at the Albion boathouse because during the pairs race some shuffling parties had entered the building and chalked all over the bottom of the boat, but the misdemeanour was discovered in time to be remedied. *The Wave* got ahead during the struggle on the turn at the island and were first back to the bridge, winning the handsome Town Cup.

Before seven o'clock hundreds of Oxford and Cambridge men got down to the meadow opposite the island for the Grand final. The crew of the *Black Prince* had taken a mutton chop and a glass of ale apiece and embarked again at seven, all of them feeling in better spirits because it could be no disgrace to them should they be beaten by a crew made up from several colleges. They were obliged to manoeuvre a little in order to prevent their Etonian rivals having weigh on their boat when the word was given, but when the boats were even they went off at a great pace and soon pulled back the Etonians' slight showing. There was a cacophonous din from the bank as the supporters ran along the meadows, and for half a mile the boats stole a foot or two from one another and then dropped back.

As they reached the corner near the poplar, the shouts became tremendous and Smyth had a faint vision of silver medals dancing before his eyes, inspiring him to put everything he had into a few strokes and trust to chance for gaining the bridge. A similar feeling must have pervaded the crew, for they suddenly shot right ahead of the Oxford Etonians and came in at the bridge with their stern just clear of the Etonians' bow. The umpire put the verdict at half a length in a time of eight minutes and about thirty seconds.

The crew passed right under Lord Chesterfield's carriage at the centre of the bridge, thousands of spectators acclaimed their victory

from the banks and nearby boats, and two Trinity men danced in a
punt half full of water close to where the *Black Prince* and her baked
crew came in. The mob forced their way into Mr Cooper's garden and
small boys looked on with awe at the evident warm state of the men,
dripping with perspiration and gulping in air to replenish their
exhausted lungs. Then they dressed leisurely and went to the committee's stand where, after signing a document binding them to return the
cup to the stewards on the next entrance day, 24 May 1840, they were
presented with the coveted Grand Challenge Cup and their medals.
They admired the cup again and read the inscriptions on the medals.
On one side was engraved 'Grand Challenge Cup Prize Medal' and on
the other 'Henley Regatta Established 1839' with a wreath of aquatic
flowers. After giving three cheers for the committee and secretaries,
the men of Trinity brought their cup to their inn, being propelled there
not so much by the action of their own feet as by the pats and slaps on
the back applied to them by an admiring people. Their room was soon
filled with old Cantabs, and in company with them and with the
unsuccessful Etonians, whom they invited in from the next room, they
quickly saw the end of half a dozen of champagne, poured into the cup
so that the bubbly was accessible only by each person dipping his
frontispiece into the silverware.

There was now a great throng in the town, cheered by the great race
and the continued advances made by the June sun against nature's
efforts at having his say. The reporter from the *Reading Mercury*
noted that although the stand on the Remenham side had been a
failure because of the inclement weather, and although the multitude
which he had expected had been kept at bay by the rain, at least eight
thousand people had attended – and his was not the highest estimate
that day. The bridge again became crowded towards ten o'clock, when
a superb display of fireworks, arranged by Mr Fenwick, was set off on
a barge moored near New Street. And none of the Humane Society's
apparatus for rescuing people in distress, which had been brought up
from London together with drag nets and the like and been housed at
Hobbs' Rowinghouse, near the bridge, had been required.

The Trinity men dined at the Star, where they found the Wadham
crew extremely happy and noisy, having given themselves up to
delight when they realized that their close race with the Cantabs had
implied a tremendous victory over Brasenose, although Wadham held
a much lower place on the Oxford river barely a week before. The

crew of the *Black Prince* roosted late, having rowed into town and found silver.

On the following morning, Saturday, 15 June, Smyth awoke at the Red Lion from a confused consideration of eight oars, medals, gunfirings and silver cups, and packed all his moveables into his hatbox. A hearty breakfast and involved calculations over the bill delayed the *Black Prince*'s departure until almost midday, when with the cup in its box in the bows, and amid flag-waving and cheering from the bridge, the men from First Trinity pulled out for London. Their hearts were lighter, though some heads were heavier, than on the previous day as they moved along the reach for the last time, and they were delayed by a huge West Country barge at Hambledon Lock. They passed the ruins of Medmenham Abbey, embowered in trees, and passed under a suspension bridge at Marlow, where a good-looking church was under construction, and saw a model of a frigate lying off someone's lawn at Maidenhead. They walked up to the great castle at Windsor and then visited the chapel at Eton, reminiscent of that of their near neighbour at Cambridge, King's. They passed Magna Charter Island and the bow end of the boat had violent cachinnations about the beauty or otherwise of the tower of Egham church, and they paddled past many little villas and spent the night at a waterside inn at Thames Ditton.

Here Wythe and Gough bribed the chambermaid to let them lie in on the following morning, delaying embarkation by an hour. Looking round as he toiled steadily at his oar, plash plashing in the bright morning sunlight, Smyth was astonished at the beauty of Richmond while Barclay craned his neck to steer a passage through the multitude of craft pleasuring about. The *Black Prince* carried her silver cup proudly past the Duke of Northumberland's Sion House, a most ungainly lump of architecture, Smyth thought. From Kew they had a tedious paddle at low water to Putney, where they disembarked to visit Mrs Avis, who had put up Smyth and Penrose with the Cambridge crew for the Boat Race. She produced champagne to drink to the cup and then filled it with flowers for them.

At Westminster they pulled from the Lambeth shore after passing the church and carried the *Black Prince* into Searle's boathouse, where the Cambridge Subscription Rooms were situated above, meeting-place of Cantab oarsmen and reading room for boating and yachting magazines. First Trinity dispersed into Westminster, Smyth towards a snug camp bed at the lodgings of his friends, the Pollocks. On Monday morning they left their medals at Makepiece's in Lincoln's Inn to have their names inscribed on them, collecting them after visiting Dollonds to see a telescope which had just been made for Cross. At Webbs they were amused by the conversation of an American who was unwilling that they should think him such, but his remarks on the majority of English travellers being purse-proud islanders betrayed his Yankee lineage. And in *Bell's Life*, published in the Strand for five pence and claiming sales of 22,000, they read about themselves and the grand regatta at Henley. They also read about a great excitement out at Chelsea, where a Mr Hampton had on the previous Thursday descended from a balloon over Cremornehouse Gardens by means of a parachute in the form of a chaise umbrella. A Russian slaver had been captured that week and taken into Portsmouth Harbour by the navy. There had been a serious earth tremor in the neighbourhood of Manchester and towns to the north, and there were reports from all parts that last week's rains had brought incalculable benefit to crops, even if not to regattas.

The paper also gave notice of the attractions of amusements in the light-hearted second summer of Victoria's reign. *Henry the Fifth* was playing at Covent Garden, a revival which was the crowning achievement of Mr Macready's management. 'The field of Agincourt in moonlight is probably the finest imitation of nature ever seen on the stage,' the reviewer wrote. Charles Kean was playing his favourite characters three times a week at the Haymarket. Some shooting galleries offered archery. There was notice of a duel between two MPs, Grattan and Lord Londonderry, and a long account headed 'Most Atrocious and Cold-blooded Massacre of Thirty Unoffending Natives in New South Wales', for which seven 'monsters in human shape' were hanged in Sydney on 15 December last.

The Marylebone Cricket Club had played Surrey and then Cambridge the previous week, and there was a preliminary announcement and the teams for the Oxford and Cambridge match now on at Lord's. William Massey, the stroke, had gone up there because he was representing his university at the crease. Boxing benefits were noticed, and a reader had asked *Bell's*: 'Did a man ever run a mile in three minutes?' No, said the paper, the shortest time was four minutes and twenty-eight seconds, by Metcalf. There were answers about chess and billiards, pigeon shooting and quoits, skittles, cribbage and the Ascot

Cup. There was an account of a policeman of P Division, Michael Maddigan, who 'thought proper to shake hands with a polar bear in Surrey Zoological Gardens, and, to his astonishment, suddenly found his digits halfway down the bear's throat.' A bone was thrown to the bear and the severely lacerated arm of the law was released. There were warnings against pickpockets at the Hampton races and an account of a citizen's arrest for same outside the Opera House in Covent Garden. A boy had been drowned in the Thames.

There was discreet remedy, one of the Trinity men found, in the advertisements for those who fell prey to the army of ladies of the town.

> Public Notice to the Unhappy [it said]. Dr Eady continues to be consulted in all cases of Syphilis Disease and derangement of general health . . . the effect of mal-practice, the free indulgence of pleasure and other causes; consumption, rheumatism, dropsies, headaches, eruptions, obstinate gleets, etc. . . . . Letters containing the description of symptoms will answer the purpose of personal consultation.

There were notices of boat races on the Thames that week – Vincent versus Antrobus for the Colquhoun Sculls today, Cambridge Subscription Room races for fours tomorrow, and on Thursday the Arundel Yacht Club's race for vessels up to seven tons from Temple Gardens to Wandsworth Meadow. There was notice of Cumberland and Westmorland wrestling at Liverpool, and a dispatch from Cape Town sent on 11 March by James Brooks before setting off for Singapore on his 142-ton schooner-yacht *Royalist* on the next part of his circumnavigation of the globe. And there was an advertisement for a sparrow shoot: a sweepstake match for a silver snuff box at Mr Hetherington's, City Arms, Hammersmith Bridge, on Wednesday, 19 June, from barges moored on the river. Twelve sparrows each. Dinner and shooting, 8s 6d.

Thus ended the first Henley, with the crews dispersing and the stewards counting the receipts and the tradespeople rejoicing at a profitable, if at times wet, week. Their town was looking good after several years of unease among the rural population, there was sense of a new age in the woods and vales round about as the new reign got started and the Great Western got nearer. Henley had changed little in hundreds of years except for some recent street widening and the improvement of buildings in the Market Place. The Queen hardly realized the extent of her domain, although it was reckoned that at the start of her reign 1,200,000 of her subjects lived abroad, most of them in her own possessions from primitive Ireland to Raffles's Singapore, and from the Punjab to the clean paradise of New Zealand, where voluntary colonization had begun in earnest. You could get a free passage and a seven-year ticket to Australia for poaching.

The population was not imperially ambitious, either. They had been militarily successful in Europe against the French, had campaigned against the evils of slavery, and devoted much energy to godliness and trade, which was on the whole successful. Especially for the young men whose fathers sent them with ample allowances to the universities and who spent their ample spare time hunting, shooting, fishing, cricketing, rowing and betting. For them there was an exciting outlook, whether in commerce, or church, army or state. There were bound to be developments. In recent years an Englishman, Faraday, had discovered an amazing process called electrolysis; two Americans had speeded the communication of life and death, Morse with the telegraph and Colt with the revolver; and now a Frenchman, Daguerre, had found that you could capture scenes of real life on light-sensitive paper. Lord Durham, much quoted for his assertion that anyone should be able to 'jog along on £40,000 a year', in soberer mood presented a report to Parliament in February 1839 – leaked comprehensively to *The Times* of London beforehand – advocating that the colonies as extensions of English society should be competent to govern themselves. And Lord Auckland, Governor General of India, had taken drastic steps to safeguard the North West frontier, to the dismay of the Duke of Wellington and the directors of the East India Company, but probably to the delight of many of the Indian nabobs who were almost a race apart when they returned to England for early retirement. Russians had been seen in Kabul, in the turbulent country of Afghanistan, and had also been supporting the Persians against the Afghans. As the young gentlemen of Trinity conquered the Henley reach for the first time, General Keane, with fifteen and a half thousand British and colonial troops, nearly 40,000 camp followers and 30,000 camels, carrying everything from soap and cigars to wine and potted meats, was looking down on Kabul, where he was about to restore Shah Shuja to the throne in place of Dost Mohammed. If anyone in Henley had any inkling of this on Friday, 14 June 1839, it would have been Thomas Gore Lloyd of India House who lived at the

Grove. Military imperialism was born in Kabul in that August, a frightened and confused infant.

Meanwhile domestic affairs were the chief preoccupation in the reading rooms at Henley, in the drawing rooms of the great houses and in the saloons of the Star, the Wheel and the Red Lion. On Sunday, 23 June, *Bell's Life* printed a correction stating that the time for the last heat for the Grand was seven minutes and about thirty seconds, not eight minutes and about thirty seconds. This, though, was most unlikely and the stewards rejected the assertion strongly, many taking advice from rowing men that such a time would be much too fast for such a distance, bearing in mind the times of other races. *Bell's* also said:

> We have received several letters complaining of impositions practised on visitors by some of the innkeepers and others. At one house in particular where Oxford men put up, they were not allowed to partake of anything in the shape of eatables but in one room, at the door of which five shillings were demanded, before the parties were permitted even to look at the niggardly cold collation. Coach proprietors charged ten shillings each for nine miles from Maidenhead (railway) to Henley. Passengers were, however, gratified by the arrangements made by the GWR. No doubling of charges by the railway.

The stewards deemed their venture a success, and thought they would hold an aquatic event again in 1840.

3

F. Weatherley encounters siren water lilies
1868: The case of the redundant coxswain

In the summer of 1867 an unusual event took place on the Seine a few miles below Paris. A large party of English oarsmen, professionals and amateurs, went there to take part in a new international regatta, managed jointly by the French and the English because the rules and methods of procedure differed greatly in the two countries. In July of that year readers of the *Manchester Guardian* were treated to generous descriptions of the procedures by an anonymous correspondent who was an undergraduate at Corpus Christi College, Oxford. He was Charles Prestwich Scott, a bright young man in his second year, who had just had a remarkable experience. He had been offered the editorship of the Manchester paper, the most valuable newspaper property outside London, as soon as he graduated, on the strength of being the owner's cousin.

His college had a crew on the course between the bridges of St Cloud and Surennes, but Scott's dispatches to his future employer concentrated more on wondrous scenes from the New World.

> Paris has resolved to have a genuine regatta [he wrote] and neither trouble nor expense have been spared to procure it. Splendid prizes, the most exalted patronage, reduced fares for the oarsmen, and free carriage for their boats, have been the baits held out to tempt competitors from every country. When to these are added the inducements which Paris itself at this carnival offers to every visitor, we cannot be surprised that the entries for the races have been larger, perhaps, than have hitherto been anywhere known.

Scott opened his report of the second day by asserting that it 'will be long remembered among rowing men, and should make either English oarsmen or English boatbuilders reconsider the first principles of their arts.' Another Oxford man who was there, Walter Bradford Woodgate of Brasenose College, thought so too. The people who particularly caught their attention were four sturdy New Brunswickers who, having beaten everything on their home waters, had brought two home-made boats some thousands of miles to show the rest of the world how to row. Among the neat boating men in strange costume, Scott reported, with high boots, long flannel coats and peaked hats, the New Brunswickers were a strange contrast, having flesh-coloured jerseys, dark cloth trousers, leather braces and bright pink caps.

> Their style of rowing is by no means in accordance with received ideas [he went on]. It consists in a short, quick stroke, pulled almost entirely with the arms, hitting the water fairly at the beginning, with a jerk at the end, and a regularly marked hang upon the chest. They row without a coxswain, bow steering, partly by an ingenious contrivance with his feet, partly with his oar. Their time is perfect and their course is straight as a die. . . .

The New Brunswickers beat Paris, Boulogne, Hamburg, London and University College, Oxford, on the Seine. 'Thus were two crack English crews, rowing quite fresh, in boats weighing about 60 lb, beaten by the tired New Brunswickers in a boat weighing 200 lb.'

The cotton merchants and the entrepreneurs in the mills and manufactories of Manchester read that the New Brunswickers were not amateurs of the usual kind, being men to all appearance of much the same stamp as our English watermen.

> Their success is largely due to their splendid condition and enormous 'grit', partly to the fact of their rowing without the deadweight of a coxswain, but also partly to the good qualities of their boats, which, though much too heavy, are keel built, stand up well at the bows, and displace wonderfully little water. The following are the names of these heroes of the day: Stroke, G. Price; 3, R. Ross, 2, S. Hulton; bow, R. Fulton. Their average weight is 11 st 5 lb, but they look more. . . .

Scott went on to note how the English watermen 'as usual stole a lead, cheating the Amsterdam boat of a clear length', and how the starter allowed this race to continue, and how the recent death of Maximilian had kept the Emperor and the Parisians away from the regatta, which was nevertheless exceedingly interesting from its cosmopolitan character. He criticized the English for indulging in one of their frequent displays of exclusiveness and unconciliatory characteristics, and praised the French for their politeness and readiness to do all that could be required of them. Woodgate, meanwhile, won a sculling race and left Paris with some notes and drawings of New Brunswickian marine architecture in his pocket and an inkling in his head of a masterstroke for next year's Henley.

Woodgate was brought up in his father's rectory at Belbroughton in Worcestershire, where he had sporting adventures on the sly, and in the October quarter of 1850 was sent to Radley, a newish school near Oxford which enjoyed a sybaritic reputation, where he messed about in boats and indulged in some mischievous deception. Competent to run errands for his father by the age of seven, the young Woodgate would make for Ruberry Hill on the boundary of Staffordshire and Worcestershire, where Birmingham prizefighters often met. The Brummagem 'pugs' were kind to him and allowed his pony to jostle to the front of the ring, and they would give him a sip of beer at the Cock afterwards before he returned to the rectory. His father's coachman recognized his talents at horsemanship and arranged for him to ride an old mare over the hurdles in a consolation scramble at catchweights after a day's racing at Redditch. Woodgate won handsomely and got a roasting from his governess for coming home late, but fortunately his reverend father was away and nobody guessed what he had been up to.

At Radley Woodgate passed in swimming and took to the river in a small dinghy, his first outing being with another boy new to the sport, with a third boy, only slightly more experienced, coxing. Then, on a half holiday, he took the old wherry from the boathouse, a craft with a high flared gunwale and low freeboard fore and aft, with old-fashioned square-loom sculls, admirably adapted, he said, to bark a tyro's knuckles. He toiled zigzag the one and a half miles to Sandford, and back again, and accomplished it while teaching himself to feather his blades in four hours, including the three-mile round trip between the school and the boathouse. The school was much more civilized than most of the day, having separate cubicles for each boy, servants to black their shoes, virtually no fagging and fresh joints of meat at dinner.

But Woodgate reckoned that the diet held back his growth. Radley allowed him under eight hours' sleep and, apart from lessons, demanded two and a half hours of football or fives in winter and in summer three miles on foot to the river and back, plus several miles of rowing. The fuel for this, after rising at 5.45, prayers, rollcall, and an hour and a half's study, was a bread-and-butter breakfast at 8 a.m., a dry bread lunch at noon, and a meat dinner at 4 p.m. Prefects got supper, others did not. The eights were allowed to buy biscuits and a glass of beer at the Sandford ferry public house. Woodgate found an ingenious way to supplement his diet. The school was on the estate of Sir George Bowyer, and the boy befriended Sir George's gamekeeper. Stone showed him how to collect rare eggs and butterflies and instructed him in woodcraft, which Woodgate turned to his own advantage. In darkest November he set wires in the runs in Radley copse. He then labelled his poached pheasants to himself and waylaid the carrier's cart which was on the way to the school, consequently receiving a surprise dinner present from the Rev. and Mrs Woodgate.

He may have been undersize for his age, but the young Woodgate was certainly tough, as could be deduced from an episode which he told some of his friends at dinner in Brasenose, Oxford, a few years later. There was a cloister passage connecting the chapel with the house at Radley, and it had a springy boarded floor exactly eighty yards long. At Whitsun in 1857 the prefects were discussing how long it would take to run a mile on the planked flooring. The topic of the day ended with Woodgate being matched to run a hundred times up and down it in an hour, a time which was to include eating two pots of jam. Greengage was barred because of delay in expectorating stones. He bolted the jam with the aid of a paperknife and a glass of water, and rubbed his right hand raw by punting himself round against the brickwork at each end. He calculated that the elasticity of the board was worth 10 per cent, while the distance was just over nine miles. He did it with about a minute to spare. He then went down to the river and rowed to Nuneham and back, giving further punishment to his right hand.

In 1858 Woodgate was in the first Radley eight to race against Eton. They lost. He went up to Brasenose and launched into a very successful rowing career, while dipping into law studies and charming his way through the high-living and jape-laden life of a young college gentleman. There was good groundwork for the events of 1868. His diet was better, for a start, although it did get out of hand sometimes. In his freshman's term he was enlisted for the college Torpid, which trained barbarously on raw steak and a run before chapel. Being under ten stone and still of effeminate appearance, he played Lady Barbara in the college production of *The Little Savage*. After dinner in hall and the performance, there was a celebratory supper on Brasenose's usual lines: oysters, dressed crab, grilled bones, poached eggs and wine, followed by a choice of four steaming punches – whisky, rum, gin or brandy. Woodgate somehow got to bed in his petticoats and attended chapel next morning with rouge on his cheeks. He probably awoke to the reek of boiling lobster, for his rooms in the college's back quad were over Tester's, the fishmonger in the High. The pair had a difference of opinion about the trade's odoriferousness, which spilled over into a ruling against Tester by the college dons when the summer temperatures made the air even higher. But Woodgate and Tester eventually became friends, the former as punter and the latter as bookmaker.

Before Woodgate began to find the delights of Radley, there had been several developments of note at the regatta. In 1843, the year in which Prince Albert became patron of the Thames Grand Regatta, started by some gentlemen endeavouring to support 'the industrious class of mechanics employed in boatbuilding' whose livelihood was threatened already by the increase of steamboats on the river, Oxford won the Grand at Henley with a seven-man crew against the Cambridge Subscription Rooms.

A new rule had come into force that year which said that nobody should be allowed to substitute for another who had already rowed in a heat, nor should any member of a club be allowed to row with more than one crew in any of the races for the same cup. This followed a cunning ploy by the Cambridge Subscription Rooms in 1842 when, as holders of the Grand, they challenged themselves by entering a Cambridge crew, planning to transfer men from there to the holding boat if the challengers lost a heat. At this time all events at Henley were challenge ones, so that the holders did not have to take to the course until the final. Substitutions did not arise in the event because the challengers reached the final to meet their 'old boys'. The other competitors, though, had shown restlessness with the Cambridge plan and had appealed to the stewards, and the result was the new 'substitute' rule passed in time for 1843.

Ironically, Oxford became the first victims in that year when their captain, F. N. Menzies, fell ill after their heat. They rowed their final with seven men and won it, being lucky to get the Bucks station and thus a little help from the Bushes Wind. When the finishing gun fired and the Dark Blue flag was run up the feverish captain was pinned to

his bed in the Red Lion in exasperation, according to a verse by Tom
Hughes, brother of the stroke man:

> Within a darkened chamber,
>   Wrapped in his tartan plaid,
> Fevered in mind and body,
>   Our captain brave is laid.
> To keep him from the river
>   They've ranged stout waiters four,
> And they've barred the windows firmly,
>   And firmly locked the door.

Oxford's supporters celebrated the victory by throwing the toll gate
on the bridge into the river. The authorities were lenient at the next
Petty Sessions.

In 1840 the course had been moved a little downstream to start
opposite the temple on Squire Freeman's Island and finish further
from the bridge, thus cutting out the need to shoot the bridge after
racing. The District Challenge Cup for fours was started that year, and
in 1841 the Stewards' Challenge Cup was introduced as a four-oared
event with the same qualifications as the Grand. The umpire, instead
of riding along on a horse as he had done for the first regatta, was
provided with a crew of London watermen to follow the races. In
1841 his boatmen almost won the Grand when they gave the finalists a
rude shock at Poplar Point. T. B. Bumsted of the London Amateur
Scullers Club became the first man to win the Diamonds in 1844, and
in the following year J. W. Conant of St John's, Cambridge, was the
first man to use outriggers at Henley. Outriggers were the talk of
watermen from the Tyne to the Thames, and one who did more than
wonder at the possibilities was an undergraduate at Trinity Hall,
Cambridge, Frederick Furnivall. With his friend Beesley of St John's,
he spent a long vacation in the mid-forties in a coal shed building
Furnivall's twelve-inch wager boat with outriggers, the narrowest
boat ever seen on the Cam. But there were earlier claims for outrigged
sculling boats on both Tyne and Cam.

It was in 1845 also that a new challenge prize for eight-oars was
introduced, which became known as the Ladies', and also one for pair
oars, the Silver Wherries. There was a dead heat in the Stewards'
between Oxford University and St George's Club, London, which was
eventually awarded to Oxford on the evidence of their coach, Arthur

Shadwell, who covered both posts with his eye. By 1847 there was always a judge at the finish, appointed by the committee.

By the time the townspeople, or rather the tradespeople, of Henley presented an address to the stewards thanking them for their 'unceasing exertions during the last ten years, in promoting the interests of our town', bringing it to the notice of thousands who compensated for injury to their trade, introducing amusement and benefits, etc., the regatta was actually at rather a low ebb. It was probably suffering from too many events for the available support. The District Challenge Cup fizzled out with no entries after 1845, but a sculling event for local amateurs was started in 1846, H. Sergeant being the first winner. In 1847 there was only one entry for the Town Cup and so the stewards hurriedly instigated a Visitors' Cup for four-oars, using the silverware of the District Cup. That year also Mr Donkin of Wyfold Court presented them with a cup which was allotted for the winners of the trial heats in the Grand. By 1850, when the Silver Wherries became the Silver Goblets, there were only fifteen entries in the entire regatta. Then came the year of the Great Exhibition.

On 1 May 1851 the Queen opened Joseph Paxton's enormous glass house in Hyde Park before an enormous concourse of persons amid scenes of triumphant enthusiasm and dazzling brilliance. It was a showcase of machinery and artifacts enshrouded in a palm-lined crystal palace, an amazing collection of engineering wonders and crafts from a country which was the workshop of the world, together with exhibits from overseas. The Queen wrote to her uncle Leopold that 1 May was 'the *greatest* day in our history . . . the *happiest, proudest* day in my life. . . . Albert's name is immortalized with this *great* conception, *his* own, and my *own* dear country *showed* she was *worthy* of it.' The first of six million visitors went to the show and Schweppes the caterer began to sell a million bath buns, and little Woodgate probably ate more than one of them on the day Radley let him out to be taken to London by his parents. There they were pleased to see that Waldrons, who owned the scythe forges in the valley near Belbroughton, won a prize for their products. Waldron paid high wages but their grinders often went to an early grave, the victims of steel dust in the lungs. The Rev. Woodgate tried to persuade them to use respirators, but to no avail.

The country warmed to the diligent pursuance of exhibiting England's glory by Prince Albert, the German who had so enchanted the

Queen in the October after the first Henley that she proposed to him when his visit to his cousin at Buckingham Palace had lasted three days. During the next few years she was persuaded by her husband's seriousness and sincerity in matters of state to allow him an untethered advisory role.

The sporting gentlemen got in on the mood of the Exhibition. *Bell's Life* that year is full of debate and controversy which fairly mask the small number of good amateurs who took to the water. On 5 January a correspondent suggested 'a champion prize of one hundred sovereigns, open to all the world', with two other prizes of £20 and £10 for second and third, should be rowed for on Henley reach on one of the two days of the regatta. He thought an exception might be made to Henley's amateur status for the great year 1851, when so many foreigners would be present, in order that the people of all nations could see England's best amateur and professional rowing. 'As many persons would be attracted by the appearance of the Durham, Manchester, Shields, Newcastle, Bristol, London and Richmond men,' he wrote, 'that the people of Henley would put down something extra towards this race.' He would give £5 and induce his London boat club to subscribe. This was countered by a letter on 19 January suggesting Putney as a better venue because, 'although, doubtless, many of the higher classes would patronize Henley, it would not be a world's regatta for most of the middle and industrial classes would be unable to witness it, whilst at Putney the assemblage would be unprecedented and extraordinary.'

By 2 February Henley had subscribed £55 and London University £25, and, said *Bell's*, the plan 'has met with the approbation of His Royal Highness Prince Albert, who has graciously been pleased to contribute.' On 9 February the challenge was announced and Oxford contributed £60. The townspeople through the brewer Brakspear had asked Stonor, now Lord Camoys and patron of the regatta, to request royal patronage from the Prince. This had been granted in a letter to Camoys from C. B. Phipps at Windsor Castle on 31 January and *Bell's* conveyed the Royal title first in a headline on 23 March.

The professionals, meanwhile, prepared for battle as correspondents suggested funds to transport them from far away to Henley. It was pointed out that it would cost the Claspers £40 for training and passage to and from the Tyne independent of their boat, and that there were steamers about three times a week from London to Maidenhead which could transport boats on their decks. On 2 March Mr Robert Davie, a moulder at Messrs Hawks, Crawshay and Co., was killed at the works by molten metal. He was in training for Henley with the St Agnes crew of Newcastle upon Tyne, about twenty-two years of age, 'a fine, manly-hearted fellow, and the sole support of a widowed mother', said his obituary. By June Richard, Robert, William and Henry Clasper were at the Feathers, Wandsworth, in training for the prize in a new boat from Newcastle and John Salter had built a boat for the Feathers' own crew of T. James, H., J. and G. Salter.

Meanwhile, controversy raged in the pages of *Bell's*. In March somebody suggested a prize for juniors, and on the 23rd a reply appeared saying that, as Henley was the scene of the best, juniors were not wanted, but what about a lightweight prize for men of 9 stone to 9 stone 7 pounds, 'as I think you will find in this year that they intend to astonish the natives'. In the same issue another response said that the letter on the subject of 'A Little Prize for Little Scullers' was a lamentable proof that the writer had not heeded previous remarks.

> The question has been much canvassed and discussed in rowing circles and I never yet heard a decent sculler approve of it. We do not want to see fifteen or sixteen men who will not enter for the Diamond Sculls scampering over the course by themselves. If ownership of a pet is the aim of such gentlemen, they can arrange among themselves to have a quiet set-to on the Lea, or in Bugsby's Hole: but do not let us have them at Henley. Do not let it be said of a man who has as good a notion of sculling as a cow has of a customs officer, 'here is a cup which I won at Henley'. Such a proceeding would be a fraud on the multitude. . . . No analogy exists in this context between gentlemen and watermen's apprentices. . . . The latter are a distinct *class* altogether from watermen, and from that circumstance can well be allowed to contend for a prize confined entirely to themselves, but there is no such distinction between what would be called the 'senior and junior' amateur.

The muffs wanted to exclude the good man and transfer the prize to an individual who 'bears to him the same resemblance that a dray horse does to a racer,' concluded the correspondent Charon.

On 3 March 'A Junior' accused Charon of resorting to abuse, but a note from the editor said, 'We do not see that there was any personality or "abuse" in Charon's letter.'

By June the Great Exhibition in Hyde Park was admitting 70,000 people a day, brought to town by cheap-excursion trains. The assemblage within the Crystal Palace had a countryfied aspect which, *The Times* said, was striking when the scene by which they were surrounded was remembered. No doubt the publishers of the *Bachelor's Pocket Book* were doing a good trade that summer, 'a complete and gentlemanly guide to all the day and night attractions of this great metropolis, accurately describing all the pleasures that possess a "local habitation and name".' Post free 8s 6d. Rowing men, however, were more concerned with the annual fête. Specials brought them to Twyford where, when the station bell rang to announce another train from Oxford or London, there was a rush of touting cabbies offering anything from a four-horse drag to a market cart, and once the fares arrived in Henley they were assailed by the rosette salesmen and the odd old gipsy crone, forecasting their winnings for a piece of silver. 'Names and colours, sir, of every boat entered,' shouted the card salesmen.

Although he had usurped Camoys as chief patron, Prince Albert was not among the throng. One aspect of his un-Englishness, the quality which many of his wife's subjects found difficult to accept, was that he was a not a sportsman. Camoys, now the vice-patron, was not there either: he was attending the court, for on finals day at Henley the steam packet *Vivid* arrived at Woolwich bringing Leopold, King of the Belgians and Queen Victoria's uncle, on a visit to the palaces, Buckingham and Crystal.

The 1850s were a decade of commercialism, years in which, as somebody pointed out, men wore narrow dark clothes and stove-pipe hats which made them look like the very steam engines they were building. There was a dreadful war in the Crimea and then the Indian Mutiny, and both the Iron Duke and the man who painted the elements of the sceptred isle, Joseph Mallord William Turner, died. At Henley there was fun but little of interest in the years Woodgate spent at Radley, except the appearance of Royal Chester Rowing Club in an eight without a keel in 1856. This club, having been formed in the year before Henley started, very much a gentleman's club, came to Henley Royal for the first time in 1855 and won the Wyfolds in a keelless boat named *Victoria*. It was the first occasion that this cup was given for four-oared racing. They won the Stewards' also. Although actually founded in 1838, Chester claimed origins which made the Oxford, Cambridge and London clubs look like whimpering infants, for nine centuries earlier King Edgar the Peaceable was said to have voyaged from his palace at West Chester to the Church of St John and back on the Dee, himself at the steerboard of a crew of eight other kings.

Chester returned to Henley reach in 1856 in an eight-oar built like the *Victoria* by Matthew Taylor of Ouseburn, Northumberland. Taylor had strong views on boat-racing and training: for example, he was once appalled at the thought of any crew in training weakening themselves by washing, and he was much influenced by the Clasper school of professionalism on the Tyne. Clasper had built the first keelless boat there, although Bill Pocock, who coached Westminster School, claimed that he had made one first which Clasper had seen when he was visiting London. Chester looked washed, but rolled their fancy boat prodigiously, slobbering their oars along the water, and then raced off with both the Grand and the Ladies', for good measure finishing as runners-up in the Visitors' and the Wyfolds and withdrawing from the final of the Stewards'. All these crews were stroked by their captain J. B. Littledale, who helped Taylor with the designs of the boats.

Such effrontery from a provincial club caused some revision of the rules. In 1857, the year in which the Great Western Railway opened its dapper little branch line from Twyford through Wargrave to Henley, the Ladies' Plate was restricted to the clubs and colleges of Oxford and Cambridge and the schools of Eton and Westminster. The Visitors' for four-oars had the same restrictions applied, and the Wyfolds was closed to competitors in the Stewards'. The toss for stations was replaced by a draw, and London Rowing Club, formed in the previous year, won the Grand.

By the sixties Walter B. Woodgate reached Brasenose, if not maturity, and he had a most agreeable time. He got on well with 'The Chief', Dr Cradock, who encouraged a relaxed and friendly atmosphere between dons and undergraduates, which was not encountered in all the colleges in Oxford. At University, for instance, screwing-up took place quite often, in which an unpopular don's oak was secured with coffin nails during the night, the prank completed by filing off their heads, thus invoking the use of carpentry to rescue the unfortunate next morning. Cradock was often to be seen watching his college's cricket at Cowley Marsh and, as the sun declined, making his way to the towpath to check on the college eight. Woodgate kept up his daredevilment while making pocket money by writing sermons, a commodity in great demand in such an ecclesiastical town. He sparred with the great Tom Sayers in a tent at Abingdon, not very successfully, and he walked from London to Oxford non-stop for a bet immediately it was laid in a public house. He and the college crew used to take the train to Abingdon and walk back as a training exercise. He got a seat in Oxford's victorious Boat Race crews of 1862 and 1863; he set his dreadful fox terrier Jenny on cats, and allowed her to accompany him to Henley where, although wearing Brasenose colours, she was unable to discriminate between supporters and did a lot of damage to Brasenose trousers on the towpath, a misdemeanour which cost her master at least half a dozen of champagne.

Oxford imposed duty and political activity on its young gentlemen occasionally. Woodgate indulged in the popular vanity of having his room, now on the first floor on No. 5 staircase, pictured with himself and his chief *intimes* posed in it. Champneys, his partner in many races, is there, and Heap, the crack sprinter. In 1863 Woodgate was a member of a crew which pulled the Prince and Princess of Wales up and down the river at the Oxford procession of boats. The royal family was still shocked by the terrible blow of December 1861 when Albert died of typhoid. He had gone to Cambridge in November to admonish his son Edward about his wayward ways, to deliver parental rebuke, and he had caught a chill which turned for the worst. His death had put an end to the heyday of his beloved wife's reign, and she had become a mourning recluse. And in 1863 Woodgate was involved with a Boat Club committee which somewhat reluctantly granted the University Cricket Club their request to wear dark blue at Lord's. Rowing and cricket were the only sports in which Oxford competed with Cambridge, apart from the minor indulgences of rackets, billiards, and Aylesbury steeplechasing, although some undergraduates were talking about starting inter-university athletics.

At Oxford Woodgate played his part in dicing with proctors and porters, and dealt a blow against the Oxford Union and fellow students of doubtful social status by founding an exclusive club, Vincent's. He and his friends objected to the Union's exorbitant terminal fee of a guinea and used to patronize Vincent the publisher's reading room in the High, which was only 13s 6d. Vincent closed his doors in about 1861 and two years later Woodgate hired his rooms and selected forty of his friends to get things started. They offered free beer, tea and coffee, which was a great advance on the Union, and they could get away from all the ghastly dry bobs who patronized the

University Book Club barge, a totally unexclusive affair which opened on Sundays and which the wet bobs resented.

It was '62 which was a fantastic year on the Henley water for Woodgate. He rowed three races on the first day and five on the second, winning the Stewards', the Visitors', and the Goblets with his friend Champneys, but losing the Diamonds in a re-row after finishing the first final in a dead heat with E. D. Brickwood. Before racing started that year he had been involved in dismantling a tradition and preventing an innovation. He was the successful ringleader of an oarsmen's revolt over the arbitrary way in which the order of racing was drawn up. They produced their own programme, which was adopted by the committee after some argument. The committee were at first more concerned with providing the best entertainment for ladies who rose late. The competitors wanted a rest between races, and theirs was a small victory for performing animals.

The innovation was a stand erected at Poplar Point by an enterprising speculator who had leased the meadow there, its effect being to block the view from carriages which parked on the bridge and along the Berkshire towpath just near it. After a boisterous dinner the evening before the regatta the University College eight and the Brasenose four ripped the stand apart with their bare hands, cheered on by townsfolk and watched by half a dozen policemen, who only interfered to prevent the resultant pile of timber being thrown into the Thames.

There were other lively incidents during the sixties. Kingston Rowing Club was causing consternation by recruiting oarsmen from Oxford and Cambridge in May and early June, and they drew Woodgate into their Grand-winning eight in 1865. To put an end to the Kingston Law the stewards ruled that 'no one shall be allowed to row or steer for a club unless he has been a member of that club for at least two months preceding the regatta,' and this was extended to three months after 1866. In that year Woodgate entered the Goblets twice, once with E. L. Corrie as a Kingston entry and once calling himself Wat Bradford with M. M. Brown. He and Corrie won the event but a new rule followed swiftly disallowing assumed names. In that year, of twenty-eight medals offered in eights and fours, twenty-seven were won by Etonians or Old Etonians, and all except two of them had been pupils of Edmond Warre at the school. Memories of Warre and the music of the Thames were kept alive as far away as the Punjab, when in

1865 officers of the Rifle Brigade at Nowshera and Peshawar sang a new song after dinner in the mess. Captain Algernon Drummond had been sent some words about jolly boating weather and swinging together by William Johnson, his tutor at Eton, and a tune for them had come to him, based he thought on a setting for Tennyson's 'Break, Break' by Blockley. He and his brother officers tried it out and got it down on paper, to their great delight.

There were two attempts in the sixties to include canoe races at Henley, but they produced scorn and scant support from the rowing men. Woodgate became the high watermark of the regatta. He had a succession of wins which was second only to that of A. A. Casamajor, one of the founder members of London Rowing Club. By the time he got to the regatta in 1868 he had already sat in ten boats which were first across the line in finals, whereas Casamajor had won sixteen events when he died shortly after the regatta of 1861. His death had caused a flutter through rowing circles at the time, theories being offered about the effect on his health of so much competition, but while controversies about the benefits of exercise grumbled up and down the rivers of England, the regatta at Henley remained in health each year after W. W. Smyth had brought the *Black Prince* there in 1839.

Smyth was now lecturer in mining and mineralogy at the School of Mines, had published a book called *A Year with the Turks* about his travels, and was married to Antonia Story-Maskelyne of Basset Down, Wiltshire. All his crew were alive except for the bow man, Walter Gough, who had died on Boxing Day in the year they had won the Grand, and Charles Penrose who died on 5 May 1868. He had been ordained and became headmaster of Sherborne. Taylor and Lonsdale were also priests, while Strickland, Cross and Massey were barristers, the latter being High Sheriff of Anglesey.

When Woodgate and Scott returned from the great Paris regatta, the one a distinguished oarsman, a spirited demolisher of grandstands and a pedantic seeker of the main chance, the other an observant and careful scribe, destined for Manchester, the most innovative city in the world, there was great controversy about the role of coxswains. There were no rules governing them, and the colleges did not like the advantage which clubs and schools had in being able to use very small boys, who could also double up in events when oarsmen were no longer permitted to do so. This came to a head in 1868 when two clubs in the same heat of the Stewards' found they had the same cox, and the arbitrator ruled that he could cox neither. The Thames Cup was founded for crews not strong enough for the Grand, and the District Goblets was discontinued.

But Woodgate stole the thunder at this regatta. Having spent a good deal of time tinkering with a steering device which owed much to the ingenuity of the men of New Brunswick, he announced that the Brasenose crew in the Stewards' would row without a cox, with himself at No. 3 steering with a wire and lever attached to his stretcher. W. Wightman Wood of University College, Oxford, protested to the stewards on the grounds that there was evidence of intention in the rules that boats should carry coxswains, that it was contrary to the rules of the university boat clubs, that it was contrary to the unwritten general law of boat-racing, and if all these failed, it was contrary to long-established custom. The law was almost certainly on Woodgate's side but the stewards wisely supported the plea of custom, hastily ruling that all eights and fours must use a coxswain. The intention of the regatta was that all competitors should meet on an equality, and the ruling was made a few days before racing began.

Woodgate then wrote to the chairman, Camoys, saying that Brasenose would comply with the condition of starting with a cox-swain but that he would jump overboard directly the race began – as well he might, since the boat contained no fifth thwart. Opinions flew as to the propriety of the affair and Woodgate claimed the precedent of the Seven Oar race of 1843. But it was clear that the stewards intended coxswains to complete the race. Brasenose chose to prove their speed if not to uphold equality or win a cup. A Brasenose man, Mr F. Weather-ley, was found, wrote one newspaper reporter, 'devoted enough to play his Marcus Curtius part' and thousands flocked to the bank to watch the fun. When they could get along the towpath, that was, for a horde of gipsies had pitched their knock-'em-downs in close and dangerous proximity to the horse barrier. The *Field* noted that their ruffianly behaviour and obscene language were most disgraceful in the presence of ladies and advocated that police should keep them from the edge of the river instead of allowing them to hold their revels under the very noses of the high-class company at the great regatta of the 'kingdom'.

As soon as the umpire bade the boats go the gallant Weatherley plunged into the river while Champneys, Rumsey, Woodgate and

Crofts set off in pursuit of Kingston and the Oscillators Club, spurred by the roar of the running crowd. Weatherley had a narrow escape, said the observant man with the notebook, from strangulation by siren water lilies before he struck out for the bank and safety. Brasenose won by a hundred yards and were disqualified immediately.

The year in which Weatherley indulged in his heroic flirtation was also the one in which W. W. Smyth was president of the Geological Society; in which Furnivall founded the Chaucer Society, one of many literary societies which he begat; in which a pregnant English lady, Emily Nickalls *née* Quilhampton, became the first woman to climb Mont Blanc and Mont Rosa in the same week.

4

Mr Punch finds a kaleidoscope with delirium tremens
1901: Health and beauty, slides and swivels,
amateurs and professionals

Anybody who witnessed Weatherley's self-sacrificing plunge in 1868 and the final of the Grand in 1901, where Leander met the University of Pennsylvania, lived through immense change, innovation and excitement, whether viewed aquatically or by a Victorian in the zenith of the old Queen's reign. The railway builders reached every extremity of the British Isles, manufacturing industry continued to grow almost oblivious to the competition that was developing in Europe, across the Atlantic and even in Japan. English agriculture was in deep depression caused by cheap imports from America, Europe and Australasia, all made possible by the great speed of railways, steam ships and the technique of refrigeration. The workers in the fields round Henley, therefore, were not knowing good times, but they could relish the growing imperialism which became a bulwark of lifestyle for all classes. The popular press and the weekly magazines brought news of relatives' life from the many outposts of empire; British ships ruled the seas and outnumbered everybody else's, British telegraphs took the world's pulse frequently and swiftly. At home on the offshore island, religious tests for academic posts at Oxford and Cambridge were abolished and women were admitted. As the ancient universities caught up with the modernity of London and Manchester, the civil-service recruitment was made subject to examination and the politicians set about putting order into municipal affairs.

This was also a period of great expansion for the public schools, supported by the prosperity of the upper and middle classes. While many rowing and boating clubs were started along the rivers and coasts, cricket and aquatics found that they were no longer the only team sports to be taken seriously by spectators. Emphasis on physical recreation for gentlemen amateurs at schools and the concentration of population in industrial towns combined to change the sporting habits of the nation. More and more watermen were driven off the rivers, and while the squirearchy and the wealthy townsfolk continued their indulgence in hunting, shooting and fishing, the working classes could turn only to kickabouts on rare open space or vicarious glory at the Saturday match.

For rowing men the seventies, eighties and nineties held three topics of major interest. Innovations in equipment changed their sport and a more rational approach to diet and fitness dispelled some of the fads which served ill health; the champions of amateurism made their voices heard against the dangers of professionalism; and closely linked with that was the threat of the foreign invader, a problem which caused the erection of the barricades before Edward became king in January 1901. And Woodgate's planning and Weatherley's leap did not go unnoticed. A presentation cup for coxless fours was held in the next year, but Brasenose eschewed the event. Weatherley became a lawyer in Bristol and took to quieter pastimes, like lyric writing. He wrote the words of 'Danny Boy', sung in many a drawing room to the tune of 'Londonderry Air'. Within five years coxswains had been made redundant in the Stewards', Visitors' and Wyfolds, thus leaving them with only the eight-oared events to steer at Henley.

In 1888 Guy Nickalls, whose mother had climbed Mont Blanc and Mont Rosa in the same week of 1868, when Guy was under two years of age, won the Diamonds. On the way to doing so he met W. Sweetman from the Isle of Wight in a heat. 'His sculling was fitted for Southampton Water rather than the Thames,' Nickalls said in his memoir of the occasion.

> Shortly after the start, about half-way up the island, I heard a bang, and a shower of shrapnel fell around me; the balls from his bearings. I offered to start again and he paddled back to the raft and got another slide fixed.

Sweetman used a patent slide which ran on ball bearings, and was not a success, but his quirky invention was only one of many attempts to improve the length of the stroke through sliding the posterior.

In 1881 Bedford School had won the Public Schools' Challenge Cup, started in 1879, by greasing the thwarts of their boat so that they could slide on them. Greasing was a well-known technique. Later a rule was introduced at Henley limiting the width of thwarts in fixed-seat boats to six inches. For senior crews, however, the slide revolution started in 1872 when most boats of London Rowing Club and Pembroke College, Oxford, were fitted with them at Henley. Their quick introduction followed a great victory on the Tyne the previous year by the sliding Tynesiders of Taylor's crew over the fixed-seat men under Chambers. There are references to partial sliding on the Tyne as far back as 1857, but it was in 1870, the year that the leather-covered metal button was developed for oars, that R. O. Birch used a slide successfully in a sculling boat at King's Lynn regatta, and the year before J. C. Babcock organized a six-oar gig for Nassau BC of New York which had wooden frames covered with leather and grooved at the edges to slide on brass tracks.

The trouble with slides was that the friction of the seat caused a lot of hard work for the legs, and it took a long time for oarsmen and coaches to perfect the technique of the leg drive coordinated with the sliding, the combination which brought a huge improvement in the rowing stroke. Because of this they were discouraged for novices for many years, many people believing that an oarsman must start out and learn on a fixed seat. The friction problem was solved gradually: Thomas Farron, an American oarsman, fitted wheels to his seat in 1877, but their size made it run too freely. Eventually slides with two pairs of small wheels on each side were developed, the wheels fitting into travellers.

It was also an American, Mike Davis, who made another innovation. In 1874 he produced a swivel rowlock, and within two years they were used on many sculling boats and sweep oarsmen were experimenting with them. Davis was an untiring inventor and in 1882 and 1883 built boats for Yale which were very long and narrow, each pair of men having a separate cockpit. The crew of 1882 against Harvard set record times for the course, rowing a shuttle-like stroke at which a rate of 44 strokes to the minute was slow, but their cox lost the race for them by poor steering. That of 1883 had a seventy-foot four-cockpit boat with a large windsail on the bow and rated 45 to 50 strokes per minute, but the men came to the race overtrained and the result was a Harvard win by a minute and twelve and a half seconds.

So Henley in the seventies had added interest for the rowing people as well as its usual pleasures for the social gathering that assembled in the town once a year. As *Bell's Life* reported in 1872:

Left and below: Head-gear and foot-wear

The umpire's view. H. Vollmer and T. Keller of Zürich, Switzerland, pass the progress board in the Double Sculls final of 1955. They lost to G. Zhilin and I. Emchuk of Burevestnik, USSR, who are on the Berks station, by half a length

The scene at the finish in 1844 by an artist in the *Illustrated London News*.
He has depicted the race going downstream instead of up

From a painting by R. F. McIntyre of the Public Schools Fours in 1884.
Boaters and houseboats were gaining in popularity, and a steam launch was
introduced for the umpire in 1869. Before that the watermen who rowed the
umpire's boat often had difficulty keeping up with the race

Above: The Island depicted as the Leander enclosure in 1893. Dr Edmond Warre and A. P. Heywood-Lonsdale are the foreground, the eights are those of Eton and Radley, and everybody who was anybody is here for posterity

Below: The Golden Days, a cartoon by Arthur Hopkins from the *Graphic*, 1891

Left and right
Cartoons of Rudie Lehmann and Guy Nickalls by Spy (Sir Leslie Ward) from *Vanity Fair*

Below
The Shoe-wae-cae-mettes. From the left: W. H. Durell, Moses Nadeau, Joseph Nadeau and Stephen Desseau. They were the first American crew to come to Henley, with Columbia College, in 1878

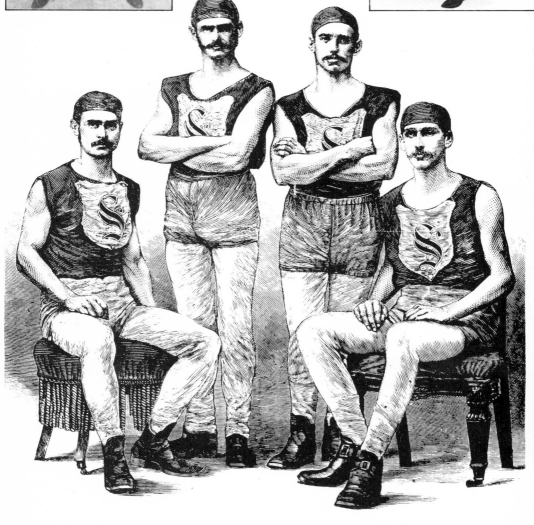

Steve Fairbairn, from the portrait by James
Quinn in 1926 which now hangs outside the
Main Hall in Jesus College, Cambridge

Royal visits
Top: King George V and Queen Mary in the
Maritana, 1912
Above: Princess Elizabeth and Princess Margaret with Sir
Harcourt Gold, Chairman of the Stewards, in 1946

Above: Edward, Prince of Wales, mee
the Stewards in 1921

MARITANA.

Above: Princess Anne in the royal barge with John Garton CBE, Chairman of the Stewards, in 1977. The barge is manned by winners of Doggett's Coat and Badge

Top picture: Princess Margaret returned with her husband, the Earl of Snowdon, in 1964. As A. C. R. Armstrong-Jones he coxed Jesus College, Cambridge, in 1949 and 1950. Here he is shaking hands with Senator Saltonstall of the Harvard '14 crew

Soviet seamen unload boats at strikebound Surrey Docks in 1955. Two days later a Soviet eight was beaten at Henley for the first time. Vancouver RC hit the headlines on both sides of the Atlantic when they led Club Krasnoe Znamia past the enclosure after overhauling them at Fawley. Vancouver eventually lost the final to Pennsylvania

What with the revised code, the introduction of sliding seats, a sweeping disregard of vested interests as represented by last year's holders, the first appearance of the 'travelling telegraph', and what was perhaps the most exceptional feature of all, two days' racing without rain – conservative Henley presented this year a startling tissue of innovations.

The revised code was a change in the rules which prevented a crew which crossed over and took the water of their opponents from being entitled to keep the new station. Now 'each boat shall keep its own water throughout the race, and any boat departing from its own water will do so at its own peril'. Crossing over was permitted, therefore, but if the crew who started on the station came up they had right of way.

The disregard of vested interests referred to the end of the challenge system. Holders of cups were now required to compete in heats, no longer having a guaranteed passage to the final. The reporter was not entirely happy with Henley in 1872, however. The racing was dull.

Why is it [he wrote] that men who are scarcely equal to winning an occasional pot at a third rate provincial regatta should think it worth their while to pay a guinea for the unprofitable privilege of rowing last in their heat for the Diamonds has always been for us a mystery not to be explained even by the inherent perversity of human nature. . . . Is the compilation of a regatta programme such a formidable task that it should occupy the combined inellects of the committee and the printer from 8 p.m. on Thursday to 2 p.m. on Friday? And why should the telegraph be closed at 8 p.m., the very time when its services were most needed?

A reporter's lot was not a happy one.

The seventies also produced interest in the regatta from further afield than had been customary. Dublin University BC entered the Grand, Ladies', Visitors' and the Goblets in 1870. They had borrowed boats and several of them had not sat in a fine racing boat before, being used to rougher conditions near the mouth of the Liffey at Ringsend. They were sick on the crossing to Holyhead and the long train journey left them with little time to spare to prepare for racing. The English critics noted that Trinity College, Dublin, as they were called on the programme, had a quick and firm beginning of the stroke but feathered high. They did well enough to win the Visitors' over University College, Oxford.

More exotic were the first Amercan visitors, in 1878. Columbia College BC of New York and the Shoe-wae-cae-mette crew from

Monroe, Michigan, entered the Stewards'. The Shoes were French-Canadian watermen of slight physique but with remarkable endurance. They could keep up a high rate for great distances and, when pressed, the stroke man, Stephen Desseau, would give a weird yell as he took the rate up to fifty. They were phenomenal champions of the West. In the Stewards' they won their heat, beating both Trinity, Dublin, and Columbia, the latter being fouled by Dublin, and then were rowed out in the final, Joseph Nadeau collapsing and London RC winning. Columbia made amends by winning the Visitors', the first foreign crew to take a Henley pot, and they were the toast of New York. They had brought with them a papier-mâché boat, a popular method of lightweight construction in America, but they actually won their cup in their other craft, a cedar one.

Another witness to the first appearance of Americans was young Gilbert Bourne, at sixteen years hardly believing his luck in occupying the bow seat in Eton's crew for the Ladies' Plate. They had a new and rather flat-bottomed boat with seats centred, designed by their coach Dr Edmond Warre, and used twelve-foot oars. They were a flyweight crew averaging 10 stone 4¼ pounds, and they were rigged in such a way as to enable them to start at 48 strokes to the minute and never drop below 42 over the course. They were beaten in the final by Jesus College, Cambridge, who earlier that day had lost the Grand final. It was a somewhat wide-eyed initiation for Bourne, and a few years later, after sitting in three more Eton eights, he realized that at that time his school crews did not really get much coaching to go with their achievements and that Warre, although by no means complacent, had not examined his own methods much since he first coached crews at Eton in 1861. He started them off well with ten days' work in a heavy clinker boat, himself standing in the stern, and from time to time took them tubbing in pairs with intensive instruction and scrupulous attention to detail, but much of the time thereafter the crews were practising without the watchful eye of a coach.

Against such opposition from Jesus, who had seven Blues or subsequent Blues on board, they had little chance, although they speculated later that if they had had slides longer than their approximate eight inches and if they had studied the art of using them effectively like the metropolitan clubs they saw, they may have done better. But long slides and metropolitan styles were abominations for Warre at that time. The boys travelled to the regatta daily and on the way home dined at Marlow, which was, according to the slight fellow in the bow, magnificent but it was not training. They were kept very quiet until their competition was finished, so they did not see much, but what Bourne remembered was Henley's first taste of the American college yell. The Visitors' final was completed by the chant of C—O—L—U—M—B—I—A ringing out over the Thames.

The Shoe-wae-cae-mettes were no gentlemen and their presence at Henley, unlike the Columbia students', did not go down well if the report in *Bell's Life* was anything to go by. The man from *Bell's*, though, devoted a large part of his report to complaints about the press box, saying that he did not agree with critics that the committee be drowned but hinting strongly that the stewards might like to give him a seat on the launch in future, and he also criticized the appalling conditions inflicted on regatta visitors by the Great Western Railway. But this is what he had to say of the Shoes:

> I did not hear their 'not euphonious yell' so cannot judge of the effect it had upon those were so unfortunate; but I saw them, both ashore and afloat, and I cannot for the life of me imagine however their entry came to be accepted. I can only say that if four Englishmen – who had to work for their living – presuming they could row well enough to stand some chance in this regatta, had entered their names, the idea would have been scouted at once. Their rowing was to my mind execrable, I never saw worse form in any crew having first-class pretensions; 'bucketting' would be a mild term in describing their stroke; the only qualification they possess is their brute strength, and when not too much pressed they rowed pretty well together. Their friends had evidently puffed them up with an undue amount of vanity, and as they made their way down to the starting post, cheered by the crowd on the banks, some of the crew did not receive the plaudits bestowed on them with that becoming modesty which is generally inseparable from true merit.

The entry of the Shoes was refused in the next year on the grounds that they were ineligible under the new definition of an amateur. The threat of professionalism, of competing with people who might race for cash prizes, was the burning topic of 1878. It culminated in a meeting of oarsmen at Putney which in defining amateur expressly excepted anybody engaged in manual labour. The Henley stewards said that for 1879 any entries from outside the United Kingdom must be made on or before 1 March and must be 'accompanied by a declaration made before Notary Public with regard to the profession of each member of the crew', and this must be certified by the British Consul, the mayor, or the chief authority of the locality.

Another Michigan crew fell foul of this rule in 1882, probably unjustly. They were four store clerks from Hillsdale BC whose chief merit was perfect timing when they rowed. They never trained out of the boat and usually smoked until the time they took to the water, but they were amateurs and American champions three times. They had a nasty professional habit, however. They wore silk handkerchiefs on their heads instead of caps. They spent three months in England, won at Marlow, were refused entry at Henley, and only secured one other match, with Thames RC, which was won by Thames when Terwilliger in the bow broke his slide. Their treatment caused resentment on both sides of the Atlantic.

The new rule, though, did not stop all foreigners from competing. It was an attempt to get some navigation into uncharted waters, for the regatta had never thought of itself as an international event. In 1880 the Germania Ruder Club of Frankfurt became the first crew from overseas to enter the Grand. After noting that 'the new regulations which forbade itinerant vendors of fruits, etc., and musicians to wander down the towpath beyond the first meadow made the banks on the Berks side more pleasant than usual,' *Bell's Life* observed that London had more difficulty beating the Germans than was expected as the latter rowed much better than they had done in a match with London four years previously, 'which proves that they are making rapid strides with oarsmanship in Fatherland.'

The writing was on the wall, if only faintly, and worries about the sceptred isle were not confined to sport on the water. At the end of August 1882 the *Sporting Times* published an epitaph which said:

> In affectionate remembrance of English cricket which died at the Oval on 29th August 1882, deeply lamented by a large circle of sorrowing friends and acquaintances. RIP. NB: The body will be cremated and the ashes taken to Australia.

Several strides in organization were made in the eighties. The old committee of fourteen was abolished in 1885 because a committee of management had taken over the running of the regatta in 1881. It was now to be elected annually by the stewards. There were twelve members and in 1885 there happened to be six townsmen and six rowing men, some of whom may have been lucky enough to witness a charming cameo on the bridge when the Radley crew for the Ladies' drove across in a four-in-hand just as the Eton crew approached from the other direction in a smarter coach. They met at the very centre and the two captains exchanged solemn salutes. The Public Schools' Cup was discontinued that year and the Town Cup had been withdrawn the years before. In 1886 the course was changed to start just below the tail of the island and finish at Poplar Point, which was a great improvement, although it still had two bends, one above the island and one by Fawley; but the length was the same and equal for both stations since the start was staggered. The bays on the Berks side had been piled off in 1884 to prevent crews taking advantage of slack water. Now the whole course was piled on both sides and a third day was introduced, so that only two crews need race at a time. The river was getting very full on regatta days, houseboats and launches extending all the way from Phyllis Court to the start.

This was particularly so in 1887, jubilee year, when a large royal party visited the event and fell foul of the luckless Guy Nickalls. In the final of the Diamonds this undergraduate from Magdalen College, Oxford, was being led by J. C. Gardner of Emmanuel, Cambridge, when the swarm of boats round the royal party's launches a hundred yards below the winning post allowed only enough space for the man on the Bucks station to get through. Nickalls, on the Berks station, smashed into the royal party, breaking his sculls and his boat. The Princess of Wales, through Mrs W. H. Smith, sent him a kind, sympathetic note of condolence and trusted that he was not hurt, but the committee never gave him the chance to re-scull the race.

However, Guy Nickalls was not put off winning Henley cups by his royal gaffe. In the years between 1887 and 1897 he won the Diamonds five times and the Goblets six times, three of them with his brother Vivian, who had two other victories in the pair-oared event with his school mate from Eton, W. A. L. Fletcher. Vivian also won the Diamonds once, and both brothers were in winning eights and fours. It was unquestionably their era, and in 1895 their father Tom presented the Nickalls' Challenge Cup as an additional trophy for the Goblets. Tom was most indulgent to his family, which included two other sons. He gave them the best horses to ride, good shooting and a fine education at Eton and Oxford. On the day of his silver wedding anniversary he took his wife and two eldest daughters to Henley, himself wearing a grey frock coat and a matching top hat, and they watched Guy win his first medal in the Eton eight, the Ladies'. The boys received their medals on the lawn of the Red Lion and were driven off in a four-horse brake to the Compleat Angler at Marlow, where their coach, the Rev. Donaldson, stood them a magnificent dinner with champagne cup. They arrived back at school at about 11 p.m. amid the banging of baths outside Etonian windows, cheering, ragging, and general rejoicings. Tom sent his son a present he acknowledged thus: 'I think I shall do as you propose and stand the eight a good dinner.'

The Nickalls brothers epitomized the men who raced for cups at Henley. Well-heeled, physically strong, grounded in the life of ancient schools, colleges and clubs, country houses, city finance houses, the Church or the professions, they led ordered lives and could devote considerable time to their sport. The entertainment which they provided on the water went largely unnoticed by the throng of Victorians attracted to the annual social gathering. Now over eighty houseboats gathered at the regatta, the Oxford colleges bringing theirs down river, the private owners vying for prime spots along the course and busying themselves with guest lists, and making sure that the office of the *Lock to Lock Times* knew where to deliver the next issue as they moved about the Thames from regatta to regatta. Steam launches towed them about, bands played on their decks and in the enclosures of the clubs which took plots by the river. By 1880 *The Times* correspondent, who was a good deal less crusty than the gentleman from *Bell's Life*, was noting that the racing seemed to be taking second place to the procession of pretty dresses which 'might almost vie with the Royal Enclosure at Ascot, except perhaps for costliness'. Competitors were almost becoming a nuisance to those paddling about in small boats, promenading in the meadows, picnicking or sitting down to luncheon or formal tea.

The occasion of Guy Nickall's clash with the royal party, when the Prince and Princess of Wales, the kings of Denmark and Greece, the Grand Duke of Hesse and others took to four steam launches after lunching at Greenlands with the First Lord of the Treasury, the Rt Hon. W. H. Smith, was described by one observer as giving the banks an appearance that might be noticed after a solitary zephyr had passed down an avenue of azaleas in full bloom.

W. D. Howells, an American, visited Henley for a day at this time from Paddington by one of the quarter-hour specials filled with people whom he thought would normally be first-class passengers. What struck him was that the English male was of more striking presence than the American: his impression was that the Englishman kept more of the native priority of his sex in his costume, so that at least at Paddington Station the outward shows were rather on the man's part than that of his demurely cloaked ladies – though the hats which these flowered at top gave some hint of the summer loveliness of dress later to be revealed. Fathers and uncles and elderly friends far outnumbered chaperons, he noticed. He wrote down his impressions of the day afterwards.

The weather had no whims; it was its pleasure neither to be wet nor hot, but of a delicious average warmth, informed with a cool freshness which had the days of the years of youth in it. In fact, youth came back in all the holiday sights and scents to the elderly witness who ought to have known better than to be glad of such things as the white tents in the green meadows, the Gypsy fires burning pale in the sunlight by the Gypsy camps, the traps and carriages thronging up and down the road, or standing detached from the horses in the wayside shadow, where the trodden grass, not less nor more than the wandering cigar whiff, exhaled the memories of far-off circus days and Fourth of July. Our own shore was sacred to barges and houseboats; the thither margin, if I remember rightly, was devoted to the noisy and muscular expansion of undergraduate emotion. . . . There was long waiting, of course, before the rowing began, but as this throughout was the least interest of the affair for anyone but the undergraduates, and the nearest or fairest friends of the crews, I will keep my promise not to dwell on it.

A hand bell announced the impending start of a race and a pistol shot was fired to start the crews. Howells, after a good lunch, was disappointed that the men rowed in their undershirts,

and not naked from the waist up as our university crews do, or used to do, and I missed the Greek joy I have experienced at New London, when the fine Yale and Harvard fellows slipped their tunics over their heads, and sat sculpturesque in their bronze nudity, motionlessly waiting for the signal to come to eager life.

But he found other compensations.

Skiffs and wherries and canoes and snub-nosed punts, with a great number of short, sharply-rounded craft called cockles, very precisely adapted to contain one girl, who had to sit with her eyes firmly fixed on the young man with oars, lest a glance to this side or that should overset the ticklishly balanced shell. She might assist her eyes in trimming the boat with a red or yellow parasol, or a large fan, but it appeared that her gown, a long flow as she reclined on the low seat, must be one of white or pale lavender or cowslip or soft pink, lest any turmoil of colours in it should be too much for the balance she sought to keep.

While all the more delicate hues of the rainbow were afloat on the stream, there was nothing of the kaleidoscope's vulgar variety in the respective costumes, said Howells.

Mr Punch saw things rather differently among the smart awnings and decks of the houseboats and the chinese lanterns of the garden of the Nook, opposite the Red Lion.

> Red Lion crammed from cellar to garret – not a bed to be had in the town – comfortable trees all booked a fortnight in advance – Lion Gardens crammed with gay toilettes – flags flying everywhere – music – singers – niggers – conjurors – fortune tellers! Brilliant liveries of rowing clubs – red – blue – yellow – green – black – white all jumbled up together – rainbow gone mad – kaleidoscope with delirium tremens. Henley hospitality proverbial – invitation to sixteen luncheons – accept 'em all – gone to none! Find myself at luncheon where I have not been asked – good plan – others in reserve! Houseboat like Ark – all in couples – Joan of Ark in corner with Darby – Who is she? Don't No-ah – pun effect of cup. . . .

Mr Howells and Mr Punch and thousands like them enjoyed themselves in their various ways, come rain or shine, while the aquatic world paid considerable attention to training and diet in order to bring entertainers to the throng for those who could be bothered with them. If they cared to look for it, the young men of English schools and universities, the students and coaches of American colleges could, by the closing decades of the Victorian age, find a lot of hints towards their art, many of them unhelpful but many of them conducive to improving performance and comfort. Much attention was paid to the design of boats and equipment, what should be eaten and drunk, what exercise should be taken, and what sort of stroke should be used to best move a boat. Some were outspoken, some were reasonable; some were deadly earnest and many managed to have a good time.

Among the scholars of rowing, for example, was Dr Warre, who ruled at Eton. He had been president of OUBC in 1858 and founded the trial eights and the University Volunteers. In 1860 as a master at his old school he was asked to coach the eight by the captain of boats, R. H. Blake-Humphrey, and did so by daily invitation for the next twenty-five years. His quiet, perfectly pitched voice instructed generations of boys to keep their feet on the stretchers at all times, praised those who applied themselves correctly and refrained from abusing those who did not. The latter would find themselves dropped from the boat. He was elected a steward in 1868 but never really liked the regatta in the years that he turned out a small army of orthodox oars, although he applied his intellectual powers to the definition of the amateur, a topic which smouldered for eleven years until it was first published in 1879. Neither did that event solve the dilemma. Warre also brought his scholarship to bear on ancient ships, oars and naval tactics. He contributed a history of boatbuilding as an introduction to Woodgate's book on boating in the Badminton Library series in 1888, a work packed with sound advice and charming illustrations of river life which gave little hint of the more mischievous side of its author's character.

Younger men, too, were active on and off the water in extending the frontiers of rowing and enlightening their contemporaries. Rudolph Chambers Lehmann for one added sharp wit and prime colour to the kaleidoscope of the era. Born in 1856, he had gone from Highgate School to Trinity College, Cambridge. He was president of the Union in 1876, took a first in classical tripos and became a barrister. He was also one of the earliest editors of the magazine *Granta*, editing it from London with the aid of Cambridge editors from 1889 until 1895. No number ever appeared during this period without Lehmann having written between a quarter and a half of it, poking fun at the Union or poetically recalling heroic aquatic feats. In 1889 he became a contributor to *Punch*, devising series like 'Modern Types', or the 'Adventures of Picklock Holes', and he joined the *Punch* staff in 1895.

Among a crowded social life, attending meetings of the Table at *Punch*, conversing with friends he met at his father Frederick's house, which was a rendezvous of outstanding figures in the world of art and letters, Rudie Lehmann found time to coach Cambridge and then to revive Oxford's Boat Race crews and entertain rowing men at his country house at Bourne End. He published a very good book on rowing in the Isthmian Library series in 1897, which set out to explain what training and style were all about. In the introduction he commended rowing as a noble open-air exercise, fruitful in lessons of strength, courage, discipline, and endurance, and as an art which requires on the part of its votaries a sense of rhythm, a perfect balance of symmetry and bodily effort, and the graceful control and repose which lend an appearance of ease to the application of the highest muscular energy. Much has to be suffered and many difficulties have to be overcome before the raw tiro, whose fantastic contortions in a tub-pair excite the derision of the spectators, can approach to the power, effectiveness and grace of a Crum or a Gold; but, given a healthy frame and sound organs immured to fatigue by the sports of English boyhood, given also an alert intelligence, there is no reason in the nature of things why oarsmanship should not eventually become both an exercise and a pleasure.

Lehmann dedicated his book to the regatta's chairman, Herbert Thomas Steward, who was also chairman of the Amateur Rowing Association and president of Leander club, and he collected for it articles by experts on everything from steering to Australian rowing. He once had a valuable lesson on steering and the coxswain's role from the Rev. Arthur Shadwell, who years before had coached and steered Oxford University by methods which left no one in doubt that he was cock of the boat. Lehmann found that the word 'coxswain' was derived from 'boy', 'boat' and 'swain', thus meaning boat-boy and someone in servitude, but Shadwell and many others did not see it that way. Lehmann met him one day in the eighties at Abney House when the owner, Charles Hammersley, spotted Shadwell sculling himself and his little bag of things down river. Hammersley recognized his Eton chum of fifty years before and called out 'Skum!', whereupon Shadwell recognized his nickname, answered meekly for a king of OUBC, made fast his skiff and stayed for a fortnight.

Shadwell treated Lehmann to a lecture on the decline of rowing. Modern oarsmen were universally of appalling ignorance modified by insane rashness. Style had perished from the land. Where were the polished feathers, the straight backs, the long and massive body-swings, and the crashing strokes of the brothers Menzies and other demigods of the past? Movements fit only for an asylum of the halt and maimed had taken their place. The sliding seat was an invention of the devil and in it was the root of all our ills. Men had forgotten the true science of boatbuilding. They ought to be screwed to their thwarts but instead shuffled to and fro like louts at a fair. Lehmann tried to demonstrate to him how a slide was used, but Shadwell was convulsed with laughter and took his place in the boat and spent five minutes showing the true style, several times falling over backwards because he had failed to adjust the straps on his feet. Too bad he had never been coached by Dr Warre who trained his boys to row without straps, but Shadwell's tour was one of force and Lehmann never forgot it even if he did not agree.

Autocratic coxes were on the decline because coaching by professionals from the coxswain's seat was on the decline, but the job of steering was as important as ever. Another Cambridge poet, Robert Henry Forster, pointed the pitfalls:

> There once was a captain who steered,
> But his second appearance is feared;
>   For two funnies, one whiff,
>   Three fours, and a skiff
> Are said to have quite disappeared.

Lehmann wrote that steering 'is no light task of endurance, self-control, and vigilance to which these men submit themselves, and gratitude should be their portion.' Recognizing that a mere twitch of the hand or failure of judgement could win or lose a race, he offered practical points about how to sit in the boat and use the rudder and emphasized the importance of judging speed and distance when it came to avoiding obstacles, turning a corner, or turning the boat round.

Preparation for rowing had blundered through a maze of opinion since the days of the first Henley, some of it ignorant, some eminently sensible. The conversation composed by Lehmann between two cynics learning the art at Cambridge had good grounds, judging by the published opinions of trainers which they might have come across.

> So they coach us and reproach us (like a flock of silly jays
> Taught by parrots how to feather) through these dull October days.
> We shall never understand them, so we shouldn't care a damn
> If they all were sunk in silence at the bottom of the Cam.

Things were not much fun in America in the early days of the Harvard–Yale matches, for example. Take Wilbur Bacon's Yale crew of 1864, a six-oar. The men rose at six and ran three to five miles wearing heavy flannels on empty stomachs. Before and after noon they rowed, hard, for four to six miles, and they ate underdone meat with now and then a few potatoes or rice, but no other vegetable. They drank small quantities of weak tea. Much score was put on losing weight through perspiration. Because water restored weight the men were given only what they could not do without, and the best trainer was reckoned to be he who could train without water. The absolute limit was one glass for breakfast, two for dinner, and one for supper. The agony of such a course when men were rowing in the hot sun was furthered by the prohibition of baths. Some coaches would permit no bathing for three weeks before a race. Thus the men often came to the race covered in boils. Edward Ferro of Harvard put the blame on the English:

> Having derived our notions of training from an old English book on proper way of training pugilists for battles in the ring, we had only the simplest kind of diet, only three glasses of water a day, no matter how hot the weather was, and no sweets, tobacco, or beer; consequently by the day of the race we were down pretty fine.

Archibald Maclaren took a much more rational view in his treatise on training published in 1866. He was involved in training at Oxford University and selected rowing to examine because he thought it was the exercise most susceptible of being influenced by a judicious system of bodily preparation, 'being at once an art of considerable intricacy, demanding long and assiduous practice, and an exercise of considerable difficulty, involving the possession – although not in equal degree – of both muscular and respiratory power.' The diet tables followed at Oxford and Cambridge and written by various trainers looked considerably more wholesome than those inflicted upon the American students. Maclaren was a sensible and sensitive observer of the human condition. The ordinary agents of health, he said, are exercise, diet, sleep, air, bathing and clothing. And training is to put the body, with extreme and exceptional care, under the influence of all the agents which promote its health and strength, in order to enable it to meet extreme and exceptional demands upon its energies. He reckoned that young men needed only about seven hours' sleep as against the ten hours advocated by many. 'The instant a man is awake, let him get out of bed. . . . Ablutions performed, let him open his windows to the fullest extent.' He condemned the pernicious habit of college bedmakers of pulling the bedclothes a yard too high and folding the overlength back again so that the chest supported twice the necessary weight. He saw that bathing both cleaned the skin and acted as agent of considerable tonic power for the nervous and circulatory systems.

Maclaren's book also pulled together information concerning exercise, rowing and diet from diverse sources. He quoted the research of the Rev. Professor Haughton of Dublin University that the work done per minute by a boat's crew varies as a cube of velocity. Thus doubling the speed requires an eightfold increase in work per minute. The Rev. T. H. T. Hopkins confirmed this by an experiment to calculate the force employed in the propulsion of an eight in racing trim at racing speed by towing a sandbagged eight behind a four, the two separated by a dynamometer – a Salter's spring balance – the four being pulled along from the bank.

Maclaren measured the rate of growth of nineteen-year-olds arriving at Oxford University, and he noted the work of a US Army doctor, W. Beaument, on the digestion of food. It was published in Edinburgh in 1838, two of the main conclusions being that individuals differ with regard to digestion and that the nutritive value of an article of food and its digestibility do not necessarily have a direct relationship with one another.

When it came to specifics Maclaren condemned the practice of eating meat 'as free from the influence of fire-heat as when it was hung in the butcher's shop'. He advocated the principle of little and often when it came to liquids. 'Meet the demand for fluid gradually under extreme conditions,' he wrote, 'like I did when traversing on foot in midsummer some of the hottest parts of Europe where, as the natives complimentarily have it, "everything was asleep or in the shade but dogs and Englishmen".' Beer in moderation is unquestionably a wholesome beverage. Wine if drunk habitually ceases to be a stimulant; let no man, young or old, habitually drink wine; but it can be a restorative from depression and a promoter of sound sleep. And 'distilled spirits, of course, find no place on a young man's table'. They are pernicious to youthful brains. In short, intemperance and self-indulgence are incompatible with health, strength or activity. Tobacco should be forbidden, but one shouldn't change a man's fixed habits suddenly. All medicines are poisons because they change the normal action of some function of the individual. Maclaren's advice was to leave all drugs alone.

I have seen men swallow food with the dull leaden hue of raw flesh with as much repugnance as if they were taking physic, bolting it in pieces with the aid of niggardly apportioned tea. . . . Yet men wonder that on such a diet as this they are assailed by diarrhoea or constipation, that boils rise in groups, that blisters canker into sores, and that wounds do not heal!

And he had a special word for the fad of his day, egg and sherry. Medical men, said Maclaren, prescribe an egg in sherry to patients as being at once a stimulant and nourishment. It has been recommended for men just as they are stepping into the boat. What will happen? The wine acts upon his nervous system immediately, whether beneficially or not is another question. The egg will remain in his stomach as egg until long after the race is over and will aid him no more than if it had been put in his pocket.

Archibald Maclaren made the amateur's lot a happier one by setting out his ideas so well, and they were translated to good effect by people like W. H. 'Piggy' Eyre. He joined Thames RC in 1868, rowing in their scratch eights in March of the next year and running with the Thames Hare and Hounds. His club had its origins in the rag trade, its original members being mainly clerks and salesmen, and there he found congenial company of an enthusiastic set of amateur swimmers, boxers and oarsmen, among whom was G. H. Vize who became heavyweight champion in 1878. Vize and Eyre shared rooms at Putney and were very ambitious; they formed a four for the Wyfolds of 1870, which the club thought was running before they could walk and was thus unwilling to help. They tubbed in the winter at Harry Salter's boathouse at the Feathers in Wandsworth. As soon as it got light enough they would walk to the Feathers at six in the morning and row hard to Putney Bridge, hard back downstream to West London Railway Bridge, back to the boathouse, dive into the barge entrance of the Wandle or into the Thames for a bath, throw buckets of water over each other, eat breakfast of cold meat, stale bread, watercress if available, and two cups of tea, and bustle off up to town for a day's work. For lunch they would have what the Artful Dodger gave to Oliver Twist, a quarter pound of ham and beef shoved into a penny roll, and often they would row again after work in the dark before another al fresco bath and supper of steak or chop with green vegetables if they could get them, and a pint of strong ale. After that they would go for a walk at top pace to harden the muscles of their legs, between four and six miles. Two or three times a week they'd go boxing in the evenings. Eyre then used to sit up until 3 a.m. with his law books on several nights a week, something which he did not recommend for training, but he had the ability to sleep or wake up any time he felt like it. There was no let-up at the weekends either. Saturday would be a row to Richmond or Westminster, and Sunday training in sculling boats. At that time there was an unwritten law at Thames that you did not row on Sunday. By this programme they made their peace with Thames by winning the Wyfolds for the club pretty easily, and the training methods of Eyre, Vize, Slater and Lowe were adopted effectively for the next fifteen years.

In the seventies they put out eights as well as fours. During Henley they stuck to the same diet: stale bread, chop or cold meat for breakfast, with two cups of tea and never coffee; meat, vegetables or salad, stewed fruit or tapioca for dinner, with a larger version for supper. They had strong beer for dinner and supper, no potatoes, butter, or cheese. Port was occasionally allowed, and by the eighties a bedtime cup of gruel or barley water had been added. Eyre and Labat had a small Apollinaris before retiring if they felt tied up. They would get up between 6 and 7.30 and run a hundred yards at top speed. At eleven they would train in the eight and in the four afterwards, and repeat the outings at 5 p.m., and after supper take a walk of three or four miles, usually to the Five Horseshoes at Remenham. There they had a go at winding the bucket in the deep well, five minutes being a good time but the record being nearer three-and-a-half. Then they would walk home to bed, singing through the woods in four-part harmony.

Their efforts paid off in 1876, when they won the Grand. They had the Bucks station, the 'Oxford Mixture' of Brasenose and University colleges had the centre, and Jesus, Cambridge, were on Berks. Eyre wrote an account of it for Rudie Lehmann.

> Hastie the stroke went off in a way that, I think, fairly paralysed the other strokes for the moment. What the rate was I do not know, but we all took it up magically and I never in my life, before or since, felt a boat jump under me like it. We cleared the 'Mixture' in less than two hundred yards, crossed them, and after a sharp tussle got the Jesus water, and were right under the Berks shore opposite the farm. That is so. The Almanack and steward's book are wrong. Then Cabby came at us with a rush. The yells of the Cantabs to him to bump us I shall never forget. Hastie jerked his head towards Bucks and Safford, losing his nerve, lugged his right string so hard that he ran us across Oxford again, and nearly fouled the bushes just above Fawley Court boathouse. When we got straight, we buckled to, and came

across gradually, got their water again a little before the corner, and won (easing down a bit, but mortal licked at the finish) by nearly two lengths. Oxford were a long way astern; but, as Jesus eased off, so did we. In the last hundred yards they came up with a rush, and overlapped the Cambridge men just on the post. I believe Bankes is under the impression to this day that they would have won if it had been a little further. Lord, what an evening we had after it.

They lodged at a house in New Street. Two of them lived in the summer house at the end of the garden, including J. H. H. Moxon, with whom Eyre used to go rambling to study plants and birds. But on this night Hockin leaned on a rose bush while making an impromptu speech, and he fell behind it with only his feet remaining to represent him. Two of the party were dispatched to the Red Lion for more supplies of champagne and a bottle was smashed as one of them reeled round a corner. He stood solemnly still, wine running down his leg and the neck of the bottle in his hand and said, 'Stop a minute. I heard such a strange noise just now, like a 'splosion.' Very poor stuff, said Eyre, but it made us laugh at the time. One does not win the Grand Challenge Cup every day, one does not indeed. At 2 a.m. the luckless Hockin awoke from the rose bush and roused the household to let him in.

It was in the year of Piggy Eyre's success in the eight that Edwin Dampier Brickwood wrote a little book called *Boat Racing* in which he paid tribute to sense in preparation for the sport, albeit with a typical prejudice to enforce his views:

The art of training has been rescued from the depths of empiricism in which it was too long suffered to dwell, and in which the ignorant prejudices of illiterate professionals, who at one time usurped the coaching of amateurs, purposely kept it. At the present time it is conducted on the principles of commonsense and hygiene, and so far from being a mystery is now nothing more nor less than an adhesion to a few simple rules.

And simple rules, of course, gave way to straightforward indulgence in times of celebration, like the bump supper or the winning of a pot. Witness Leander Club's festive evening after taking the Grand in 1892 when they sat down on 11 July at the Ship, Greenwich, to a twelve-course table that groaned with all that was fashionable in the land.

Despite health and efficiency in rowing, rumours persisted in aquatic circles about the dangers just as they had done in 1839 when Smyth

The Ship. *Greenwich.*

The Leander Club.

WINNERS OF THE GRAND CHALLENGE CUP, HENLEY, 1892.

LE MENU.

TORTUE CLAIRE   TORTUE LIÉE
GRAS VERTS AU JUS

CARRELETS ET SAUMON SOUCHÉ
WHITEBAIT
RISSOLES DE HOMARD   PETITES SOLES FRITES
BOUDINS DE MERLANS À LA DANOISE
ANGUILLES ETUVÉE À LA BORDELAISE
TRUITE GRILLÉE, SAUCE À LA TARTARE
OMELETTE DE CRABE AU CORDON BLEU
WHITEBAIT À LA DIABLE
SAUMON À LA NORVÉGIENNE

TIMBALES DE FOIE GRAS À LA LUCULLUS

EPAULE D'AGNEAU GRILLÉE ET HARICÔTS VERTS

CANETONS RÔTIS ET PETITS POIS VERTS

ASPERGES EN BRANCHES GLACÈ

CAILLES RÔTIES ET SALADE À LA FRANÇAISE

JAMBON GRILLÉE Á LA DIABLE ET SALADE DE TOMATES

GELÈES AU VIN   MERENGUES À LA CRÊME
DAMES D'HONNEUR

POUDING À LA NESSELRODE

GLACES
CRÊME AUX FRAISES   EAU DE CITRON

Dessert.

PÉCHES, NECTARINES, FRAISES

W. T. BALE, *Proprietor.*

LUNDI, LE II JUILLET, 1892.

and the crew of the *Black Prince* first went to the regatta. Except for
the odd individual case, however, nobody produced much evidence
for oarsmen enjoying only a short, active life. In June of 1869 Warington Smyth, hero of the first Grand, wrote to Dr John Morgan of
Manchester Royal Infirmary:

> I rowed in *every race* during my whole career at Cambridge, not even
> omitting the Autumn Races between Captains and University, and for two
> years in the University crew on the Thames against Leander and Oxford.
> My University Crew of 1839 was reckoned the best, for many years before
> and after. . . . I have led an exceptionally physically active life, and having
> to inspect the Prince's minerals in Cornwall, do my climbing on the ladders
> for one or two hundred fathoms against most competitors, whence I trust I
> am sound in wind and limb.

This was in response to Dr Morgan's questionnaire sent to all Blues
from 1829 to 1869 to take the pulse of their health. Morgan published
the results in a fat volume in 1873 to deal with the rumour still
persisting that the participants in an Oxford-to-London time trial had
met untimely death through their exertions. He exhaustively inquired
into the 294 men who had made up the fifty-two crews which had
contested twenty-six races to 1869, finding thirty-nine of them dead
but the great majority in excellent health. The sample, said Morgan,

> would not, as is too often the case with athletic champions in lower walks
> of life, be ensnared into the convivial excesses of decayed prize-fighters or
> the pot-house orgies of acrobatic heroes. . . . Bodily culture is the antidote
> to insanity and the recreations of casino and music-hall.

Twenty-one years after the questionnaire, on 19 June 1890, Sir
Warington Wilkinson Smyth died while sitting at his desk at 5 Inverness Terrace in London. He was seventy-two and was marking exam
papers for his students at the School of Mines. For seven years he was
chairman of the Royal Commission into accidents in mines and the
means of preventing them, and he had been knighted after the completion of this task in 1887, Jubilee year. He was survived by his wife,
Antonia, and two sons.

Morgan's painstaking inquest did not blow away the shadow of
death. Lehmann found it necessary to include a chapter in his *Rowing*
called 'A Recent Controversy' in which he examined the cases of three
young oarsmen who had died recently. Messrs Cotton, Stretch and
Balfour had all been coached by Lehmann and he produced as much

evidence as he could to show that they had been perfectly fit when under his care and that the sport had not contributed to their deaths. Cotton died of consumption, Stretch of appendicitis and blood poisoning, and Balfour of influenza and blood poisoning. Lehmann was partly writing in response to a controversy in the *St James's Gazette* about the health of athletes, which centred mainly on oarsmen and from which sprang a subsidiary issue. Mr Sandow, eminent weight-lifter and 'modern representative of Hercules' as Lehmann put it, claimed that, if given Cambridge men to train according to his system, and provided they also spent some hours a day getting instruction in rowing, he could guarantee a crew the like of which had never before sat in a boat. His method entailed allround muscular development which could be accompanied by complete permissiveness in matters of eating, drinking and smoking. Lehmann did a hefty demolition job on Sandow and illustrated the chapter with pictures of a variety of oarsmen's torsos, claiming that they were eminent performers, weeds and giants all.

The decade of the 1890s saw the regatta progress with its social whirl depicted faithfully by the artists of the *Illustrated London News* and other journals. The stewards tinkered with the course: in 1891 arrangements were made to measure boats and draw the longer ones back at the start to make the bows level and ensure that each crew rowed the same distance. In 1894 they reserved the right to hold preliminary heats where events were heavily subscribed, instead of extending racing to a fourth day. They brought their laws of racing into line with changes made by the Amateur Rowing Association. And in 1897 they made minor adjustments to the course to eliminate the advantage of the Bucks station in a prevailing south-westerly wind. In the previous year the town council agreed to the lease of the enclosure near the Nook on the Berks bank to Leander Club of Putney for £25 per annum. The condition for the club was that it must spend £2500 for the erection of residential and boathouse premises for completion by 24 June 1898. This was duly done and in the same year significant events took place in Ireland. The Rowing Club and the Boat Club at Dublin University amalgamated to move from Ringsend to a new boathouse at Islandbridge, on the Liffey to the west side of the city. Upholding the honour of Old Trinity was to get new strength with good training water away from the roughness of the Irish Sea. Rowing at sea, incidentally, was of some interest in England. In 1885 Willy

Grenfell stroked an eight across the Channel, though the crew almost went under two or three times, saved by their foresight in carrying jam pots on board for use as bailers. Criticism of the foolhardiness and ill-preparation of this expedition brought letters to the *Field* describing the circumnavigation of the Isle of Wight in a day by a four-oared galley, a distance of about seventy miles and three times as far as from Dover to Calais. This was followed by an account by A. B. Mayhew of Ventnor RC of how he had sculled round the island in pretty bad weather one day in 1881.

The stewards made another significant move in 1893 when they entered an agreement with the Union des Sociétés Françaises des Sports Athlétiques exempting their clubs from sending entries before 31 March, which was to be the pattern for agreements with other governing bodies of the sport overseas. The political question in rowing which obsessed the late Victorians was the definition of an amateur, and closely bound up with this was the threat of foreign invasion, no less, which was fanned on the English side by confused notions of nationalism. If men do not row 'they will in many cases do a great deal worse: hunting, riding, steeplechases, tandem driving, billiards, and the like' was the comment of J. F. Bateman back in 1852 when he was lamenting 'the unfair clamour which is sometimes raised against boating and boat clubs'. The supporters of all kinds of sports believed that they were germane to the English character, that they were a key factor in the society which had become the richest that the world had ever known, and there was a strong tendency to suspect that foreigners were not always capable of subscribing to notions of fair play.

In the year after Woodgate and Weatherley tested the stewards' judgements by defying them and setting further changes in train, the Earl of Wilton published a work which glorified hunting, horse-racing, coursing, archery, yachting, rowing and music as the native pursuits of the English which gave them a freedom unique in the civilized world. A guest in one of the hundreds of houses which catered for the leisured classes might have plucked it from the library and read passages like this:

> In tracing out this general outline of the nations of Europe [which all lived under varying degrees of tyranny or at least non-participation in the affairs of government by even the likes of Wilton] my object is to show that where there is no spirit of freedom there is no inherent love of sport

nor of manly pastimes; and the converse may with equal truth be asserted, that where there is no inherent love of sport and manly pastimes, there can be no spirit of freedom; or it would seem impossible but that some of these nationalities would have ere now asserted their personal rights and achieved their own liberty.

[He goes on:] Let us take the great powers of Europe; in none of them is the liberty of the subject understood as we understand it. The conscription, the passport system, the gagging of the press, entire exclusion from all share in the government of their country. These conditions, all of them utterly at variance with freedom, are at the root of Continental legislation. The youth are educated under a military system which takes every school and every individual of that school under the control of the State. Not a game nor a pastime exists. . . . Gymnastics are encouraged on the ground, like boxing among the Russians, that they fit the youth better for soldiers, for which all alike are intended. Where is the courage that would excel in the hunting field? Where is the daring that tempts the yachtsman to brave the ocean's storm? These are elements that form the character of a free people, for which, if we look to the Continent, Echo may indeed answer, Where?

Echo, though, was not so smug. There was a good deal of courage, skill, energy and daring bound for the waters of Henley reach, both from the dark lands of Wilton's Continent and the country cousins in the Americas, and a taste of what was to come occurred not many years after the publication of his oeuvre. If Wilton had been around when the Shoe-wae-cae-mettes and the Hillsdales appeared, he would have seen the English sporting character at work. Before the deluge, however, came the question of the laws, the great amateur-versus-professional debate which Rudie Lehmann ably observed from his stance as a writer and a coach.

From the 1820s onwards there had been trouble at both Oxford and Cambridge about the use of watermen to coach crews, and in particular to cox them. Lehmann himself was coached by a boatman in the Kingston RC crew with whom he rowed in 1880, but the practice was dying out because of the decline in numbers and influence of the professionals and because of opposition to the notion of mixing professionals with amateur crews. The old dictum

> Row and work, boys of England, on rivers and seas,
> And the old land shall hold, firm as ever, her own!

was adhered to only on a basis of class. In 1878 a meeting of prominent oarsmen was held in Putney, at which the representatives of most of the prominent clubs wrote the following definition:

> An amateur oarsman or sculler must be an officer of Her Majesty's Army or Navy or Civil Service, a member of the Liberal professions, or of the Universities or Public Schools, or of any established boat or rowing club not containing mechanics or professionals; and must not have competed in any competition for either a stake, or money, or entrance fee, or with or against a professional for any prize; nor have ever taught, pursued, or assisted in the pursuit of athletic exercise of any kind as a means of livelihood, nor have ever been employed in or about boats, or in manual labour; nor be a mechanic, artisan, or labourer.

This, as Lehmann pointed out when discussing it, was not much good as it attempted to define both who is an amateur and who is not, and many cases are not covered by both approaches.

But it was also based on the notion, not with reason to many, that artisans gain a physical advantage over gentlemen amateurs when it came to muscular contest because of the bodybuilding which may ensue from their work. Lehmann exploded that theory by pointing out that bodily labour of another sort is more often than not a disadvantage to the intending oarsman. Skill, quickness and precision count more than mere muscular strength unless the latter is acquired by oarsmanship.

In the next year the Henley stewards had a go at a definition themselves, coming up with a negative one which was more explicit:

> No person shall be considered as an amateur oarsman or sculler who has ever competed in any open competition for a stake, money, or entrance fee; who has ever competed with or against a professional for any prize; who has ever taught, pursued, or assisted in the practice of athletic exercises of any kind as a means of gaining a livelihood; who has been employed in or about boats for money or wages; or who is or has been, by trade or employment for wages, a mechanic, artisan, or labourer.

As the stewards were drafting their rules, the London clubs set up the Metropolitan Rowing Association so that they could form representative crews from among their members to race against foreigners and colonials in challenge matches on the Thames, for there was fear that there might be a crisis in the future if a club like London RC could not boat a strong enough four from within itself to repel boarders.

In 1882 this association became the Amateur Rowing Association, extending its borders and setting itself up as the governing body of the sport. It established its own definition of an amateur, brought up to date in 1894, and drew up rules of racing to be observed at regattas, though Henley never came under its jurisdiction. The definition was very similar to the stewards' version, the main difference being that steerers were referred to specifically as coming under the rules, that people who were or had been engaged in menial duties for wages were disqualified, and that anyone disqualified as an amateur in any other sport was disqualified. Lehmann argued that the ARA, by reading its amateur definition alongside its rules of racing, which said that no mechanics, artisans, etc., might compete in a regatta under ARA rules, had, in limiting its definition of professionals to those who earn their living in or about boats, created three classes of oarsmen – amateurs, non-amateurs who were not professionals, and professionals.

Before this revision of 1894 the 'manual labour' bar led to trouble. In 1890 the National Amateur Rowing Association was set up by clubs who were not happy with such a clause. The NARA's rules were otherwise very similar to the ARA's, but the revision of the ARA rules in 1894 did nothing to heal the rift, and the minority voices on the ARA, which included Lehmann's, got nowhere with their objection to the discrimination against artisans, mechanics and labourers who in everything bar their means of livelihood could meet the terms of competing as an amateur.

And at Henley, as the century drew to a close, there were many who were very suspicious of the amateur status of the foreign and Empire invader. Rudie Lehmann was troubled greatly by this also.

Dr Warre fails to repel boarders
1901: Foreigners fail in the Grand while oarsmen rout the Little Englanders

The great attraction of the regatta of 1901 was the University of Pennsylvania, the latest challenger for the Grand from overseas. In 1900 the Club Nautique de Gand of Belgium had lost to Leander in the final. The *Field* reported the arrival of the Philadelphians on 22 June:

> The University of Pennsylvania eight reached Henley shortly after midnight on Wednesday, having travelled by special train from Birkenhead. The *Waesland* in which they crossed the Atlantic from Philadelphia arrived at Liverpool on Wednesday afternoon, the weather having been fine during the voyage, and the crew in good health. They have brought two paper boats with them, fitted with seats which slide up a slight gradient and are fixed down the centre of the craft. Swivel rowlocks are used, and the oars are rather short and heavy, with small handles and very broad blades. . . . Naturally after their voyage they did not show to advantage, but making all allowances the impression was that they were not more formidable opponents than those who have previously come from America. They are not quite together, and seem to miss the first part of the stroke.

When the *Field* had reported in March that Pennsylvania were coming the Rowing Editor pointedly remarked in print that if Laffan's Agency telegram giving the news of the entry was true and Pennsylvania had declined the stewards' invitation to send a four as well as an eight, then this looked like Henley touting for foreign entries. This brought a sharp riposte from H. T. Steward, the chairman, who wrote that Henley had never touted for foreigners and had not done so for Pennsylvania.

The Times reported that Pennsylvania

> sends a crew which has been very successful in America. The men, though not specially big or heavy, are very muscular and in splendid condition. Their style of rowing is quite contrary to the approved methods in this country, and is much the same as all the crews which have come from the USA. Their stroke is very short and there is no body swing. . . . Their system of training is also opposed to that in vogue in this country, in being on teetotal principles. They are allowed no liberty, and are kept to their quarters almost as strictly as prisoners.

And the *Field* had dug out an unusual problem for the Americans.

> As Ellis Ward, their professional coach, performs his duties in America from a launch and cannot ride either a horse or a bicycle, they were in some difficulty as to how they were to receive instruction. This has been overcome by the SS *Hibernia* being brought into service, and all the coaching is done on the reach below Temple Island.

The regatta rules forbade launches on the course, but an Englishman took pity on Ward's difficulty, got permission for him to use a boat well away from the course, and secured the use of the *Hibernia*. This was Theodore Andreas Cook, who was the captain of Radley who saluted Eton on the centre of the bridge in 1885, and by this time interrupted his career as a journalist on the *St James's Gazette* to act as timekeeper at Henley. To do this he invariably wore a panama hat, won in a bet off Joseph Pulitzer, the American newspaper proprietor, who had employed Cook in the nineties as tutor to his son Ralph. Cook had had a marvellous few years taking Ralph to St Moritz and other fashionable resorts of Europe, where they tried their hands at skating, curling and the Cresta run, and then he had got involved in journalism through Pulitzer. At one time Pulitzer's *Sunday World* published a full-page picture of Cook stripped to the waist and sitting on an old copy of the *Century Dictionary* on the platform of a railroad station, where with the aid of the station broom he was captioned as: 'English university man showing details of his college stroke. No relation of Bob Cook of Yale. Says our boys will never beat it.' This was part of Pulitzer's successful circulation war on the New York Sunday paper market, and reflected great public interest in the different 'strokes' of college crews.

Anyhow, Cook did Ward a favour by finding the *Hibernia* for his use, and he went along on some training outings for the ride. To his great surprise Ward hardly said a word except to whisper hoarsely through his megaphone when Cook went to the stern of the launch to talk with some American friends who were aboard. Cook found out later that Ward thought his passenger had been specially delegated by Leander or some other English club to tell them what Ward said and impart to them the secrets of the 'Pennsylvania stroke'.

Pennsylvania's quarters were an inn on the top of Remenham Hill, an important location for them because Cornell and Yale, both recently in Henley, had stayed in houses near the river and complained of the effect of the enervating valley on their performance. Ward may have had his suspicions about the likes of Cook, but his crew were careful to do their practice in the open, giving out the time of every trial, in order to conduct themselves well in English eyes and avoid the criticism levelled at their predecessors. Anglo-American relations in sport had not been good, particularly in 1895 when a London athletics team in New York accused the Americans of packing their team by producing two, three or four runners to compete with each of the English competitors. In the same year Lord Dunraven, challenging for the America's Cup in *Valkyrie III* against Mr Iselin's *Defender*, accused the American spectator boats of interference, and the challenger of putting ballast aboard the *Valkyrie* during the night. He retired after the third race, all of which caused fury in New England.

In 1895 also, at the start of a heat of the Grand, Cornell went off and Leander did not, the result of a misunderstanding. The umpire Willan had his eyes wholly on his visitors to see that they got fair play, so he told Theodore Cook afterwards, and he did not hear the Leander cox say 'No' in response to his 'Are you ready?' The wind was blowing off the Bucks shore and the Leander men's pleas with it. One or two of them took a stroke as Cornell streaked off along the island, while the rest sat still expecting Colonel Willan to call the Americans back. Eventually they were too far ahead to be recalled, and Cook blamed the fact that they did not stop on their professional coach, Charles Courtney, for they would only take orders from him. They were accused by the English press of shamefully violating the traditions of the course by not stopping and offering a re-start. They did not allow a decent show of courtesy to interfere with their speed as a crew. English justice was done in the next round when Trinity Hall of Cambridge pulled past Cornell at the Mile Post and got a verdict of 'Easily' after the American crew broke up in disarray and exhaustion by the time they reached Phyllis Court.

Cornell first acquired a bad name in England because of the exploits of their Stewards' Cup four who were defeated in the first heat of 1881. When students and faculty gathered in Ithaca to see their men off to catch the National Line's *England*, all good wishes went with them for their European tour – Henley, the Metropolitan regatta at Putney, a race in Vienna for a prize of $1000 against the Austrians! None of them could have suspected that the medical student in the stroke seat of the four, John N. D. Shinkel, had been in negotiation with a saloon keeper in Ithaca by which he would win the first race in the Visitors' and then lose subsequent races, the conspirators gaining a large sum at long odds.

The first thing that went wrong for Shinkel was that the new committee of management decided that the rule compelling foreign entries to be made by 1 March must be enforced. Cornell had sent a cablegram to the regatta on 25 May saying 'Cornell University fours entry Visitors' and Stewards' delayed through misunderstanding. Will you accept now? Passage engaged for Saturday next.' The crew arrived and tendered formal entry on 15 June, and several English clubs petitioned the stewards to let them row, with support from the press. By the casting vote of the president the stewards overruled their management committee and allowed participation in the Stewards' but not in the Visitors' on the grounds that they were a university crew and not a college one.

The *Cornell Era* reported that the press of England and America almost universally denounced the stewards' action.

> We cannot expect fair play from the *New York Herald* as its aquatic department is run by a Columbia man. Our president Andrew D. White has certified that all gentlemen including the substitute are members of the Cornell boating organization, in full regular standing, and are amateurs.

The *Saturday Evening Herald* said:

> The stewards of Henley regatta seemed extremely anxious to avoid competition. On two distinct occasions they have treated American entries in a very shabby manner – making regulations without giving due notice thereof, and tricks of that kind. American oarsmen can outrow the world today, and only want an opportunity to prove it.

The *New York World* believed that 'Britannia rules the wave at Henley but only because she will not waive the rules.'

After this Cornell were knocked out of the Stewards' by finishing third behind London and Thames. Piggy Eyre of Thames remembered that well, because in the morning his eight got knocked out of the Grand by London in a gruelling race, and he and the stroke of London, Frank Playford, lay exhausted on the lockers in the boathouse a good half hour after everyone else had left. Playford and Eyre turned out for a heat of the Stewards' and just below Remenham Cornell and London fouled, and they all went back for a re-start. Cornell got an early lead but were overhauled by the others. To make up for not starting in the Visitors' they arranged a private match against Hertford College, Oxford, on the following Saturday. Hertford had won the Stewards' and had an easy victory after the Americans hit the bank twice. At the Metropolitan regatta they were again defeated by London and Thames, one newspaper claiming that Cornell could have got a better place 'had the stroke oar done his duty'. For all that, they were gaining on Thames towards the end of the race.

And so to Vienna, where, when the crew had set up a lead of four lengths over Vienna Rowing Club after a mile on the Danube, Shinkel slumped over his oar. A doctor on the bank examined him and unhesitatingly pronounced him fit, and his colleagues accused him of feigning a faint and selling the race. There had been little harmony outside the boat for the whole European trip, Shinkel attempting to take over the captaincy and management of the crew from the appointed manager, Chase. The editor of *Sports-Zeitung* in Vienna told the crew that he could give them evidence that Shinkel had sold the race, there being a discrepancy of 1500 florins in the rowing club's accounts. Accusations began to appear in the Ithaca papers as well, and the students had a miserable journey back home via England as they watched Shinkel sleep on his purse at night and failed to get explanations from him about various meetings before they had left for Austria which now looked suspicious. And so they returned to a New York autumn of discontent and messy argument.

Shinkel was but a ghost for the 1895 crew from Cornell. As they lost to Trinity Hall supporters of both crews took to vulgar chanting, 'Cornell! Cornell! I yell Cornell!' being met by 'The Hall! The Hall! I bawl The Hall!' In that year Nereus Boat Club of Amsterdam

University became the first foreigners to take the Thames Cup. In 1896 Yale got a better reception than Cornell. W. L. Alden in *Pearson's Magazine* said:

> I am glad to hear that Yale University intends to send a crew to Henley, for the Yale men know how to row, and are free from the delusion that the main object of rowing a race is to win a prize. Unfortunately that delusion is rather common among American sportsmen. The Cornell men were a prey to it when they rowed over the course last year without an opponent. From their point of view they were right. They were declared to be the winners, and that seemed to them vastly preferable to being beaten in a fair race.

Bob Cook brought Yale to Henley. In 1873 he had spent three months on the Tideway and at Oxford and Cambridge and taken some of the ideas he saw back home. He grasped the essence of fixed-seat sweep-oared rowing, strove to make a race between Harvard and Yale over four miles the climax of their rivalry on the water, saw the value of developing a broad base of oarsmen at American colleges, and advocated the introduction of the amateur coach to hold off the artful tricks and jerky strokes of the professional scullers.

He was not successful in all of these things, particularly the last. At Henley in 1896 he introduced more length and stride into his crew during their three weeks of practice under the critical eyes of the English. They were beaten by Leander, but Cook, like Courtney before him, returned home with a few more ideas, and a trend developed in America for adopting, or at least adapting, the English style. Despite their fate at Henley, Cornell and Yale were riding a crest in the United States, particularly at Harvard's expense, and in the autumn of 1897 Rudie Lehmann arrived on the Charles River to try and put things right. Harvard rowing was in crisis and Francis Peabody suggested that his old friend at Trinity should be asked to come and coach. At the time Lehmann was finishing coach for Oxford's Boat Race crews and had coached the recent Leander crews, including the men who sent Yale packing at Henley and those who had been left on the start by Cornell. And Lehmann was a true gentleman amateur, living up to the reputation by refusing remuneration for his labours, which pleased the president of the college, Dr Charles W. Eliot.

In two seasons Lehmann achieved much, though not quite in the expected direction. He coached in autumn and returned when the ice melted in spring, leaving the men in the meantime to their old methods of rowing machines, practice tank, weights and running. The condition he had made was that he could only teach the methods he knew, so the crews were Anglicized, rowing in boats which were side-seated, allowing longer oars inboard and outboard, had fixed pins or tholes instead of swivels, and slides of sixteen inches, shorter than those to which they were accustomed. His every move at Harvard was followed by the press, particularly the campus newspaper, the *Harvard Crimson*, and rowing quickly gained in popularity. What he was trying to do was to introduce some of the life he had known all the year round at Cambridge, England, to Cambridge, Massachusetts. While many American critics derided the Englishman's ways, both Courtney and Cook welcomed his presence. He urged the students at Harvard to set up a Union similar to that of which he had been president at his *alma mater*, he addressed the Harvard alumni of New York making only modest claims for his 'new stroke' and appealing for funds for a new boathouse, and he attended a dinner in Washington laid on in his honour for his services to rowing and amateur sports by Teddy Roosevelt. He visited Groton school and a fifteen-year-old wrote home to his parents: 'Mr Lehmann, the English coach, gave us an informal talk on rowing. . . . As you probably know, he is about the greatest authority on rowing in the world.' His name was Franklin Delano Roosevelt.

Neither of Lehmann's two Harvard crews distinguished themselves against Cornell and Yale. But in the following years his achievement in uniting the factions at Harvard, and re-introducing fun to the Charles River, began to pay off. There were trial eights, the men were allowed calves-foot jelly and sherry while cooling off after a row, and the college and its schools and classes could muster twenty eights by the time Lehmann had finished. He acquired two prizes himself, an honorary degree bestowed by Dr Eliot for bringing 'the best traditions of manly sport to Harvard from a sister university', and a fiancée, Alice Davis of Worcester, Massachusetts, who was tutoring his friend Peabody's daughters after a thorough grounding at the nearby Radcliffe College. He had turned forty and was thinking about expanding his bachelor's house at Bourne End to cope with family life. In the year that Rudie and Alice returned he made his last appearance in Marlow RC's eight, and he gave the club a racing eight as a present.

In 1897, Lehmann's first season at Harvard, there was more trouble with foreign professionals. Edward Hanlan Ten Eyck, christened Edward Hanlan after a famous Canadian professional, won the Diamonds in record time of eight minutes thirty-five seconds for Wachusett Boat Club of Worcester. But he came to England with his father, who coached him, and they fell foul of Henley's customs. Son and professional father were even seen dining with some English professionals.

Ten Eyck was fortunate to have got to Henley at all. A four from Winnipeg were having difficulty with their amateur status because the stewards spotted that one member, Osborne, had spent a short time four years previously working in a lumber camp as an inspector and accountant. After submitting letters from his doctor and his former employer, the Winnipeg secretary wrote to J. F. Cooper, the Henley secretary:

> Should your committee still be of the opinion that Mr Osborne is not eligible we would ask your consideration for our position caused by the great distance that separates us, and request that you will kindly cable the following message – 'Galt, Winnipeg. Unsatisfactory,' in which event we will reluctantly write to you withdrawing our entry, otherwise the crew will leave here on the 1st June.

Winnipeg came, beating Utrecht and losing to New College, Oxford, in a semifinal. Ten Eyck's entry in the next year was refused.

The *Field*, the country gentleman's newspaper, was by this time the most prominent rowing paper since *Bell's Life* had capitulated to the *Sporting Chronicle*. In 1896 it ran a leading article advocating that Henley be closed to all foreign crews on the grounds that it was unsuited as an international occasion. It had been founded as a British regatta, a meeting place between colleges and schools and a few other like-minded clubs and was just another date in the oarsman's calendar, whereas aliens thought of it as the major objective for the year in the absence of an international regatta. Thus the competition, argued the *Field*, was unfair, for the British took the sportsmanlike view that the regatta was a meeting of old friends, not a place where special measures had to be taken to defend certain trophies.

The Pennsylvania oarsmen, or at least their managers who looked after them on Remenham Hill, were probably aware of this widely held attitude. Their countrymen had had a rough time over amateur status and Henley's code of behaviour. They were anxious to meet Leander in the final of the Grand, and were under no illusion that Leander was merely another club who happened along to see their friends. Leander crews had had mixed fortunes, but it was well known that the club recruited almost exclusively from the best oarsmen at Oxford and Cambridge, a policy which enabled them to put together very strong eights almost at the last minute, only three weeks before Henley, and to defend the honour of old England.

In April, shortly after Penn had announced they were coming, the *Field* ran a long leader advocating that British crews prepare to repel the invader and again deprecating the effect that foreigners had on the regatta, imposing unfairness on British oarsmen who might like to enter for more than one event. In the spring the Americans announced the setting-up of their own Henley on their Thames River, Harvard, Yale, Cornell, Penn, Columbia and the Boston clubs all being involved. An ex-president of OUBC wrote to the *Field*:

> After many years' trial and failure to give satisfaction to the oarsmen of England as a fair course for their skill, culminating on the last day of the regatta in 1900 in really drawing lots or tossing up for all the challenge cups – for the Berkshire boat had no earthly chance – it is much desired by nearly the whole rowing community that in the first year of our King and of the century the alternative course may be tried, or that we may revert to the old line, finishing near the bridge.

In June of 1901 the Amateur Rowing Association committee presented a silver cup to Rudie Lehmann on his retirement as honorary secretary. A famous oar-maker, E. Ayling, died at Brighton just before the regatta after a long illness. The usual crowd flocked eagerly to the regatta once more, leaving the London of the new King by the specials from Paddington, taking their minds off the war, but being unable to ignore the daily column of casualties, deaths and illness from South Africa. Some clutched the very first edition of the *Tatler*, a new society and dramatic paper, Henry Irvine and Ellen Terry were playing in *The Merchant of Venice* at the Lyceum, and Sarah Bernhardt was in *Tosca* at Her Majesty's, and Charles Hawtrey in *The Man from Blankleys* at the Prince of Wales. Major-General Baden-Powell was suffering from the effects of malaria which he contracted on the west coast of Africa. There was a huge military exhibition including tableaux of British and French army types at Earl's Court, and a huge naval exhibition at Crystal Palace.

You could hire single broughams fitted with india-rubber tyres. A crop of wine and spirit merchants were given royal warrants. The *Lusitania* ran aground before dawn in fog at Seal Cove, Newfoundland, and 500 Montreal-bound passengers were taken ashore. Geo. Wright and Co. had upwards of 200 billiard tables in stock from 50 to 200 guineas. There was anxiety in Simla on account of the lateness of the monsoon.

The man from the *Pall Mall Gazette*, the London evening paper, turned out for a dip on 4 July.

> A plunge is the rightful beginning to the orthodox Henley day [he told his readers]. Most of the crews came out about ten o'clock for gentle exercise. On the towpath I made an heroic attempt to interview a member of the Club Nautique de Gand. It was not altogether a success, because his English was on a level with my French, and the curious sounds we produced in trying to become intelligible to one another made the two boats within earshot row away in a hurry.

His later dispatch said:

> It is a glorious midsummer day. Only the gentlest of zephyrs stirs the flags into life. The scene is absolutely perfect in its gorgeous beauty. The trains from town are filled to overflowing. The landing stages above the bridge look like Southampton docks on a busy day. To get a family party, with its impediments, safely on board demands the training and organizing ability of a transport officer. Still, it can be done as the continuous procession of boats pouring through the arches of the bridge proves. . . .

By half past eleven there was a fringe all the way along the booms dense enough to give Leander a rousing cheer as they paddled to the start. The Americans' reception was no less hearty.

> Mr Fuller, who came over with the Philadelphians, told me that they came over to row Leander, and not the Belgians. They want to take the Grand away from the holders, and no one else.

The following day was cloudless and shimmering and the man from the *Pall Mall Gazette*, refreshed from his morning plunge, watched the Belgians mournfully packing up their boat as the crowds gathered for the finals. The boat

> after the manner of Kipling's mountain gun is built in three bits. It was rather a melancholy sight, like the coffining of their high hopes and gallant ambitions. The Belgians are a very hardy and workmanlike crew, and insist on doing all the work that concerns their boat with their own hands.

So the boys from Philadelphia met the men of Leander – C. D. Burnell, the strongest sweep in England, Dudley Ward, C. J. D. Goldie, Etherington-Smith and others. The Americans led for the first part of the race, fell behind, came back at Leander, and lost, amid a scene of enthusiasm 'that has rarely, if ever, been paralleled at Henley'. The American Society in London gave both crews a complimentary supper at the Cecil Hotel on the 25th, and Dr White of the university gave a speech which expressed the visitors' cordial feelings towards the regatta.

After that the rowing world spent the rest of the year in politics. On 6 July the *Pall Mall Gazette* published a letter from 'A Woman'.

> Sir – let me lift up a voice which was drowned in the vulgar carnival of heartless and overdressed women – I blush for my sex – who were flirting and eating strawberries and cream while the Empire was burning in South Africa. Every pop of corks drawn from bottles of champagne sounded to me like the knell of England's fame. It was not, however, against this ostentatious display of wealth – drawn I have no doubt from South African mines – by callous pleasure-seekers that I wished to protest. My mission to Henley, I need hardly say, had no connection with that so-called sport, which appeals to the basest love of brute force in its most revolting form, and excites the passion for ascendancy which will ere long leave England where Babylon and Rome are left. I went to distribute leaflets demonstrating the heartless brutality of my country, denouncing the corruption of its Ministers and the outrages of its khaki-clothed butchers (how much more sincere was the cruel red of the blood-stained mercenaries in former days!).
>
> And what was I destined to witness in prosecuting my thankless and fruitless errand? Let me tell you. Eight poor lads from the great Republic across the Atlantic bending, beaten and exhausted, over their oars! Was there any sign of sympathy in that mob of 'smart' people for the vanquished? No, men and, I am shocked to say, women – to outward appearance delicately nurtured – went mad with the lust of ascendancy. They cheered and exhibited every token of exultation; and I thought of the poor lads in that boat – who had left mothers and sisters in America and I knew, as if I could read their hearts, that there was branded there an indelible hatred of their conquerors, and of the unsexed women who gloated over their defeat. I looked into the future, and I saw a progeny of stalwart Anglo-Saxons breathing the free air of a Republic, growing up with feelings towards England which will yet bear a bitter harvest.
>
> That is the result of your Jingo craze for 'supremacy'. This pride with the defeat of your rivals is inconsistent with the elementary principles of

Christianity: it encourages those passions which, in the noble words of your one genuine humanitarian, is 'making South Africa a hell-upon-earth'. That is what you mean when you recall not with shame and remorse, but with a degrading pride, the saying of the Duke of Wellington that the battle of Waterloo was won on the Playing Fields of Eton. And at Henley one understands. – Yours, etc.

Was this undergraduate impersonation or the real thing? It was difficult to tell, but it brought an expected response. On 9 July 'Slowboy' wrote:

Sir – with reference to the letter headed 'Henley 1901' may I suggest that it was rather inconsiderate of you not to add an editorial footnote to explain that the letter was intended to be humorous. Personally, I had to read it through twice before I realized that it was really a joke, and I am sure that many of your readers, more hasty than myself, must have missed the point entirely. – Yours, etc.

The editor's note under this said: 'We are sorry, but the joke did not seem to require annotation' and was followed by a letter from 'Another Woman'.

Sir – let me also lift up a voice, which was nearly drowned at what a malicious female (?) calls that carnival of heartless and overdressed women, Henley 1901. I blush for my sex. My mission to Henley – please accept my assurance – was to have a jolly good time; to share if possible in that magnificent power granted to all true-hearted English men and women, for seeking relaxation from a gnawing trouble – in this case prolonged by the unyielding and unrighteous mind-rulers of the ignorant Boers and renegade cosmopolitans still foolishly opposing 'The Empire' in South Africa. How the American oarsmen – praise them – will laugh when they see 'A Woman's' (?) letter! It has been predicted that when English national games cease to interest the Briton the race will cease to be 'supreme'. When! The games of our Empire's youth build up the brain, let us remember, as well as the body. On again reading over 'A Woman's' letter, I once more, in her own words, say 'I blush for my sex,' and I blush for her the more because she expresses such thoughtless thoughts against the country she considers good enough to live in – Yours, etc.

The English did not, then, lose their sense of humour even in the face of alien invasion at Henley and troublesome Boers in South Africa. The Philadelphians went off to race Dublin University at Killarney, where they won easily, but not before a question was asked in the House. Mr Murphy inquired of the Chief Secretary for

Ireland whether he was aware of the Pennsylvania-versus-Dublin race in July on the Lakes of Killarney and if, in view of the fact that this event would cause a number of visitors from America and other countries to visit Killarney, he would give directions to the police authorities at Queenstown and elsewhere to desist from asking the names and examining the persons and luggage of such visitors under the plea of searching for arms. Mr Wyndham replied that arrivals at Queenstown were politely invited by the constabulary to give their names and destination. The police did not examine persons or passengers' luggage.

Foreign invasion was the issue that really came to a head after the defeat of the students from Pennsylvania. As soon as the regatta closed there was a renewed campaign by respected rowing figures whom the Americans called the 'Little Englanders' to impose a ban on foreigners. Dr Warre, the headmaster of Eton, wrote to *The Times* reiterating that the amateurism of Henley was threatened by the stewards' acceptance of foreign entries. 'If the result of Friday's race had been different,' he said, 'whatever we might have thought we could not utter our thoughts without inviting the disagreeable retort that we did not know how to take a beating.' He said he had nothing but admiration for the Americans who came to Henley at great expense. But without going into the larger argument over the very desirability of international contests in sport, 'I most earnestly desire that our amateur oarsmanship may be preserved from the deadly inroad of professionalism, which is already making a business of so much that ought only to be pleasure, and threatens to crush the life out of the sports of "merrie England".' Let us restrict our Henley pots to the United Kingdom and set up a proper international regatta elsewhere, if that is thought desirable.

C. J. Bristowe of Trinity Hall was quick to reply. He pointed out in a letter in the *Field* – from which the *Field*'s aquatics man heartily disassociated himself – that it was good for oarsmen to have foreigners at Henley because, for example, while Americans could learn about English training methods, the English could learn a lot about American scientific methods from them. Had the Grand Challenge Cup ever been intended to be restricted to domestic crews? The stewards probably never thought about it, but how could they be expected to bar foreigners after letting them compete for so long? Would they let the standards fall? Would they keep colonial crews out? In any case, did not the press overemphasize the Britain-versus-foreigner aspect of the clashes, and was not the ARA formed for the purpose of producing crews if necessary to beat foreigners? And should not the stewards consult them about the problem? The Americans, who were not consulted, could point to the fact that every college crew of theirs beaten in the Grand or the Stewards' had not met equal competition as Leander crews were national in all but name.

John Edwards-Moss in a letter to *The Times* used precisely this argument to support the ban on foreigners. The grounds of this well-versed critic were that the Henley course, although admirable for a regatta, was not reliable enough to produce fair conditions for international competition, and that the Leander–University of Pennsylvania contest was representative neither of university rowing nor of national rowing. That is, their status was unequal. He made the assumption also that Penn spent their whole season training for this one competition.

By this time W. H. Grenfell MP had proposed a motion for a special general meeting of the stewards that

> this meeting, . . . while fully prepared to promote the establishment of an international regatta upon a proper course and under suitable conditions, is of the opinion that Henley Regatta does not provide either a proper course or suitable conditions for international competitions.

He then proposed amendments to the rules which had the effect of restricting entries to the United Kingdom, and for the Goblets and Diamonds to British subjects domiciled in the UK.

Battle raged in the pages of *The Times* and the *Field*. Dr Warre agreed to second Grenfell's proposals and a third steward, Rudie Lehmann, the ex-Harvard coach and ex-secretary of the ARA, expressed support. So did Woodgate, president of Kingston RC. The ARA had been opposed to foreigners at Henley in the past, maybe because it saw the possibilities of a new international event on the Thames. Now it brought Grenfell's motion to the notice of its leading member clubs and suggested that they might discuss it and make their opinions known. Eventually a long and lucid article in the *Fortnightly Review* by Theodore Cook set out the arguments. He ranged through the foreign successes and failures and pointed out that only four foreign crews had won cups at Henley. They were the

Dutch sculler Ooms (1892) and the American Ten Eyck (1897), neither of whom Cook considered to be proper amateurs, the Columbia four who won the Visitors' when it was an open event in 1878, and the Nereus BC eight which took the Thames in 1895. And was our rowing at its last gasp? 'Does the whole scheme of British oarsmanship depend upon the perpetual presence in this country of certain ounces of inscribed silver?' he asked. There had been many attempts to wrest Henley's pots from us, all of which had failed, and furthermore the ARA had dropped its original aim of forming representative national crews. Meanwhile, there was growing interest in international regattas in Europe, there being events in Hamburg and Amsterdam, and had not an English crew defeated the world in Paris in 1867 before this argument had arisen?

Furthermore, Cook outlined the difficulties of starting an international regatta which Woodgate was so keen on. Would foreigners come to it if they had other opportunities abroad and if they were told in no uncertain terms that they were not wanted at Henley? The iconoclasts had ranged far and wide, suggesting abolition of the Thames Cup, a special cup for foreigners at Henley after which the winner would race the Grand winner over the championship course, criticizing the Americans for training too much and the English for training too little. Lehmann wanted to leave the colonials eligible, which Cook applauded, but he thought Lehmann's view of Henley to be a pleasant picnic rather than a regatta for first-class racing.

> If Dr Warre's restrictive principles are carried a little further I see no reason why Henley in time becomes a quiet little gathering of stewards' friends to whom a tasteful selection of family heirlooms can be annually distributed, without too much exertion on the part of the recipients at the time or previously.

He dismissed the argument that multiple entries were threatened by foreigners. There was little to be said for the pot-hunter. If one horse wins most of the races, he asked, is this proof of strength of the sport? And the participation of overseas crews had encouraged the stewards to improve the course, even if this process could be carried further. The adherence of the American system to professional coaches might be regrettable, but it would take a long time to change it, and in view of that should we deny ourselves twenty years of American participation? Cook summarized his opinion of building a barrier round Henley: 'An English crew which cannot beat all comers under present conditions for the Grand Challenge Cup does not deserve to win it.'

On 22 November R. G. Gridley, secretary of the ARA, forwarded the results of the members' canvass on Grenfell's proposals to J. F. Cooper, the Henley secretary. The stewards' special general meeting took place shortly afterwards and the *Field*, a little mournfully, reported the proceedings. The Cambridge college captains and others voted unanimously against the proposals, the committees of Twickenham, Royal Chester, Molesey and Leander clubs all declared against Grenfell, some unanimously and some by majority. A meeting of forty-five at Kingston voted unanimously against, presumably without the attendance of their president, Woodgate. London RC polled all its members by post and voted 280–92 against Grenfell, and at a meeting in Thames the vote went 125–38 against Grenfell. Only OUBC supported Grenfell, but with a sting in the tail – 'Committee decide against foreign entries provided they can row other than Henley.'

The stewards at their meeting considered an amendment moved by Colonel Makins 'that in the opinion of this meeting it is inexpedient that any alteration in the rules of the regatta be made at present.' After protracted discussion Colonel Makins's motion was carried by nineteen votes to five. For once the *Field* did not add its opinionated rider. The stewards, and the leading rowing men, agreed with Cook's estimation in the *Fortnightly Review* that

> so far foreign entries have neither been invited nor discouraged. To say that they must be done away with now because the founders of the regatta never thought them probable may be compared to abusing a railway train because there were no steam engines in Eden, or to complaining of a clock face because the hands have moved from 1839 to 1901. Henley has never been 'constituted'. It has – like all our best institutions – grown gradually from precedent to precedent into the regatta that we know.

6

Bob Herrick's Bostonians have a champagne party
1914: Americans storm the citadel after a royal
occasion

When Robert F. Herrick shepherded his Harvard crew on board
the White Star liner *Olympic*, sister ship of the ill-fated *Titanic*, on 20
June 1914, the argument about foreigners at Henley was quieter in
the rowing clubs and in the papers but was still being played out
dramatically on the water. Grenfell returned to the attack in that year
in his chapter on rowing in *English Sport*:

> The greater the competition, especially if international rivalry be added,
> the greater the danger of sport becoming professionalized. Amateur row-
> ing in England has hitherto been remarkably free from this spirit; it has
> been pursued as a sport and a recreation, and valued as an end itself by
> those who love hard physical exercise, healthy emulation, and generous
> good fellowship.

Viewed from the early years of the reign of King George, the
nineties looked like the golden age of English rowing. Eton had
established unrivalled superiority among the youngest competitors
and spread tentacles into the universities and the metropolitan clubs.
They reached the final of the Ladies' Plate twenty-one times between
1878 and 1913, winning it fifteen times, and between 1896 and 1905
Leander won the Grand eight times. It was after that that foreigners
began to run off with the silverware in earnest, Belgian crews taking
the Grand in 1906, 1907 and 1909, and Sydney Rowing Club, on
their way to the Olympic Games, winning it in 1912 before the eyes
of the King and Queen and Princess Mary. The Club Nautique de
Gand had first come in 1900 and the home crowd little suspected the
danger as they put their boat in the water, took off their trousers to

reveal that they were wearing shorts underneath, tossed their cigar butts into the Thames and rowed off for a practice wearing sock-suspenders.

Before the Edwardian era was out the writing was being applied to the wall by several hands, Piggy Eyre remarking that 'undoubtedly the Tideway rowing clubs had a very uphill and ceaseless struggle against the forces of ease and enjoyment which had so insidiously encroached on the battlefield of British manliness.' The Rev. Dr Warre, the architect with R. S. de Haviland of the Eton way of rowing, had retired as headmaster in 1905 and been elected provost. He delivered weighty lectures to the OUBC at their time-honoured temple of rowing, the University Barge, which were published in 1907 under the title *On the Grammar of Rowing*, in which he pointed out that although great changes in boats and their fittings had taken place in the last half century, the art of rowing was still the same, full of manly endeavour, full of self-sacrifice, full of delight. . . . Theodore Cook applied his intense chronicler's mind to the attributes of those who became eminent in the sport. They were, he decided, the simultaneous call made by training and racing both upon the highest physical capabilities and upon those qualities of head and heart which manhood most rightly values.

> The fact that a man's individual excellence was almost worthless unless it could be subordinated to the harmony of the crew was a great incentive to combination, comradeship, to a friendliness that began in the mutual trust of human endeavour, and lasted, in many cases, through the less persistent but more irritating tests of afterlife.

Few rowing men disagreed with him, even if they were less inclined to savour their sport with a furrowed brow. While the provost of Eton was lecturing the undergraduates of his *alma mater* on Accidence Part I and II and Syntax, fresh air was breezing along the distant Cam, largely at the insistence of a big and strong Australian, Steve Fairbairn. He was born in Melbourne in 1862 into a family of powerful brothers, their father being a Scot who was playing the fluctuating market of sheep stations and silver mining. At Geelong Grammar School Fairbairn was a superb allround athlete – footballer, cricketer, runner and oarsman – and as a teenager he was fascinated as two of his elder brothers returned from their time at Jesus College, Cambridge, flushed with their successes at the traditional

English rowing style. Each had controversial arguments with the locals and each was converted to Australian style. Fairbairn himself went to Jesus in 1881, his first exploit being to paddle a canoe from Putney to Henley in twenty-three hours for a £1 wager if he could do it in under twenty-four hours. He never got his £1, but he had sent his clothes on ahead by train and turned out at the regatta in a top hat and frock coat, which was definitely not the form in those days. It was now eight years since boys at Radley had been allowed to wear straw hats to cheer their crews at Henley, leaving their tall hats at school, though the change there had been accompanied by considerable protest from some quarters. A friend from college lent Fairbairn some slacks for the regatta and shortly afterwards he and his cousin, F. W. Armytage, walked to Inverness wearing slouch hats and knickerbockers and covering a great many miles each day.

Fairbairn was a popular man at the college. When he went up to get his law degree at the Senate House there were over a hundred men imitating Jesus cocks a-crowing and the applause deafened him to the words of the degree. He won the Wyfolds in 1882 and the Grand in 1885 in Jesus crews and the Stewards' for Thames in 1886.

After the win of 1885 the coach, Tom Hockin, went off to Marlow because he was afraid the police would single him out as a rowdy. Sure enough, he was arrested next day and accused of throwing a horse and cart off Henley bridge, which pleased him greatly since he had not done it.

In 1904 Fairbairn returned to active coaching at Jesus and his influence began to spread along the river, perhaps because he had time for getting the best out of men rather than for seeking the best men. He believed that rowing should be done easily, that if something could not be accomplished in reasonable comfort it was not worth pursuing. 'There is a boat. There is an oar. Move the boat. Your natural way will be the best way.' That was his maxim, one among many, and his influence quickly put Jesus back near the top of Cambridge rowing.

Fairbairn met Robert Henry Forster, a scholar of St John's, who took a first in Classical Tripos in 1888, and in 1910 they founded the Forster–Fairbairn Trial Pairs. Forster had been a powerful Lady Margaret man, but he put down the lighter side of his sport for the readers of the *Eagle*. He wrote wonderful stories about the conversation between the college boats after their day's exertions and deduced his own principles, for example, for pair-oared rowing:

> Keep your hands and tongue steady, your temper cool (the splashing will probably prevent any other part of you from becoming overheated), and divide the responsibility of making the boat roll with the give-and-take impartiality of a boundary commission.

Forster put forward a romantic definition of rowing which he admitted was vague but which must have brought some of the more pompous gentlemen down to earth: 'Seeking fame at the end of an eight-foot spruce.'

The ideas inspired by men from Jesus took time to spread, but they certainly caused excitement. For example, Magdalene College were on an upward graph on the Cam and they planned the season in the Lent term of 1907 with relish, according to the secretary George Mallory.

> What great things [he wrote in the minutes] are now expected of this Jesus method of rowing! The style of the captain, the style of the secretary, the style of the stroke, all imaginable styles except that peculiar to Mr Rogers, all are to be blended in an homogeneous, ergocosmic device, the ingenious and possibly ingenuous Quintessence of a Facile, Indefatigable Compendium. We are to have a Jesus coach. Goldsmith has said: 'God will provide. But alas, how fickle, how selfish the Theocracy!' A fortnight has passed, and still no god to coach us. And so perforce we must go to the Hall, and get some sturdy unintelligent to 'bid him forward, breast and back as either should be', and teach us to shove it along by sweat and swearings, with all the horror of the ancient Swinck Misspent. And yet when he is secured he makes us row not a whit differently from the elegant, divine way, the way we rowed at Henley. He is none of your cursing, blustering, hell-for-leather, body-swing-overdone-at-all-costs, stupendous-recovery fellows at all. He is shy and rosy-cheeked, modest as any maiden, and makes a considerable effort to be sensible when sober and obscene when drunk. And so we become a very decent crew and go up three places.

Magdalene's enthusiasm was the more remarkable because a few years previously the college had a reputation for affluence, not rowing prowess. It was said that six or eight pairs of hunters were an almost daily sight and that no undergraduate ever dined in hall on the occasion of the Cesarewitch, the Two Thousand or the One Thousand Guineas.

At the start of the twentieth century Henley decided that foreigners were here to stay but the regatta still championed amateurism. A special stewards' meeting in December 1902 decided that

> no eight-oar, four-oar, or pair-oar crew shall be allowed to compete if, within four weeks prior to commencement of the regatta, the crew shall have been coached – or controlled – by any person not considered an amateur . . . under the general rules.

An attempt the next spring to extend the rule to scullers failed, but there were no American crews that year to race or to witness the publication of the labour of love compiled by Herbert Thomas Steward, the chairman, *The Records of Henley Royal Regatta*.

That same year, though, spirits ran hard and high, this time for the Irish. Trinity College, Dublin, met Magdalen College, Oxford, in a heat of the Ladies' at eleven o'clock in the morning of finals day. They lost narrowly and one of their men vomited for two hours after the race and had to be doped with brandy for their final of the Thames Cup. Mick Leahy, one of the crew, recalled that they were a sad and sorry lot as they were driven up to the start in two one-horsed phaetons for the five o'clock final against Kingston. After a gruelling three-quarters-of-a-mile Kingston cracked up and Dublin won easily, and the Leander crew, who had won the Grand, helped them from their boat and said that if the Trinity men cared to join their club they would be glad to have them. 'If we cared!' Leahy said. 'There was no greater honour we could desire.'

The Dubliners were coached by Rudie Lehmann among others, and they had to keep their wits about them during their long training rows from Islandbridge to their old rowing grounds at Ringsend, carrying their boat round the weir and then rowing under the bridges to Dublin Bay.

> When the lads of the village saw us coming [said Leahy] they lined the bridges and dropped anything from pebbles to brickbats on us as we shot the bridges. Down at Ringsend we realized what our forefathers had had to contend with, rough water, planks, dead rats, and big ships, or at least big to us in an eight.

One of their coaches, Andy Jameson, sent them a case of champagne and that night the crew did not know much of what happened on earth. Leahy and Arthur McNeight, the number four man, determined to put out all the lights in Henley High Street. They took one side each and each had two crewmen to hoist them up the standards to the gas jets.

> We had nearly completed our mission [Leahy recalled] when the Henley police got into action, but we got the last two lights out, leaving the street in darkness, and then ran. I have painful recollections of scaling a high wall studded with glass, which removed the seat of my trousers and a largish portion of my tail. Arthur, the long-legged devil, escaped unhurt.

In 1904 W. G. East, retired sculling champion of England, was offering his formula for maintaining the country's supremacy with the spruce in an advertisement. 'For rowing men I know nothing better than Oxo for building up and stamina. I recommend it to all whom I train. It keeps them fit and prevents staleness.' There still remained staleness about the politics of the sport, however, particularly after the regatta of 1905. Vesper Boat Club of Philadelphia sent an eight for the Grand who were tainted with the brush of professionalism when they arrived. They were defeated by Leander in a semifinal, and the American press attacked the management of the regatta after the crew had returned home. The stewards investigated the allegations and announced in 1906 that the National Association of American Oarsmen (NAAO) had failed to inquire properly into the status of the crew and that its members had received money payments and that the cost of sending them to England had been met by public subscription. The committee banned Vesper and the members of the crew from further entry at Henley. W. A. L. Fletcher tried to get all American crews banned, but failed.

The way back for Americans was laid open fairly quickly, however. In December of that year it was decided to include the Henley definition of an amateur in the agreement which must be signed by national bodies who sponsored crews from overseas. The only countries left in the club after this ruling were Canada, Belgium, Germany and Holland, but the NAAO was able organize itself and comply by the time Herrick's men from Harvard were ready to set sail in 1914. At least by having one rule for everyone, instead of relying on each country to write and enforce its definition of an amateur, the system became less open to wrangling, but many foreign entries were dismissed along the way and maybe a few pots kept at home.

Before Harvard's attempt to set right the Grand defeats of those Americans who had gone before, there were some strident and jolly times. In 1906 they sent their eight over to race Cambridge on the championship course at Putney, a meeting arranged hastily at Harvard's request after they had defeated Yale. F. L. Higginson fixed it up by visiting his old Harvard coach, Rudie Lehmann, at Bourne End, and Lehmann gathered the scattered Light Blues and got both crews training on 6 August, a month before the date of the fixture. A race between the winning Boat Race crews from opposite sides of the Atlantic had occurred only once before, between Oxford and Harvard in fours in 1869, after which Charles Dickens had addressed a splendid gathering at a dinner in the Crystal Palace.

The English papers recorded every blink of an eye of both the crews in 1906 from the moment they took to the water at Bourne End, and all the oarsmen had a capital time with their host and hostess. Since his marriage Lehmann had built a library and a children's wing on to his house. He had started the Fieldhead Boat Club there to turn out crews for Maidenhead and Goring regattas, and he had just been elected the Liberal Member for Market Harborough. The family's literary and political friends, and especially the rowing ones, dropped by for weekends or motored up or punted down for the day, particularly on Sundays, and James, the butler, had a high old time being grand in the dining room for their benefit. The rowing demigods and dynasties lounged in deck chairs and recounted old feats of glory, the house guests puffed Havanas in the library and glanced through the bound volumes of *Punch* or Chambers' various encyclopedias, with which there was a family connection. Rowing trophies were on top of the shelves, and portraits of Rudie's parents' friends Robert Browning and Wilkie Collins, Rudie's father and Rudie himself hung on the walls, done by his uncle Rudolf. All the young men had a taste of late-summer Edwardian life, and Cambridge won the race.

At about the same time the venue for the annual autumn regatta and international races at Shanghai was moved to the Ch'ing Yang Chiang waterway at a spot near the new railway bridge over the Siking reach. The chief engineer of the railway, A. H. Collinson, found the place and suggested that everybody should travel the forty-five miles or so out of Shanghai at the time of the Chinese mid-autumn festival, and Duncan Glass named the place Henli, which translated into Chinese as 'Abounding Prosperity'. The banks closed early on race days, and there were several calamities during the racing, the most spectacular being T. H. R. Shaw's leap for the deep from Scotland's eight when his oar snapped twenty strokes after the start. There were swimming races and people swimming between houseboats and a good sing-song afterwards with rousing choruses of 'The Belle of New York', about a lady of doubtful reputation.

In 1908 all foreigners were banned from Henley – and all natives from Henli – on the grounds that the Olympic regatta was to take place there shortly afterwards. The ban was announced before the Belgians won the Grand in 1907, and before Henley was decided upon instead of Putney as the Olympic course. But it looked bad to the rowing public, stopping the defenders of the prime trophy from defending and restricting any taste of the Olympic water to all but the host crews. However, the furore in the press abated when the Belgians said that they could not defend the Grand while they were preparing for the more important event. The course was extended by 270 yards downstream and 60 yards upstream for the Olympic regatta, making it a mile and 880 yards. Countries could enter two crews in each of the four events – eights, fours, pairs and sculls. The selectors picked the winning Boat Race crew, Cambridge, for the eights and set about picking a Leander crew as a long-stop. This turned out to be a glorious swan-song for Guy Nickalls, who had just decided to retire from active rowing at the age of forty when he was called upon.

Guy got a letter from the selectors in January 1908 asking him to get fit and race in scratch crews at Putney. He had a word with his wife, who had been putting up with his long absences while he was coaching Magdalen, Oxford, crews, and accepted, that night giving up beer, spirits, wine, potatoes, pastry and sweets. He ran a mile before breakfast every day. The crew came together gradually, being known as the 'Old Crocks' or the 'Ancient Mariners'. Both they and Cambridge avoided Henley regatta but they practised there for six weeks before the Olympic regatta on 29–31 July. Nickalls had scant regard for what he saw of the English crews of the regatta except his own superb Magdalen four, winners of all three four-oared events in 1907 and retaining two of them in this Olympic year. As he trained and coached and watched, he saw D. C. R. Stuart stroking Cambridge in 'what they were pleased to call the sculling style' and W. A. L. Fletcher, champion of banning foreign crews, experimenting on his Christ Church crew with Belgian rig, oars, measurements and an exceedingly poor imitation of their style. Those who blamed the English style, thought Nickalls, should have known that it was the oarsmen who should be blamed and not the orthodoxy. Christ Church won the Grand over the boys of Eton, but in Nickalls's estimation they were a crew unworthy of any Grand medals.

So A. C. Gladstone, B. C. Johnstone, Nickalls and Don Burnell, who described the orthodox forward position as rubbing shoulders with the inside of one's knee, came to the Olympic regatta. F. S. Kelly, who had set up a record in winning the Diamonds in eight minutes ten seconds in 1905, was also in the crew. According to Guy's brother Vivian, Kelly hated training and spent his whole time playing the violin, on which he was a wonderful performer. The crew was completed by R. H. Sanderson, R. B. Etherington-Smith and stroked by H. C. Bucknall, with Cockie Maclagan coxing. Their average age was twenty-nine years six months, Nickalls being nine months into his forty-second year. They beat the Hungarians, then the Canadians, and met the Belgians who had dismissed Cambridge, sculling style or not, in the final. Nickalls said that he had never been beaten by a colonial or a foreigner, and he wasn't going to be in his old age or his last race. They won the final comfortably, and his Magdalen crew won the fours over Leander. J. R. K. Fenning and G. L. Thomson of Leander won the pairs and H. T. Blackstaffe the sculls.

The Olympic regatta was a civilized affair for spectators. Paddington was now only fifty-five minutes away by train. They had a choice of the Lawns Club, the Empire Lawn and Stand, or the Grand Stand Enclosure, the first charging twenty-one shillings a day including lunch, champagne cup and afternoon tea, or ten shillings and sixpence without the food. There was an important development for campers and picnickers for a new and wonderful Thermos was on the market, advertised in the *Lock to Lock Times* as keeping hot drinks *hot* for twenty-four hours and cold drinks *icy* cold for many days. There was a quart Thermotot jar for food available also. Lighting could be effected by Aladdin, a thousand candlepower at a halfpenny an hour, burns ordinary paraffin. Also, if you believed Dr J. Collis Browne, most medical problems were solved, for his Chlorodyne 'acts like a charm in Diarrhoea, Cholera, and Dysentery – the best remedy known for Coughs, Colds, Asthma, Bronchitis – effectively cuts short all attacks of Spasms – the only palliative in Neuralgia, Gout, Rheumatism, Toothache.' Sophisticates smoked

Turkish or Egyptian cigarettes. Regattas were advertised at Marlow, Hampton Court and Ditton, Shepperton and Halliford for tradesmen's, watermen's and cabmen's events, Reading, Wargrave and Shiplake for skiffing, and Laleham for punting. Hotels offered all manner of delights, some of them having garages and pits for the maintenance of motorcars as well as making carriages, horses and boats available for hire. You could buy a forty-five-foot launch for £150, or a punt and two paddles and four cushions for £10, you could hire or buy houseboats, eat *al fresco* at waterside inns, buy Parian White to clean buckskin, kid and canvas, and get Sicilian Lemon Zest which, with a drop or two of the liquids from its twin bottles, made lemonade.

In such a year ended the remarkable rowing career of Guy Nickalls. He raced eighty-one times at Henley, drawing the Bucks station and the Berks station forty times each and the old centre station once. He won sixty-seven of them, lost twelve, dead-heated once, and scratched once. And was only beaten by Britons. That year also Edward Hanlan died, the Canadian sculler who became world champion. Toronto turned out for the funeral and an island in the Lake Ontario was named after him. Jack Clasper died as well, and was buried at Lower Putney cemetery.

In 1911 another event attracted the attention of rowing's gentlemen amateurs. Jesus College sent a crew to compete with the Belgians on their own water, a courtesy which no other club had seen fit to pay to the foreigners who had most recently made inroads into Henley's prime silverware. The coxswain, Conrad Skinner, had the time of his life, and winning the race at Terdonck was only the half of it. He found that from the first to the last in Belgium there was incredible enthusiasm for English ideals of sport, and the race was the primary topic of conversation and the press. English reaction to the idea had been, according to the diminutive Skinner, at best kindly. Jesus were held to ridicule by many for taking a college crew to race the Belgians on their own waters, greeted with the cynical indifference which David evoked by his hardy challenge to Goliath of Gath. The Belgians, he found, reacted rather differently. Invitations were lavished on the men from Jesus. If they entered the opera the *prima donna* stopped in mid-air and the orchestra struck up 'God Save the King'. A set of postcards of the race sold 170,000 copies in a week. A special march was composed by Coutelier for the banquet and played by the 4th Lancers' band, and 10,000 people waited outside for a glimpse of the crew.

J. D. Barnard wrote a poem, with apologies to the late Poet Laureate, which appeared in *Chanticleer*. It began:

> Alektor the Cok,
> Of fowls the chief,
> The prince among roosters
> That crow in the morning,
> With his good crew
> Of Jesuit oarsmen,
> Sallied forth
> In the May of springtime,
> Crossed o'er the straits
> To the land of the stranger,
> To vanquish the victor,
> To conquer the mighty.

And it ended:

> Boldly this band
> Of tried and true oarsmen
> Went forth o'er the sea
> To the land of the stranger:
> Challenged them loudly
> To contest of racing.
> No recreants they:
> They gladly gave answer
> And brought out their long ship.
> Keen was the struggle:
> Ship against ship
> Started off at the signal.
> Keenly they strain
> For the honour and glory,
> The glory of triumph.
> Hard rowed the strangers,
> But vain was their prowess;
> Away and away
> To the goal of the racecourse.

> Honour the victors, and
> Honour the vanquished.
> Great was the contest,
> The contest of heroes,
> Of Briton v. Belgian.

Later in 1911 Henley saw some excellent racing, and members of London, Thames, Vesta, Twickenham, Molesey and Staines clubs could see from a new stance. They were all members of Remenham Club and they opened a bungalow in a superb position along the course, the only place from which both the start and the finish could be seen. Previously they had shared a lawn with the Grosvenor Club of Piccadilly. They did not get anything like the little Winnipeg crew of 1910 rowing a fourteen-stone German crew to a standstill in the Stewards', but they did see a dead heat in the Goblets in the record time of eight minutes eight seconds between two Thames pairs, Beresford and Cloutte and Logan and Rought. They tossed for the verdict, Beresford and Cloutte going through to the final. This course was adopted because they all had to row again in Thames's crew for the Stewards', which they won. The pressures of competition at the regatta, which had caused it to be extended in 1906 to four days with finals on a Saturday, had also begun to restrict the legality of doubling-up. Club crews were allowed to enter both the Thames Cup and the Ladies' but were required to scratch from one or the other before the draw.

In 1912 the course was changed slightly. It was a further attempt to deal with the Bushes Wind. The whole course was moved seventy-three feet and the piles on the Bucks side were moved ten feet nearer the Berks side, giving less width for the crews but less shelter from the wind on the Bucks station. The stewards had a much larger talking point, though. On finals day two thousand white-frocked children from Henley and district lined up near the station to cheer and catch a glimpse of the special passengers on the 11.25 special from Paddington. There was plenty going on in preparation for its arrival. In the enclosure someone was putting chairs first in a semicircle and then one behind two and admiring the effect. Bill East was out for a test run in the state barge with her crew of scarlet and gold watermen, stroked at an easy dip and bucket by Bossy Phelps. At the town landing stage workmen were putting down a red carpet, and on the road towards the station an awning was being erected by men who were late for the job but who were clearly out for a record.

All this was observed by the man from the *Manchester Guardian*, who also spied out the land:

> For seriously minded people who had not spent the night on the river with the madcaps the day at Henley began with getting the best position along-

side the booms under the wall of Phyllis Court, or as near them as possible. In that position one would be able to lie and watch the racing down the straight channel between the piles and at the same time loyally observe the King and Queen.

He noted that the station had lost its identity behind flags and shields and awaited the royal party with a dignity peculiar to decorated stations.

> Earlier one had fancied the King in the race between him and the sun, but the sun was there first. The light morning breeze died away, the big elms dripped and the water glistened like diamonds when pole or paddle broke its glassy surface. The pierrots and nigger minstrels pushed their boats with no regard whatever for paint or patience, and they made their wild music and wilder wit among the gay folks who lined the booms in all the colour variety of a herbaceous border.

Sharp to time and accompanied by five launches crowded with officials of the Thames Conservancy, the royal barge put off the landing stage. King George, in a dark blue flannel suit and a homburg-panama, and the Queen and Princess Mary in blue took their places among the buff and stuffy cushions of the great gilt boat. They were led ashore by Lord Desborough, formerly W. H. Grenfell, in comfortable time to see their neighbours Eton College beat Jesus College in the final of the Ladies'.

At the lunch break the press of boats crackled apart like drifting ice floes, paddling downstream in search of a shady nook for a picnic and another view of the royal party as they were boated to Greenlands, home of W. F. D. Smith, beyond the start.

> One turned to lunch amid the distant threatening of thunder and the first spots of rain. It did not last long. There was a scurry for shelter or mackintoshes, and then life went on as before. The conjuror conjured, the pierrot sang, the luncher lunched, and the sulky sun thus snubbed came out again and chased away the thunder clouds before the pageant returned.

The King and Queen followed the Grand final on the umpire's launch, *Maritana*, steered by Pat Labat of Trinity College, Dublin, and Thames RC, seeing the Australians from Sydney beat Leander by three-quarters of a length. The Australians' participation on the way to the Olympic Games in Stockholm had almost been disallowed because Hauenstein worked as a policeman, but it was decided that he was an amateur.

Leander looked rough beside them [reported the *Manchester Guardian*]. Our English drive, swing and recovery are too individual to harmonize like the clockwork action that can be extracted from the school of long slides and broad blades. But this is to drift into theories once more: what the King saw was that the men who could shoot and ride could also row.

He also saw Logan and Rought beat Beresford and Cloutte in a re-run of the previous year's Goblets final. The Queen gave away the prizes before catching the royal train back to Paddington. The evening was warm and close and the punts lingered on the river. 'There are some who hold that, whatever may be the merits of boat racing, the real Henley begins at twilight when the heat and burden of historic days are done.' So concluded the *Manchester Guardian*'s report of George and Mary's day out. Tiny Ernie Arlett was born in Henley that day, christened George in honour of the King and Ernest after Ernest Barry, a professional who was a great friend of Ernie's father. The standard from the royal barge mysteriously found its way to Australia.

In 1913 C. McVilly came from Tasmania to win the Diamonds but was received in silence by the crowd at the prize-giving because he was 'washing' his opponent Pinks in the final. Australia had gone overboard about Henley, for by this time there were or had been Henley regattas at Yarra, Torrens, Brisbane and Parramatta. In 1914 the Harvard Junior Varsity crew arrived. They were the second Harvard crew, the first being ineligible because they were coached by a professional, Jim Wray. Alumni at Harvard had been working for some time to get American crews eligible again for Henley because there was much talk in Boston of trying to capture the Grand. Everything seemed to come together that year: there was a good crew practising for the Union Boat Club in Boston, mostly Harvard graduates, and for the first time the second varsity boats were eight-oars instead of fours. At the 'American Henley' on 16 May at Philadelphia the Union BC came second to the Junior Varsity crew, with Annapolis, Yale and Syracuse behind them. The Union club were given the go-ahead for Henley and the Junior Varsity were told that if they defeated Yale's second crew at New London they could go too.

Bob Herrick replaced Wray as coach for the statutory month before Henley and the Union crew also got an amateur, E. C. Storrow, in place of William Haines, the club professional. Herrick's daughters remembered the time well. They were at New London staying at the Griswold Hotel. Harvard always seemed to win in those days, and a Republican was in the White House. What more could a girl ask? The crew defeated Yale and left by the night train, boarding the *Olympic* next day. Herrick's daughters saw little of him on the voyage since he was trying to keep both the brothers Middendorf in sight at once – a difficult task.

The crossing was favourable. The crew had a walk before breakfast and a mile-and-a-half run round the deck in the afternoon, followed by a swim. At Plymouth on 26 June the Customs officials insisted on tasting the water in the carboys which the Harvard party, fearing the English drinking water, had brought with them. They arrived at Henley that evening and were quartered at Roslyn House, while their graduate crew arrived several days beforehand and were at Sonning. The Harvard boys had only two days of practice before the start of the regatta. Herrick tried to get the officials to arrange that they would not be drawn against Union in the first heat, but they very properly told him that Harvard must take their chances. They drew Leander.

James B. Ayer of the Union BC, entered in the Diamonds, described the ambience of the place for the *Harvard Graduates' Magazine*:

> Near the finish of the race-course, and opposite the town, were the large tents shared by all competing oarsmen except those of Leander. . . . Here was the rendezvous, days before the races, for gossip and criticism; for all crews must leave by one landing and must row over the course in order to get their daily practice, inasmuch as the upper and lower locks are not more than three miles apart. Thus there is no opportunity for seclusion; all practice is viewed by hostile as also by friendly eyes, and the proof of this close inspection is not wanting; for the inquisitive oarsman may read the very next morning in the *Sportsman* or in *The Times* what impression he has made upon his rivals, friends, or critics. He will even find that his crew has been measured over measured portions of the course; if it has stopped a few feet short of the mark, even this will be noted in the summing up of the 'usefulness' of the crew, accompanied with an estimate as to whether the men were 'all out' or only 'taking paddling exercise'.

The Union BC's reception was not of the boisterous kind, said Ayer.

We were not met at the station by a band or given a dinner every evening. But our hosts tried to treat us like one of themselves, and that spelled perfect cordiality without exuberance. Among the pleasant incidents were the full privileges of Leander club, complimentary tickets to all of the enclosures, both public and private, on the days of the regatta, and an interesting Sunday trip.

Ayer also noted that the articles in the morning papers were evidently prepared with thought by men who knew rowing. Union did not make a favourable impression on the water, with short strokes and lacking in pace, but both Union and Harvard were praised for their quick hands-away and Harvard for their greater body swing. Ayer beat Gould of Jesus in the Diamonds and then lost to the eventual winner, the giant Italian, Giuseppe Sinigaglia.

Herrick was coaching Harvard from an old white horse that was used in turn by several coaches. The horse stopped and started automatically with the crew it was accompanying. For a couple of days Herrick felt much of a stranger among the forty or fifty coaches who travelled the towpath, but gradually the ice was broken and he made many friends. 'My experience is typical,' he said. 'The English wait a bit, and then if they take you on they take you on all over.'

This year the boat tents were guarded for fear of attack by suffragettes. It was not a happy time in the outside world. The papers were full of the burial arrangements being made for Archduke Ferdinand, heir to the Austrian throne, and his wife who had been assassinated in Sarajevo on 28 June. On 1 July *The Times* celebrated the seventy-fifth anniversary of the regatta by printing a list of world affairs in 1839, remarking that 'houseboats diminish, motor boats multiply, to the grief of all other users of the river'. On 2 July a great sensation was caused just before the lunch interval when a boat went down the river with bills advertising that Joseph Chamberlain was dead, and in the afternoon Prince Henry and Prince Alexander of Teck were witnessing the completion of unmitigated disaster for the English in the Grand. There were eight entries, four from home and four from abroad, including Winnipeg who greatly resented being referred to as foreigners and claimed to be an Empire crew. Harvard raced Leander and beat them by about a length in the fastest time of the day. The Canadians from Winnipeg beat Thames, Union beat London RC, and Harvard's next-door neighbours at Roslyn House, Mainzer Ruderverein of Germany, beat Jesus. Four English crews knocked out of the Grand in a day, and the next was a little hung-over for the hosts.

> Long after the rain had ceased gusts of wind would sweep across the water fluttering to showers the drenched leaves of the overhanging chestnuts to the discomfiture of adventurous picnic parties [said the *Manchester Guardian*]. On the whole, if one belonged to a club, it was best to stay there and watch the races from the smoke-room windows with a return to the fireside during the intervals for a welter of anecdote and reminiscent rowing 'shop'. . . .
>
> The Pegs carried our hopes; where England failed Empire might succeed. They looked a likely lot of men but so did the lithe young men from Harvard, who recked nothing of our strange climate and paddled their boat down as though they might at any moment time their rhythm to a song. . . . Likely enough there was something very different in their hearts as they lay at the stakeboat. Thenceforward they could have heard nothing but the megaphoned instructions of their cox and the heartening shouts of their supporters . . . by the time a college cry was half performed the boats – a flash of shooting canvases and plugging blades – had gone out of hearing. Half a mile and still level. . . .

Then Harvard moved up and won, and Union defeated the Germans. The headline in the *Boston Globe* next morning said: 'Only Americans left for Grand Challenge Cup Final at Henley.' This was certainly a Bostonian way to wake up to 4 July, Independence Day.

When Harvard defeated their graduates by a length and a quarter in the final the world got on with its business. There was a strike at the Woolwich Arsenal, rumours of the assassination of Huerta of Mexico, and all leave for troops had been cancelled in Bosnia. The *Pall Mall Gazette* said:

> The Grand has gone to America, the Diamond Sculls to Italy. Are we downhearted? Not a bit of it! Why should not the eight of America's largest university be able to beat a scratch Leander crew? And why should not a burly Italian, with all Lake Como to scull on, be able to beat the best of our men who can find time for training? We have just got to learn the lesson that we have no inherent and indigenous superiority in sport, and that, if we wish to retain or regain our position, we have got to work for it.

An advertisement in *The Times* of 7 July said:

> In loving memory of British Rowing, which passed away at Henley on Saturday July 4th. Deeply lamented by many sorrowing followers, who hereby place their regret on record.

At least Leander beat the Germans in the Stewards' and the weather improved for the end of the regatta. The *Manchester Guardian* said that the crowds would have carried away the memory of a brilliant picture. From whatever point one watched it the scene, moving yet composed, changing yet ever the same, was always a delight. On the same page the paper printed an article on the soda fountain and how to make egg flips at home, and launched into the new fashion in hats:

> The sudden change from last year's very large hats to this year's very small ones has caused a good deal of wastage among people whose ideas of frugality do not permit a whole set of new hats every year.

In August the *Field* reported that there would be a collection on the 22nd – sponsored by the mayor, the chairman of the stewards and the secretary of the ARA – for the Belgian Ministers' Relief Fund for the Sick and Wounded as a token of admiration from Henley-on-Thames. The paper commented:

> The heroic defence of the Belgian nation has commanded the admiration of the world but nowhere has the gallant conduct of the Belgian army aroused more enthusiasm than amongst those who have in happier times watched the Belgian crews competing at Henley regatta.

And in December Jack Clasper's son-in-law, Fred Rough, died in Oxford, where the suffragettes who burnt his boathouse almost ruined his business.

7

A *fair wind for Steve*
1939: The war of the running slide

'Just when we may see it all again no one knows. Our wish and hope is that it may be soon.' Robert F. Herrick's expression of faith appeared in the official American rowing guide shortly after he witnessed his university win their second Grand Challenge at Henley. It was 1939 and already most of the Englishmen whom the Harvard men met were struggling into uniform for another off-the-water confrontation with Germany. Herrick was sad that the ranks of 1914 had been so devastated – in 1919 Theodore Cook listed 272 English and Empire oarsmen who fell during the war, 188 of them ex-Oxford or Cambridge. Lieutenant G. S. Sinigaglia of the Italian Army, winner of the Diamonds, was killed in July 1916. The Harvard 1914 crew were mercifully all intact, but Herrick learnt that four of the fine German crew from Mayence who were billeted next door to the Americans at Henley on that occasion had been killed, and one was badly crippled. The stern four of the Jesus crew who had gone to Belgium in 1911 died, and Jesus College's Belgian relief fund collected £800. Mick Leahy of Trinity Dublin, the man who put out the lights in the High Street, lost a leg.

In 1939 the stewards broke with tradition by touting for entries from overseas to celebrate their regatta's centenary, and Harvard decided late in the spring that they would send the university crew if they did well enough. Timing was again very difficult, because the race with Yale was on 23 June and Henley's first day was 5 July. After their customary hard winter on rowing machines until the ice melted on the Charles River in mid March, they had a good season, only Cornell beating them, and under the professional coaching of

Tom Bolles they won the Yale match. They were the pick of a huge club whose activities were now way beyond the participatory achievements of Rudie Lehmann's short era. This year the Harvard boathouses contained thirty-five eight-oared shells, five eight-oared barges and seventy-one other boats.

The professional coaches' rule had been dropped by this time and Bolles's crew were accompanied to Henley by a party which included Herrick, now president of Union BC in Boston, and Bill Bingham, director of athletics at the university. Bingham was impressed with the dedication and the humour of the men. At the banquet at Red Top, Harvard's boathouse at New London, celebrating the win over Yale, no one smoked and after dinner Bolles said, 'Since the crew has voted to go to the Henley, let's go determined to win.' Every man was in bed before midnight, and at ten the next morning the crew pushed off with a new stroke on board. Jack Wilson, a sophomore from the Junior Varsity crew, got his seat because Bill Rowe, the regular stroke, was off to get married. The crew stayed at New London doing hard practice until the evening of 27 June and the next day they boarded the French liner *Normandie*. They took four rowing machines, and the ten men – there were two substitutes with the crew – had two fifteen-minute workouts. Bingham knew the price the crew was paying when they went off to bed at 10.30 each night as the band struck up and beautiful girls appeared in shimmering frocks.

They arrived at Plymouth at four in the morning and had a noisy incident while changing trains at Exeter because the oar box wouldn't fit into the luggage van of the GWR. The oarsmen grabbed it and tried to force it in. Eventually one Jim Shand came to their rescue by promising that he would get the oars to Henley by 6.30 that Monday, and at 6.20 the crew saw a van coming over the bridge with Shand sitting triumphantly on the oar box. There were two days left to use their oars in practice before meeting London RC on the Thursday. They settled into their boarding house on Vicarage Road and began to explore. Bingham was surprised to find that the circus-like boat tents had a sprinkler system, while Herrick noted that they were again under guard, this time not in expectation of suffragettes but of the Irish Republican Army, who could have done much damage with a box of matches.

The Harvard men were well prepared, except for Tom Bolles who had never coached from a bicycle before and had to learn pretty quickly to yell through his megaphone while avoiding all the obstacles of the towpath. They defeated London in their first race without trouble, but had a harder time against Jesus, who had put Leander out in the first round to the surprise of the pundits. Jesus started at a great rate but failed to unnerve the Americans, who caught them by halfway and earned their place in the final with clear water between them and the Cambridge men. The other finalists were the heaviest crew, the Argonauts from Canada, and Harvard beat them quite easily. They carried the trophy, presented to them by the Duke of Kent, back to Vicarage Road and Captain Talbot placed it on a table in the centre of the room. Talbot and Wilson, Stevens and Kernan, Gray and Pirnie, Richards and Fowler and coxswain Shortlidge looked long at the lists of names on the Grand, particularly at the 1914 list – Saltonstall, Talcott, Meyer, H. S. and J. W. Middendorf, Morgan, Curtis, Lund and coxswain Kreger – and they wondered if someone would be looking at their names on the cup in 2039.

The Thames Cup had an all-American final in which Tabor Academy beat Kent School, and the Americans witnessed the start of a new event in 1939, the Centenary Double Sculls, which finished fittingly in a dead heat between J. Beresford Jr and L. F. Southwood of Thames and G. Scherli and E. Broschi of Trieste. Beresford and Southwood had won Britain's only aquatic gold medals at the 1936 Olympic Games in Berlin, coming out of retirement to do so, and in 1939 they were aged forty-one and thirty-six respectively. As the Double Sculls was not a challenge event, the stewards decided against a re-row of this dramatic race and all four men received medals.

The Americans certainly enjoyed themselves. Bingham reported back to the *Alumni Bulletin*:

> The Royal Henley Regatta is something for oarsmen to boast about. In my opinion it is the best organized and best conducted athletic event I have ever seen in any sport. The color, the atmosphere, and everything about it is athletically inspiring. The shells are housed in five huge tents. There were 144 entries and the oars of all these crews seem to have all the varying shades of the spectrum, and it is a beautiful sight to see them stacked row after row in front of the tents. But even more inspiring is to see the skull caps worn by all who ever rowed, and who make the Henley a rendezvous. . . .

He saw many men over three-score years wearing the colours of famous rowing institutions, and all expert critics.

The course was a mile and five-sixteenths, said Bingham, and leave it to the British to pick such an unorthodox distance. It was straight as a rule. The crews knew what time they were racing, and when a race was scheduled for five minutes past three it started.

If your watch read 3.08 your watch is wrong and you reset it. I have never seen a contest where the officials adhere so faithfully to the time schedule. At four o'clock all rowing ceases for 45 minutes for reasons obvious to all who have been in England.

The shells started from chutes with the bows even and a rope was held on each side between the bow and number two man, and when the signal to 'row' was given the rope was pulled out. Bingham also told the Harvard alumni that although he had never seen a group of boys more determined to win and more willing to pay the price of abstaining from smoking at Red Top and from high living on the *Normandie*, he had never laughed more in a two-week period than on the voyage from the Thames at New London to the Thames at Henley. He did not say what happened on the return trip.

Herrick, too, enjoyed himself immensely, wandering about the banks where he used to ride on the old white horse. He told the folks back home what to expect of visits to the regatta. The English were very particular as to their costumes. They wore shirts with elbow sleeves, flannel shorts, and generally socks matching the crew colours with neckcloths to match. On shore they wore high-coloured blazers in college colours and embroidered with insignia. On the days before the beginning of the regatta one saw more rowing than anywhere else in the world. It was unusual for a crew before the regatta to spend as little time at Henley as Harvard had had to do when they disembarked at Plymouth at 4 a.m. and spent the evening rowing seven miles. Most crews arrived about ten days before battle commenced, and everyone coming down the course was generally accompanied by a shouting crowd of supporters.

There were constant good-natured off-hand brushes between crews who were not going to compete later. One would come alongside and say 'Will you take us on for a minute?' – and away they would go on a wild spurt. Herrick recalled an occasion when his crew were challenged by a boat of boys wearing rather girlish-looking straw hats with bright pink ribbons, pink socks and a generally dainty appearance. Lady Clare of Oxford, he thought they were.

'We of course accepted the challenge thinking we would eat them up. At the end of a minute Lady Clare were well ahead and we were wiser.' The dainty crew were actually Clare College, Cambridge, and Herrick watched their successors win the Ladies'.

He also describes the arduous day of the spectator. At the finish are enclosures for which people buy tickets. On the Berks side is the stewards' enclosure, which is official, somewhat expensive and most attractive. There are rows of chairs along the water's edge, restaurant tents and a bar. Then comes the general enclosure, less expensive, and one or two club ones, and then the open meadow which in many respects is the best place from which to watch. There is no crowd there and most of the races are pretty well over by the time the crews get halfway down.

When a race is started a cannon is fired so that spectators are warned that a race is on. Suddenly there is a surge towards the edge of the river, a clapping of hands, and the crews appear, generally one rowing rather cheerfully and lazily, and the next all tired out, just getting over the course. There is a chorus of 'Well rowed' for both winners and losers, and everybody goes back to the chairs. At each quarter of a mile there are targets on high posts which are moved so as to indicate which crew is ahead at that point and the approximate distance between them, so that with glasses the progress can be watched pretty well to the finish. But a great many enthusiasts are well down river watching at critical points like the Barrier and Fawley. During practice time groups of old oarsmen will sit for hours, with time records covering years and stopwatches, making predictions from their calculations.

Racing is up river, against the current, and regulating the flow at the weirs reduces the current as much as possible. They make it as nearly as they can without current, says Herrick's report, but current is inevitable if there has been a lot of rain. 'The result is that very fast times at Henley are often credited to a very dry year in which they say there was no current.'

He describes, too, the draw, which Harvard had arrived too late to witness.

> Quite a ceremony is made of this. The Grand Challenge Cup is placed on a table with the names of the crews written on the slips inside. The stewards then draw as from a lottery box and each is assigned to the Berks or Bucks side of the river.

He does not mention another ceremony which usually took place. The watermen had a darts match in the Carpenters Arms, Oxford versus Cambridge versus Tideway, and victory was celebrated by fifteen men supping from a huge chamber pot decorated with crossed oars. This once occurred outside the public house when a party of nuns were being conducted over the bridge, a pretty sight.

After the regatta Herrick got a letter from an English coach who was also a steward, who wrote:

> Your Harvard crew was a great joy to watch. One sometimes gets a good thrill out of watching a good *race*, even if the rowing is bad, but it is good *rowing* that always thrills me most, and your crew was as nearly perfect as possible in some of those rare refinements of style that are essential to great pace. The prolonged feather against the wind and the lightning entry into the water were points on which we always insisted in this country, in the days when English Rowing was 'rowing' and not slide-shuffling.

The letter went on to extol the virtues of the correct use of the slide and to state that the perfectly balanced rhythm which allows the boat to run fast and smoothly between the strokes had vanished in England.

> All of these points were exhibited at their best by the Harvard crew and must have been carefully thought out and admirably taught by your coach. I have spent a good deal of my time in recent years trying to tell the rising generation that their methods have got worse and worse ever since Steve Fairbairn began to teach his pernicious doctrine that each young man should take the easiest and sloppiest way of doing things. There are two cardinal principles which all here have been ignoring, *viz*: That if they want to win against all comers they must realize that good rowing is, in the first instance, difficult to acquire, and not keep looking out for the 'easy' way; and that it is *between* the strokes that the faster boat travels faster than the other, and they must row each stroke so as to send the boat spinning along between the strokes, and that therefore a good 'finish' is essential. Well, I hope that our boys will take a lesson and mend their ways, so that next time you come there may be a two-foot victory either way, in decent weather, in record time.

As he dined and drank with old friends and new acquaintances, and mused on the sad losses of the rowing community which he first met while relieving it of the Grand in 1914, Herrick would have heard many stories and learned of many developments between then and now in the sport which he loved.

There were notable deaths. Judge Woodgate, prankster, perpetrator of unemployment among coxswains, and distinguished author of orthodoxy, died in 1920. The Rev. Dr Warre, an even higher priest of the English style, a muscular Christian, who commanded enormous respect much further afield than Eton and Oxford, also passed away. The cheerful recorder of the teaching of Jesus at Magdalene College, Cambridge, George Mallory, perished while leading the final assault on Mount Everest in 1924. Rudie Lehmann, the poet who went to *Punch*, and Sir Theodore Cook, the chronicler who became the distinguished editor of the *Field*, both died. The wit and scholarship which these two, the first a Liberal and second a crusty Tory, had brought to rowing were incomparable. And Guy Nickalls, old man of the 1908 crocks who was never beaten by a foreigner or a colonial, died of injuries on the evening of 8 July 1935, after a collision at the Leeds–York crossroads. He was.heading for a fishing trip at Glen Shiel after watching a four from Zürich win the Stewards' on 6 July. 'Thank God I have been spared to see what I believe to be the finest four of all time,' he told his son Gully after the race. Nickalls had been whisked to the United States by a group of millionaires in 1913 to coach Yale, which he did until 1916 and again in 1920 and 1921, imposing the Nickalls style with variations, with controversy and some success. In between he fought in France with the Lancashire Fusiliers. He called his autobiography *Life's a Pudding*, from W. S. Gilbert's lines: 'Life's a pudding full of plums, Let us take it as it comes.' His son finished it for him and it was published in this year, 1939, a ramble of directive and anecdotage.

Woodgate was in the fray until the last. Almost before hostilities ceased in 1918 there was a letter in the *Field* advocating the revival of the regatta, and one was arranged hastily for the next year, though not for the usual cups because of the abnormal circumstances. Canadians in khaki were rowing from London RC at Putney in 1918, and New Zealanders from Thames. There was a regatta on Regent's Park lake for blinded soldiers that year. In 1919 at Henley special cups and categories were offered, though not apparently to veterans from the National Amateur Rowing Association, who could not enter for the King's Cup given by George V, which was won by the Australian Army. The King supposedly vowed never to attend the regatta again until something was done about the rule. In 1919 also there was a bold attempt to get the finances of the regatta on a surer footing by the founding of a stewards' enclosure, inspired largely by Harcourt Gold. It was this that Woodgate objected to, saying that it would squeeze out the rowing men, but his view did not prevail in a climate in which the revenue from houseboats had virtually ceased and in which clubs were making the running. Three hundred subscribers were elected that year, a regular source of income rain or shine, reduced rates were offered to competitors, and Herrick learned that the membership was now 700, much to the stewards' pleasure. They had acquired a large supporters' club, which had no powers at all in the running of the regatta.

The regatta returned to normal in 1920 in more ways than one. Vesper entered J. B. Kelly for the Diamonds, sponsored by the American Rowing Association, which had replaced the National Association of American Oarsmen. There were various versions of what happened to Kelly's entry, one being that he was refused because the rule banning Vesper was still on the minute book, and another that he did not qualify under the Henley amateur definition because he had been an apprentice bricklayer. Whatever the reason, Kelly was not allowed to compete, and the Diamonds were won by Jack Beresford Jr of Thames. Two months later he lost the Olympic sculling final at Antwerp by one second – to J. B. Kelly, the American amateur. The two men later became great friends and Kelly told Beresford that several stewards had been sounded out about his Diamonds entry and he had been advised to send it in. Two days before he was due to sail, his passage booked and his boat boxed ready, he received a telegram which said: 'Entry rejected; letter follows.' He never got the letter.

The next year Beresford stopped in the Diamonds final to wait for his opponent, the Dutchman F. E. Eyken, who had hit the booms. Eyken eventually won by a length and a half, but Beresford took the title from 1924–26 and competed in the next four Olympiads. In 1923 an experimental shortened course was tried, eliminating the bend. It was exceptionally hot and cloudless for the regatta and Dr Mick Leahy from the Trinity 1903 crew was there to greet the men from his college, paddling up and down in a sculling boat. Bobby Steen, Trinity's spare man, kept fit by sculling from Leander twice a day, and he was accompanied by Leahy, now a powerful-jawed medical man, who was talking of changing to psychiatry, and who had rowed for Leander after he lost his leg. The crew stayed at Cecil

Harmsworth's house opposite the finishing post, with punts laid on. Steen got into the boat when one member went down sick, and they went out of the Ladies' to Clare in their first race. They saw D. H. L. Gollan of Leander, a deaf mute, beat two Americans in the Diamonds and lose the final to M. K. Morris of London, who collapsed at the end. And they went to the Phyllis Court dance on Saturday night, finishing up by throwing pebbles at their coach's window at 6 a.m. on Sunday morning when looking for somewhere to sleep. Major Denroce and his wife Melene were not pleased by this intrusion but made armchairs available in the drawing room of their rented house.

Things were pretty lively at the Red Lion that night as well, and Vivian Nickalls and his friend Jack Bellamy got caught up in an excitable and bibulous crowd who were trying to do damage to the inn because the manager was a German. The crowd were ejected and Nickalls and Bellamy went outside to prevent further destruction, according to Vivian's own account of the incident. 'Bellamy was a useful man with his fists and we held the Red Lion for about quarter of an hour until a cordon of police was drawn round the mob,' said the veteran of the Goblets and of the French and Italian fronts. The presence of the police increased the antagonism of the crowd, so Nickalls promised the inspector that he would disperse the crowd if the constabulary withdrew. This they did. 'I asked them all to go away before they were locked up, whereupon they obligingly made themselves scarce,' he told his friends. On that same evening Bellamy persuaded Vivian to take a job coaching the Tigre Club near Buenos Aires. He had coached abroad before, at Detroit Boat Club for five years and then at the University of Pennsylvania for two.

The experimental straight course was deemed a success and the banks were cut along the island and the Berks shore to restore the full length for 1924's event. The rules for the Ladies' Plate were altered to allow Trinity College, Dublin, to continue to enter crews for it once they found themselves in the Irish Republic instead of the United Kingdom. There was an entertaining finish in the Goblets when G. O. 'Gully' Nickalls, son of Guy and nephew of Vivian, and R. S. C. Lucas sank by the enclosures after springing a leak caused by do-it-yourself carpentry at the start and then waiting for their opponents when the latter hit the booms. The trailing crew offered a re-row but had crossed the line first, and the committee said that that must be the result.

The do-it-yourself carpentry was the official version of the accident in C. T. Steward's Henley Records, and it was true that Lucas never embarked without a hammer and a file on board, but Gully put the blame on their boatmen. Before the race he had removed the forward bulkhead in order to move Gully's seat nearer to the bows, and failed to replace it. On the first stroke Gully's stretcher broke away and gashed the side of the boat and the water was able to fill the cockpit and the bows, so that by the time they reached the enclosure the canvas was under water and they suddenly stopped with spectacular effect, the bows going down and the stern rising ten feet into the air.

The Red Lion had another incident in 1927 when R. T. Lee won the Diamonds and that evening stepped up to a drunk who was annoying ladies dining at the hotel, lifted him clean off his feet and dropped him out of a window. Fortunately the fall was not great. The number of entries at the regatta was worrying the stewards by this time, and in 1928 they forbade double entries in the Ladies' and Thames Cup and restricted the numbers in the Thames to thirty-two and in all other events to sixteen. Four years later they forbade competitors from taking part in the Grand and the Wyfolds at the same regatta. In 1929 there was the unprecedented occurrence of two dead heats, one between Argonaut BC of Canada and London RC in a heat of the Grand, and the second in a heat of the Goblets between G. C. Killick and J. Beresford of Thames and H. R. Carver and T. R. B. Sanders of Third Trinity. A lady in the enclosure on her first visit said through the hubbub: 'A dead heat? How dull!' London won their re-row but lost the event, while Killick and Beresford persevered to win their final. In 1938 the stewards extended their holdings as landowners, buying all the part of Lion Meadows which they did not own already.

In 1938 Joe Burk of Penn Athletic Club won the Diamonds against Len Habbitts of Reading in a time which knocked eight seconds off the record set up by the fiddler, F. S. Kelly, in 1905. Burk returned in 1939 and won again, and the Duke of Kent remarked that he must be getting used to them when he presented Burk with the Diamond Sculls trophy. 'I've seen them before,' Burk said. He and Herrick travelled home on the same ship, sharing their impressions and their memories, and they had much to talk about.

Herrick's trans-Atlantic trips between the Harvard victories of 1914 and 1939 spanned an era when the gospel according to Steve spread from Jesus to the world. It was not accepted universally, and much of the controversy caused by it arose from mistaking it for doctrine when it was an approach, more a means to effective athletic performance than an end in itself. The ideas of the colonial from Geelong nurtured on the Cam had certainly kept aquatics on the boil since the 1880s. Fairbairn went to Jesus in 1881 and got a Blue in his first year. He introduced longer slides there, initially for the trial eights of 1885, when he and Muttlebury set to work on the boat with screwdrivers. Longer slides and more leg, according to Rudie Lehmann, who wrote later about another occasion:

> Muttle at 6 is stylish, so at least the *Field* reports;
> No man has ever worn, I trow, so short a pair of shorts.
> His blade sweeps through the water, as he swings his 13.10
> And pulls it all, and more than all, that brawny king of men.

Steve strengthened riggers, campaigned for the adoption of swivel rowlocks and was a sworn enemy of the fixed seat. He did not bother his law lecturers much but had the useful knack of passing exams. He sat in four Blue boats, five Cambridge May boats for Jesus, and once rowed the university pairs with the coxswain and won, Steve pulling the cox round the long bend to get a lead and the cox having to do the work on the shorter one. 'Well steered,' said the cox at the end of Steve's bend, and he replied, 'Shut your mouth and row.' He was head of the river at Cambridge several times and raced in the Goblets at Henley four times, reaching the final with his great friend, A. M. Hutchinson, in 1898. All of this was after a terrible accident during his second time out sculling at Cambridge. That day he had won the hammer throw and putting the weight at the freshmen's sports. He had a head-on collision with another sculler, the other boat striking him within an inch of his spine. Two feet of its bows broke off and were left sticking into Steve, and he reckoned that he had a blood cyst for thirty-five years after this as a result of the doctor not getting all the bits of wood out of his back. It caused him a lot of pain and nervous dyspepsia, to which he was a self-confessed martyr ever onwards. But it didn't sap his strength or his enthusiasm. A picture of him holding in his arms the cox with whom he won the university pairs hung in the Jesus boathouse until it was burned down in 1932.

The superb rowing record of Jesus from 1875–85 declined sharply until Steve returned from Australia. He returned to active coaching in 1904. Sir Arthur Quiller-Couch's introduction to the 1928 Jesus history says:

> In this quiet C staircase of the front court of Jesus I look up to a beam recording that (if the time of war be omitted) for eleven good years I have been privileged to dine in the hall wherein – constant as Horace's ancestral plate – there has never lacked a trophy or trophies of oarsmanship. . . . While we remain a family . . . the gods who preside over the hearth and the oar shall adorn the hall of Jesus perpetually.

And the authors, Brittain and Playford, say: 'No greater personality has ever devoted himself with such unflagging interest or such inexhaustible energy and patience to the promotion of the welfare of oarsmen!' Such a statement, written as it is by Jesus men, may be questioned by many, say the authors, but chief among his critics are those who have never felt his magnetism because they have never been coached by him. 'It is well known among Jesus men that his very presence on the towpath, even though he may say nothing, is sufficient to make a boat go well and fast.' Be that as it may, the family certainly backed its most famous son. By 1928 a dozen Fairbairns, including three Armytages who were their cousins, had rowed in first boats for Jesus.

The style which Steve was accused of perpetrating differed from the orthodox English in two main respects. First, the orthodox style caught the beginning of the stroke with the shoulders, opening up an angle between thigh and rib as quickly as possible when the blade was dropped vertically into the water. Steve advocated driving the blade into the water and letting the slide take care of itself, which should result in a swing of the body simultaneous with an even drive of the legs through the stroke, driving the boat through the water. Secondly, orthodoxy said that the blade was whipped out of the water to be followed by a swift recovery up the slide while the boat was running, while Steve said there should be a swift withdrawal of the blade from the water by means of a quick flick of the wrists down and away – the hands-away which feathers the blade automatically – but that the oarsman should lie back at the finish and take plenty of time in starting his recovery. The hands should be above the knees before the slide starts moving evenly back. Steve was a teacher who had time for all shapes and sizes. He thought his methods could produce crews in less time than orthodoxy, which seemed to presuppose some discomfort and required conformity to a model. However brilliant the result, and results were not always brilliant, orthodoxy saw no merit in unorthodox methods. Steve wanted oarsmen to think for themselves.

His opponents, like Bob Herrick's correspondent, thought his crews ragged, his men sloppy and his outlook lazy. Others perceived that either style done well produced much the same result of neat and fast crews. The disciples saw Fairbairn as an optimist who was ready to praise and who didn't yell all one's faults at one across the water, as the bearer of infectious enthusiasm, as a tuner of an oarsman's mind to think positively about what he was doing, and as a supporter who was anxious to make the best oarsmen that nature would allow. Anything done well is done naturally and easily, Steve would say. It was this magic that brought his method from the Cam to the Tideway, where he first revived Thames's flagging fortunes, in 1923 giving them their first Grand win since 1889. Then, after falling out with Jack Beresford Sr and others of Thames's heavies, he moved to London. Archie Nisbet, a Cambridge graduate from Pembroke and captain of London in 1924, had extracted a promise from Steve that if ever he left Thames he would coach London, and, a few years later, as soon as Nisbet got wind of the argument which resulted in Steve's nominee not being elected captain, he followed Steve back to his hotel and held him to his promise. London had not won a Henley cup for many years but they accomplished successes in the Grand, Stewards' and Thames in the early thirties, and Nisbet was inspired for life as well as for rowing by Steve's teaching.

Fairbairn's gospel spread into lucid little books called 'Chats' and 'Notes' and 'Secrets' about rowing, and their fame and his disciples had travelled far and wide by 1939. He was often at the college in the thirties, as omnipresent, one undergraduate remembered, as the Virgin Birth at a theological college. Alistair Cooke from Blackpool did not pull for Jesus, he jumped for Jesus. But his chief recreation was moping over warm beer in damp rooms waiting for the college bell to chime eleven when, confined to barracks without the other sex in sight, he listened to dance music on the wireless. Echoes of Babylon while waiting for the vacation parole! Meanwhile, for the majority of the college who were dry bobs like him, there were the dreaded bump supper nights. Claude Elliott was Cooke's tutor and was responsible for most of the Australians who made up the crews. He always arranged to be called out of town on bump supper nights and a few days later had to face the ordeal of sending down a drunken Australian or New Zealander who had insulted his landlady or ravished her daughter on the upper river. Relief from the revels of head of the river came on a Sunday dawn when it was possible to stroll round the college without being peed on by a Herculean Stryne or tumbled on by a thirteen-stoner falling out of a tree.

Philip Carpmael was an undergraduate there too, a wet bob from Oundle who achieved a seat in the Blue boat despite its adherence to orthodoxy. He graduated to London RC where he was once in a dramatic final of the Stewards'. London were leading Pembroke College, Cambridge, at the time when Howitt, their stroke, caught a crab and went overboard. A second man jumped in to rescue him and the remaining pair, of whom Carpmael was one, put up a decent fight for the rest of the course. Later that year a London eight went to Henley-on-Yarra under the coaching of Dermot St John Gogarty, and Carpmael was on board. His Cambridge experience made him a supporter of Steve and he was sufficiently open-minded to take part in experiments with the syncopated style. This, the rowing stroke of the jazz age, was effected by seating men in a boat in pairs with enough space between them to allow each pair to engage in a different part of the stroke at a given moment. Thus the pairs performed in a roundel, pulling in relay so that there were blades in the water all the time. It was more sound in theory than in practice but London's short-lived experimental crew, using six men in an eight, was the talk of Putney's pubs. Of wider interest to Carpmael, however, were the two outspoken debates in *The Times* in which orthodoxy versus Fairbairnism was acted out by a cast of distinguished coaches who could argue that black was white, and did.

The intricacies of the stroke were argued at great length for the breakfast-table edification of the readers, and the second debate, which arose when the Football Club of Zürich won the Grand in 1936, had F. I. Pitman, the chairman of the management committee, claiming that the Swiss crew's style had no vestige of Mr Fairbairn's teaching. In a heat the Swiss met an incredible crew from Tokyo University who were on their way to the Berlin Olympics. They weighed a little more than ten stone per man and beat Quintin before meeting Zürich. They pulled 48 strokes in their first minute but the Swiss under-rated them and ran their boat, coached as it was by correspondence, to a six-length victory. Leander failed to hold the Swiss in the final, and Pitman said in his letter:

> Their style is really founded on that of the Continental crews they have rowed with and against, especially the Germans, who for many years past have been coached by Tom Sullivan . . . [Steve's] reputation must stand or fall by the rowing of the majority of the English crews at Henley regatta this year, ninety per cent of whom are unfortunately following his methods.

Steve, who had been accepted sufficiently by 1928 to be elected a steward, claimed that the Zürich footballers and athletes had learned rowing four years before from one of his books and that they were less influenced by German methods than Pitman claimed. Eventually, after memories of the Rev. Dr Warre and claims that England's appalling performance was down to Steve's influence, while foreigners, our pupils, were beating us at our own game, the Zürich coach, Arthur Dreyfus, wrote to say that he had translated much of Steve's work into German and those were the methods which he used. Remember, Dreyfus said, that mileage makes champions. One correspondent, Napier Shaw, made references to a Second Trinity crew, a club which took its boats off the Cam a hundred years before.

However it was defined, the doctrine spread. Not, maybe, always to good effect, but always with enthusiasm. The England of George and Edward was a little more disposed to criticism than the Victorian climate in which Steve and his brothers were brought up. Steve was typically colonial in the independence of his thinking, but he retained reverence for the Old Country's views, particularly for its inherent feeling that it had *the* expert understanding of sports and games. Years after coming to live in England he spoke, to Hutch and others, of the consequences of what he called 'too close settlement'. But in the estimation of his son Ian he 'was as little arrogant as he was sincerely convinced that somehow or other he had learnt the truth about rowing and owed it to other men to teach them that truth.'

Steve's worldwide correspondence and weekly letters to the captain of Jesus from his sickbed in a London hotel ceased in 1938. No more was he a familiar figure at Henley, his massive frame jammed into a chair by the river and his faithful friend Hutch standing silent beside him as Steve chatted on about rowing. His influence had spread its tentacles to waters all over the world and found many friends and disciples, as well as enraging the high priests of English orthodoxy.

Not surprisingly the history of Jesus College Boat Club published in 1928 was dedicated to Fairbairn. He shared with royalty, it said, the distinction of being known chiefly by his Christian name.

And just as English history would appear inexplicably different if we were suddenly told that William the Conqueror's first name was James, so the history of rowing would somehow appear to us in a peculiarly different light if we found that Steve was really an Algernon or a Herbert.

The crews from his college used to bow their heads at Henley's grace time and say 'To Steve'. He was buried in the Master's garden, gone but not forgotten, as can be seen from the letter which Herrick received. His portrait hung in the college with Cranmer's.

Steve's ideas, whether good or bad, caused controversy, and his mark lived on in other ways too, for in 1926 he had started a Head of River race on the championship course from Putney to Mortlake for the metropolitan clubs. In 1929 he started the Fairbairn Cup race on the same lines, rowed, against tradition, downstream on the Cam. The winner of the Tideway race gets a handsome bust of Steve to guard for a year, fashioned by an Oxford Blue, George C. Drinkwater. As it stands on its tall column, it seems to be saying 'Mileage makes champions', another of Steve's maxims, and it attracts crews from far outside the metropolis.

As they sat on the deck on the Atlantic swell Bob Herrick and Joe Burk discussed the coaches they had seen at work at Henley. Herrick remarked that Tom Bolles thought the English not as effective as the Americans because of inferior methods of training, but Herrick himself thought fewer English crews had the exaggerated rigid upswing of the shoulders that they used to have. They seemed more aware of the importance, long realized in America, of having a little shove left in the legs at the end of the stroke, very bad, but although Fairbairn gets the blame for that, he certainly never taught it. On balance, said Herrick, he thought Fairbairn's revolution had done the English a lot of good. Certainly the English lines which he later quoted when writing his Henley story for the American official rowing guide would fit Steve's philosophy a little better than that of orthodoxy, although the latter doctrine would not deny it:

> Not the laurel, but the race;
> Not the quarry, but the chase;
> Not the hazard, but the play;
> Make us Lord, enjoy alway.

8

Jack Kelly Jr opens his account
1946: Survival of the fittest

> When shall I see the Thames again?
> The prow-promoted gems again,
>   As beefy ATS
>   Without their hats
> Come shooting through the bridge?
>   And 'cheerioh' and 'cheeri-bye'
>   Across the waste of waters die,
>   And low the mists of evening lie
> And lightly skims the midge.

John Betjeman's wish was granted for oarsmen in 1946, when the midge skimmed lightly and the prow-promoted gems reappeared in full cry after the regatta's second enforced interruption due to hostilities with Germany. Some who had witnessed the victorious Grand challengers from Rudergesellschaft Wiking, Germany, giving Nazi salutes in the Stewards' in 1937 did not return in 1946, while many others came back as war heroes, like Alan Burrough, who had lost a leg when his tank was blown up near Tripoli and who appeared fitted with an artificial right leg as captain of Thames in his club's Stewards' four.

As soon as the war in Europe ended in May of 1945 preparations were made for a regatta, and an impromptu event was held that summer as a curtain-raiser for the real thing. On Saturday, 7 July, races were held over a shortened course for scullers, all-comers eights, and schools, crews racing three abreast and special cups being awarded. Enough space was cleared for spectators by moving a lot of the timber stored on regatta land by the Ministry of Supply. *The*

Times published a picture that morning of Jesus College men watching Eton pulling away from the pontoon, captioned: 'The first important rowing regatta since the collapse of Germany will take place at Henley today. . . .'

On the same day a historic ceremony took place at the foot of the Victory Column in Berlin when the Union Jack was hoisted in company with the flags of the Allies, witnessed by generals, officers and men from Britain, France, the United States and the Soviet Union. Mr Churchill, the Prime Minister, was resting in the South of France before going to the Berlin conference. Lord and Lady Astor entertained nearly four hundred staff and relatives from the Commons at their home at Cliveden to thank them for their kindness during Lady Astor's time as an MP. In perfect weather the Royal Australian Air Force beat the Army in a disappointing game at Lord's. A hundred Canadians were arrested at Aldershot after restive scenes over delays in their repatriation. There were new disturbances in Syria but the Japanese were being flushed out of Burma. The British troops who had arrived in Berlin found that the Russians had not arranged any accommodation for them, accounted for diplomatically as a Russian administrative error. King George VI and Queen Elizabeth returned from a three-day visit to the Isle of Man by a Dakota of the RAF, while Queen Mary and Lady Cynthia Colville visited the Royal School of Needlework and the Officers' Families Fund clothing branch in Exhibition Road. On the Sunday the Dean of Canterbury, Dr Hewlett Johnson, was received in the Kremlin by Marshal Stalin, and *The Times* reported that a dentist had identified Hitler's jawbone and a bridge of Eva Braun's in the remains of the bunker, and carried advertisements for forthcoming Lagondas, and hints on keeping food fresh in warm weather from the Ministry of Food. And propaganda from Lever Bros. on preparing for the return home of the boys:

> No wonder Julia shouts hurray!
> Her sweetheart's home on leave today,
> And frequent washing in the past
> Has made his favourite stockings last.

Water will do if you can't spare soap, said the Lux washability bureau.

They were sad times and glad times, glad to be alive and free, indulging once more in the pleasures of the river, sad to remember those who could take part at the most only in spirit. Some came back from the Dam Busters and the wooden horse, others mourned lost friends and comrades. One young woman got leave from the Ministry of Defence in Oxford to join her father for the revival. In the twenties she had sculled with him in a skiff or their double over the course every day during the regatta fortnight, taking to the water in shorts. Old ladies thought she should be suppressed for going out in shorts – a public scandal. She knew a good sculler when she saw one, like Jack Beresford Jr or the deaf and dumb man Gollan, who failed to win the Diamonds seven times and never beat Beresford, but helped Thames RC win the Grand and the Stewards' in 1927 and 1928. And she knew who else could spot a good crew, like John Beresford, Jack's father. She watched him walking up and down the towpath muttering to himself from about three weeks before the regatta to two or three days after it. She met him in the stewards' enclosure with her parents and knew that he thought, lived, breathed, ate and drank rowing. He couldn't speak of anything else. In 1945 she came back to her parents' riverside house, devastated by the fate of the prewar world she had known in France, reluctantly to the regatta, and had a remarkable experience.

Everybody was babbling, she recalled, and there were women in pretty dresses, ice-creams, and boats on the river and all the sort of things that you thought didn't exist any more. The maroon went for the first heat of the sculls and there was dead silence. Coming up the course, you could feel the silence. From the start, gradually; it was like something living. No race. So, of course, we got to the edge. I don't know if I was going down in the umpire's launch, I often did. I used to interpret for French or German visitors. From the start to the finish, it came down at the finish, one dove. . . . I've never seen anything like it. Nobody spoke. Nobody could speak. It was so dreadful, in a way. . . . Somebody said – it may not have been true – that a man who'd entered the sculls had been killed just at the end. And then after the dove came down at the finishing post the judge was so upset he put the flag down. And everywhere there was silence – Phyllis Court, on the course, the stewards' enclosure. And then we heard the gun and the race did come up, and everybody was too shaken to take much notice. The starter said that this bird went up, it may have been a gull but they said it was a dove, a white dove, and it came down at the finish and the judge put the flag down.

That was the communion she received that day. Others who were there do not confirm it, but that is not to say that it did not happen. Each may have experienced that regatta to celebrate peace in their own way. As they got their sport started again they could, perhaps, reflect on Edmund Blunden's rueful thoughts of but a year before during the struggle for the desert in which Alan Burrough for one was involved.

> There are those who may think [Blunden wrote in *Cricket Country*] that there is something after all in this matter of cricket, football, and generally the Englishman's love of sport and games. I will leave it to some future philosopher of theirs to probe into the other side, that of attitude to the variations of success and failure; for not the least striking thing in this North African war is the fact that our defeats did not at all defeat our temper. It is a priceless source of strength, this infallible 'insouciance', and it has not been uninfluenced from those games where even mighty Hammond and Bradman sometimes find themselves walking back to the pavilion without a run, and smile as they go; and the million are of their way of thinking too.

By 1946 the Japanese had surrendered also, and the regatta got back to something like its normal self. The cups for the Grand and Thames and the Diamonds were recovered from J. P. Morgan and Co. of New York, who had been looking after them, and the Stewards' Cup was returned from Switzerland. There was only one large boat from overseas, an eight from Zürich in the Grand who lost the final to Leander, but there were several foreign scullers and a pair from Uruguay and another from Denmark in the Goblets, and a Brazilian crew in the Double Sculls. Trinity College, Dublin, reached the final of the Ladies' Plate, but had travelled with some difficulty and trepidation. Having won the senior championship in Ireland they decided to come, though they thought they might be received badly as non-combatants. They contacted Josh Collins, who had sent them a modest bill each year for looking after the boat that they kept in England, and asked him to make it ready, not knowing what sort of condition it was in. Edwin Solomons, a Dublin stockbroker, bought them a set of oars and a member of Lady Elizabeth, a boat club largely composed of Trinity's old oars, finished his quest for accommodation by finding a camping site in the rectory field at Remenham.

They travelled from Dublin by boat and train bearing oars, bell-tents, and a lot of fodder because food was rationed in England and they did not know whether they would get any at all as Republicans. They were met by old members at Henley station and trekked down the towpath with their baggage to their site within hailing distance of the start. Ladies appeared from Remenham houses with cooking appliances and Leander members made a special point of welcoming the Dubliners.

The crew camped and trained wide-eyed for the two days before the regatta started. Their shell was in excellent condition, much better than the ones they had back home on the Liffey. The new oars were a delight, the boat was moving fast. They were fascinated to see so many of the famous names of rowing out practising, and they watched Jack Kelly, the bricklayer who had not been allowed to compete, coaching his son from a motor launch, using an electric amplifier, the wonder of the age. They met Kelly and he invited them to join him in Leander, where he reminisced about the Earl of Iveagh, a former competitor, and introduced them to his son, Jack Jr and his daughter, Grace.

The Kellys had brought some rations as well. Young Jack, a well-grown crewcut sailor with the US Navy, was seen passing the Red Lion on most days carrying a joint of beef under one arm and with a beautiful blonde on the other, most of those who saw him not realizing that she was his sister. He had just turned nineteen and, ever since he could remember, his father had told him that he might go to Henley and win the Diamond Sculls. Being of Irish heritage the old man had really wanted to win England's big race, and having been denied the chance he wanted his son to win it even more than winning the Olympic title. His constant talk of Henley influenced his son's life and caused junior to set his goals towards obtaining a pineapple cup.

Also up for the regatta were the crews from Jesus College, Cambridge. Their Thames Cup boat was stroked by John McKeown, who had witnessed the peace regatta the year before as a schoolboy, a bloody-minded schoolboy who had reached no rowing heights at school and was wondering if he would forsake the river for ever on going up to Cambridge that October. He saw the Jesus crew, which looked highly unusual to him, and was surprised that they did so well. He joined the club and found to his astonishment that he was rowing in the first eight in his first term, and became a rabid convert. He and some of his friends were not all naturally good oars but they found that the club took immense trouble to train them, and none of them were left feeling unimportant. They found a sense of identity at a time when outlets outside academic life were few and far between, and their fanaticism bred a cockiness on which they thrived and which made them unpopular in other parts of the college. So here they were, relaxing between outings at a comfortable small hotel in the High Street, the cox keeping himself down by shovelling malt in the high temperature of Brakspear's brewery and their strains being cured by a former member, Dr Joe Bailey, who was adept at throwing muscle-bound oarsmen bodily across a room of his near-by house.

Racing conditions were hard, with a strongish stream and a variable wind, but the regatta was blessed with fine weather as Trinity, Dublin, and the Jesus Ladies' crew set off together from Leander for the start of the final. McKeown's crew had been eliminated by King's College, London, from the Thames, and so they were in good voice to support their clubmates. The Trinity boys were nervous, the more so because the Princesses Elizabeth and Margaret were to present the prizes on their first public engagement without their parents in attendance. Trinity's run in the heats had seen off St Edward's School, Queens' College, Cambridge, Magdalen College, Oxford, and then Bryanston in the semifinal. Tension mounted in their tents at Remenham and when resting there they had been disturbed repeatedly by the maroons which were fired from the island to tell the enclosures that a race was under way and to warn boats to clear the course. They paddled down to the island and lay off it, watching with mounting apprehension the royal passengers on the umpire's launch. But they soon dismissed all thoughts of royalty as the umpire started the race. They led Jesus, then were caught, then led again by six feet at Fawley, trailed by six feet at the mile, and then spurted several times to no avail, the Cambridge men winning by just over a length. It was the most exhausting race that Alan Browne, number seven man in the Trinity boat, could recall. The Cambridge supporters were frantic on the bank, and when a great invocation of 'Jesus!' arose from the enclosure, the wife of a top-level Russian diplomat who was of the orthodox persuasion almost fainted with shock.

Leander beat the Swiss in the Grand and Jack Kelly was not treated to watching his son receive the coveted Diamonds from a royal princess. Junior reached the final but met more than his match in

Séphériades, the Greek European champion who was sculling for the Société Nautique de la Basse Seine, France. The losing finalists lined the steps from the riverside to the prize-giving site with the winners on the other side, and the royal party thus passed between Jesus and Trinity. Browne watched with mixed feelings as his opponents got the Ladies' Plate from the happy pair of girls in pink hats and pale blue dresses, distributing shy smiles to those around them. Later, though, he met the Jesus crew and got on well with them, and lost himself in the flowing champagne of Leander and the pink haze of the regatta dance. He remembered the fairground in full swing, the grey toppers and the moth-eaten blazers, and the stroke of the crew disappearing into the darkness with Princess Zagina of Albania whom he chanced to meet.

The stewards' barge was moored to the booms on the Bucks station and on it Leslie Jeffries and his orchestra played a selection from *Show Boat*, Doreen Lundy sang 'Begin the Beguine,' and Raymond Newell, famous baritone, sang 'Yeomen of England' and the 'Eton Boating Song' to that tune written up the Punjab. The BBC Light Programme broadcast the concert, but not the renderings of 'Brian Boru' and 'The Sash my Father Wore' by the men of Trinity outside the dance tent. They had warmed to the English welcome which transcended politics, at least from Leander to Remenham, where lightly skimmed the midge.

9

Vladimir Kuchmenko blows hot and cold
1955: The Russians come and lightweights make their mark

In 1954 the Russians first came to Henley, drawing as much curiosity as if they had stepped down from the moon, and a year later an industrial dispute brought matters back to earth. Between the day when Princess Elizabeth handed the cup named after her to Bedford School on 6 July 1946 and the appearance of the Soviet crews on Henley reach, the struggle between the English and foreigners continued, conducted now almost entirely on the water and not in the press. The legacy of Fairbairnism lived on, manifest in the crews of Cambridge Jesuits and other disciples of Steve. The attention which JCBC paid to its freshmen was paid back in loyalty and hard work as John McKeown recalled. Before the forties were out the college won the Ladies', the Grand, the Head of the River race, and every major event on the Cam. Chris Barton, their stroke of 1948, stroked the British Olympic crew that lost only to the Americans that year. The club laid down arduous training and believed fanatically that mileage built champions. All their Henley crews rowed at least a thousand miles in the year preceding their entry, reckoned to be about double what any other Cambridge college did. The staple of this was long trips from Cambridge to Ely, supported by excellent college dinners even during the time of severest rationing and supplemented by meagre purchases of what was available under rationing or black-market cakes from the market place. They tasted like sawdust. During this time the Cambridge crew kept a cow which they used to visit for sustenance during training runs, and McKeown became a fan of the ecclesiastical establishment when one of Archbishop Fisher's sons, a fellow undergraduate, prevailed upon his father to persuade the Labour Government to double bread rations for students, from one loaf a week to two.

Fuel shortages accompanied food shortages, and in the severe winter of 1946–47 McKeown's hair froze as he crossed the court from bath house to rooms. One scuttleful of coal was the weekly ration, enough for one evening's fire. The river froze and skaters did the course to Ely, and when the ice cleared a little the boats were fitted with ice-breaking covers over the bows so that training could be done. Even then the boats kept running up on the ice and the crews were constantly backing them off and breaking their blades on the floes.

The Fairbairn ideal was kept alive in the club by Freddy Brittain and Percy Bullock. Brittain was the social centre of the club, eccentric, scholar and college historian, ceaseless propagandist for Steve, using earthy humour, quick repartee and legion *obiter dicta*. Freddy was their St Paul and Percy their evangelist according to McKeown, though to his mind Freddy outdid the saint in originality and interest. Percy came armed with the master's slogans, was never at a loss on coaching problems, and soon put you right if you showed the stiff, unnatural, boat-stopping ways of the orthodox.

Freddie and Percy trod the boathouse boards like some vaudeville act and sent their milers out, humble as cockerels. McKeown's best memory is from the Cambridge coxless fours when the Jesus second boat, which he was in, was sent for slaughter before mighty First and Third Trinity, the club which had emerged from a wartime unification of Trinity's two surviving clubs. Second Trinity had ceased to function a hundred years before, so now the three were one. Their crew contained a Blue and three trial caps and were coached by Peter Haig-Thomas, principal Blue Boat coach. The Jesuits, having been told that they would do well if they were beaten by only a few lengths, rowed right through their opponents who then gave up. Haig Thomas was enraged and furious, accusing his men of training on gin.

John Garton, who rowed in several Eton crews in the thirties, was president of OUBC in 1939 and competed that year for Magdalen, Oxford, in the Stewards' and for Beverley Club in the Goblets, remembered the contrast between the English and the Americans in the years after the war. The Americans looked about three times as big as anything we had. 'Our chaps looked as if they'd been through seven years of war with no decent steak. They looked anaemic, puny.' But what McKeown remembered is the toughness which men could harbour within them. He could throw up regularly after a course and then row another later in the day. He saw a Jesus bow man, D. C. Bray, race the Grand final of 1947 with a temperature of 101°, a circumstance which would not have found favour with the master.

Certainly crews from abroad soon got back into the lists of title holders and the record books after the war, but it was only in the Thames Cup that foreigners increased their influence at the expense of the home teams. The first American crew to win the Thames were Browne and Nichols School from near Boston in 1929, and they were followed by other private schools from the United States, Kent from Connecticut winning in 1933 and 1938, and their close rivals Tabor Academy in 1936, 1937 and 1939. Kent and Tabor returned in 1947, Kent being the winners with a crew in which only one boy was under twelve stone. Kent had been the first American school to come to Henley when they entered the Thames in 1927, a dream which the founder of the school, Father Frederick Herbert Sill, made come true. He had been a coxswain at Columbia University in the nineties and began visiting England during that time. Later he founded Kent by a five-mile stretch of the Housatonic River, which was carefully chosen for the rowing facilities which it afforded, and then, when standing on Henley bridge in the rain in the non-rowing season of 1921, he vowed that he would send a Kent crew to the regatta within ten years. The priest and teacher from the Order of the Holy Cross was also considering wider aspects of Anglo-American contact on that day, and his idea came to fruition after a cool start at Henley.

He was in trouble with the stewards for using a coaching launch in 1927 and nobody spoke to the boys from Kent for five days, but they got a warm reception at Mr John Nugee's house at Radley. Out of that contact grew the annual exchange scheme run by the English Speaking Union for boys and girls in private British and American schools.

The heavy school crews kept on coming to the regatta, joined by St Paul's, Concord, on their first trip in 1954. There was also a sight new to Henley, however, the other edge to America's sword. Where the young giants failed the lithe student lightweight crews often succeeded. They came neat and fit, and equipped with enough technique and grit to deal with most of the home-grown products, who tended to be club second crews or college crews who were thought not good enough for the Ladies'. The Thames Cup got very popular, elimination races having to be held in most years to get the starting number down to thirty-two, and spectators were treated to some great races by this lightweight class of oarsmen which was unknown in Britain. The times taken also crept very close to those for the Ladies', which had always been regarded as senior to the Thames as well as being older. The Ladies' was partially weakened by the introduction of the Princess Elizabeth which was rowed over the full course from 1947 and was attractive to some of the best school screws. The list of winners for the Thames from 1947 to 1955 showed clearly what had happened there. Heavyweights from Kent School won it twice, and lightweights from the universities of Princeton, Pennsylvania and Massachusetts Institute of Technology won it twice each. In several cases Americans were the losing finalists. The only British crew to win were the Royal Air Force in 1953.

It was probably these big American schoolboys who made an impression on John Garton when he compared the quality of beef-steak on opposite sides of the Atlantic, and the crewcut hulk of Jack Kelly Jr, whom everybody seemed to know and dislike. He returned to the Diamonds in 1947, this time a towering University of Pennsylvania student weighing nearly thirteen and a half stone, accompanied by his parents, Grace and his other sister Lizann. He was booed by spectators, but his father said later that in a crowd that size you always find somebody who doesn't like somebody else. Kelly Sr thought that the antagonism was caused by the fuss that the newspapers made over the special rations that the family wisely brought with them. England was austere, and Mrs Margaret Kelly packed canned milk, dried eggs, sugar and canned meats. They brought a dozen bottles of Capon Springs Water in case the change of water caused dysentery, and Shor's restaurant of New York, whose owner was a family friend, sent six steaks in dried ice to the Red Lion, where they were cooked. Photographers lined up all their bottles of water and cans, quite a display for the deprived English, though the Kellys noticed that none of junior's opponents seemed to be undernourished.

Kelly had an easy passage to the final against Ben Piessens, the Belgian champion (12 st 12 lbs), then Holloway of Henley RC (13 st 12 lbs), Bert Bushnell of Maidenhead (11 st 3 lbs), and an easy final

against Fronsdal of Bergens, the Norwegian champion (12 st 2 lbs).
He thus delivered up his father's dream and did it again almost as
easily in 1949. In between he sculled for his country at the 1948
Olympic Games. The regatta was held at Henley over a shortened
course of about 1880 metres against the stream, which facilitated
three lanes. During Kelly's semifinal there was what he described as a
tornado, a headwind in a hail storm. He stopped dead in a gust,
which appeared to be providence according to one rain-drenched
spectator. The weather added about two minutes to the time taken
for the race and while the English sculler Anthony Rowe almost
stopped as well, the Uruguayan Eduardo Risso came through them
both. Risso lost the final to Mervyn Wood of Australia. Kelly had a
much better year in 1949 when, as well as taking the Diamonds, he
beat Risso by about eight lengths in winning the European title in
Amsterdam. He reckoned that he was in superb condition that summer, an Olympian a year too late.

British crews picked up two gold medals at the 1948 Olympics.
The most remarkable was that by Ran Laurie and Jack Wilson in the
coxless pairs. They had won the Goblets back in 1938 after which
they both spent nearly ten years in the Sudan, returning on leave in
time to win the Goblets again in 1948 and with them the Olympic
selection. Then they took the gold medal. Bert Bushnell and Richard
Burnell, son of that 'strongest sweep in England' who got a gold
medal at the Games of 1908, won the Double Sculls. No father and
son had ever won gold medals in any sport in the Olympic Games.
To celebrate the regatta the Drill Hall on Friday Street was turned
into a museum and gallery of rowing, treasures being lent from all
over the country.

In 1949 Harcourt Gold got a knighthood for services to rowing,
the regatta had a record 156 starters, and the stewards restricted the
number of starters to sixteen in all events except the Thames and the
Wyfolds, in which thirty-two were permitted. Schools were forbidden to compete with the same crew in the Ladies' and the Princess
Elizabeth, being obliged to scratch from one or other if they made a
double entry. Members of the stewards' enclosure were more comfortable now that additional space had been made available, for the
luncheon tent had been moved to Selwyn Meadow, across the
Remenham Road near a charming old pavilion called Barn Cottage.
The stewards had bought the field in 1947.

The dream of a small Belfast boy came true in 1950. Paddy Kemp was taken to the pictures by his parents in wartime Belfast and saw a bit of film about the Diamonds. From that day his ambition was to race for them and try to win. At 3.45 p.m. on Wednesday, 5 July, he was on the Bucks station alongside John Pinches and eight minutes and fifty-five seconds later he was still sculling, just a length and a quarter behind Pinches, who was already across the line. Pinches was defeated in the next round by a young Dutchman from Trinity College, Dublin, Robbie van Mesdag, who went on to the race of his life. He was more than two stone lighter than his countryman Neumeier, and the reporter from *Rowing Magazine*, first published in the previous December, gave van Mesdag a palm for gallantry.

> The Dutchman from Dublin is a highly temperamental sculler. His needle at the start was so obvious that it was almost a harpoon and along the island he appeared to make every kind of error. Yet in spite of his rough sculling and frequent washing out he managed to keep a consistently good run on his boat.

For the whole course barely half a length separated them. Van Mesdag stuck to his man, got his bows in front and kept them there. He won by three feet and could not get out of his boat. Next day he lost the final to Rowe who took a three-length lead and sat comfortably on it.

That was half an hour after Harvard won the Grand for the third time in the university's history. Tom Bolles and the crew flew to London from New York on an American Overseas stratocruiser and they settled in at the Hermitage and practised in the *Robert F. Herrick*, a much-admired Pocock shell. The boys were interested to compare the long layback of the orthodox crews with the more sit-up style of the American crews and the 'catch it with a running slide' of those influenced by Fairbairn, but Bolles thought that the styles were less evident than in previous years. He told the *Alumni Bulletin*: 'The extreme orthodox and Fairbairn are gone now and, in my opinion, a better style is emerging.' The English style may have been beginning to jell but the Harvard crew was causing comment from the bankside sages: 'All arms and legs,' said one. 'A veritable machine,' said another. 'Definitely quee-ah,' said a third. Against Lady Margaret the Americans experienced what they expected from an English crew – a fast English start to build up a fatal lead, followed by a running-out of gas. They were interested to see the way that Lady Margaret short-ened up the orthodox stroke when under pressure, leaving out the long reach and the layback. It seemed that bodyswing was for practice but sitting-up was for racing. Harvard beat the Dutch students from Njord in the final, and cynics speculated about whether their call-up papers would come, for after 1914 and 1939, what next? The crew were in fact three days behind cue, for American marines had already landed in Korea on behalf of the United Nations. One who was called up eventually was Jack Kelly Jr, who by 1951 was at sea on a destroyer and then came home next year to train with Navy oarsmen for the Olympic Games which were held in Helsinki. He was beaten at the post just as he had been at the 1948 Games at Henley.

Bicycles on the towpath upstream of the Barrier during the regatta are likely to be stopped by the police, said L. D. Williams, the secret-ary, in the letter to competitors. There was serious vandalism too, that year, when the statue of the two-faced goddess of Temple Island was smashed and drowned. *Rowing Magazine* took on the role of the thunderer.

> Selfish folly seeking a vulgar notoriety impelled some oafs to remove her from her pedestal. . . . It was not an action demanding pluck, since the nearest police were over a mile away. . . . No college crew was at hand to defend her as they would their banner. . . . The island is inhabited by one old woman of 91.

A shameful act, but there was no hint that a college crew might, just might, have perpetrated the deed. There was still a lot of stiff upper lip about Henley; the committee of management may have kept an eye closer to the developments in their sport which began to affect their institution, but their discernment was not always visible to the growing crowds in their enclosures or more particularly to the com-petitors who turned up from places which would never have been represented before the Second World War. They had to turn their attention to the possibility of seeding, to the amateur definition, to the growing number of contestants, to parking cars, and to the pos-sibilities of television.

On the face of it, however, things went on much the same. In 1952 Sir Harcourt Gold died shortly after the regatta, ending a steward-ship of forty-three years. He was a modest man, who had devoted hours to administrate others' pleasure, and it was he who had thought of the idea of the stewards' enclosure and set it up in the twenties. Gully Nickalls wrote in *The Times*:

> At a very early age I fell under the spell of his gaiety and infectious good humour, as did men from all walks of life, whether it was his loader in the butts or his caddy on the links.

So the Russians came in 1954. They telephoned first to inquire what the standard times were for the course because they did not want to make fools of themselves. People travelled from miles around to see them as if they rowed on their heads or faced the front. They brought with them the mystery of the unknown. As a nation the Soviet Union had only ventured into the Olympic arena in Helsinki in 1952, where they had made a considerable mark. Until then they had taken an insular view of sport since their revolution in 1917, keeping much to themselves and their kind as they worked out their philosophy of physical and artistic education. Thus Soviet athletes in any discipline had been seen but rarely, and Henley's society waited eagerly for their coming while not being too anxious to actually associate with them. Gully Nickalls went to see them in their lodgings at the behest of the committee to answer questions and explain the rules. From the jokes he told later and the attitude he struck it would not have been surprising if the Russians expected him to umpire while looking backwards. They had a good dinner and sank much vodka, while he explained patiently through their interpreter that they could not have three men on the finishing line, and explained that the English don't cheat. 'They seemed convinced,' he wrote, 'that by hook or by crook we should deny them the victory they deserved.' Nothing, presumably, was further from the thoughts of the Jesus and Lady Margaret crews, London and Thames and Leander, as they waited for their names to be drawn from the cup later in the week, even if they all wanted the fight to be a fair one.

Gully Nickalls's hand-across-the-Iron-Curtain mission was interrupted by some loud explosions. On investigation he found that the English crew living next door to the Russians were throwing fire crackers over the wall. Bloody fools, thought Nickalls, and he went round to deliver a few well-chosen words to the culprits, who desisted. A chip off the old block was Gully, remembering how uncle Vivian had dispersed an angry crowd outside the Red Lion in the early twenties while the police melted into the background.

The firecrackers stopped, the Russians raced and maybe little boys and girls dared each other to touch them as they carried their boats to and from the water. Their eight, Club Krylia, was a national crew and was easily the best in the Grand, beating the Danes in the first round, Thames in the semifinal, and Leander in the final. Their four from Krylia won the Stewards' against the RAF in a strong headwind and knocked another Soviet crew out on their way to the final. Their pair won the Goblets and the late Tom Nickalls's Challenge Cup. Their sculler, Tukalov, lost to Vlasic of Yugoslavia in the first round of the Diamonds, and their double scullers also went out in the first round of their event, beaten by Marsden and Fox of London. Nobody had known how fast they were or anything about them. They came on a ship, not down from the moon, and won some and lost some. Massachusetts Institute of Technology took the Thames Cup, Vlasic won the Diamonds, and Schriever and Stebler of Zürich the Double Sculls, so six of the seven open events went overseas.

The next year a game of brinkmanship was played out between the Russians and the stewards, which resulted in the latter making a large concession and taking liberties with established rowing custom in order to keep crews in a race. Indeed, the confrontation was not the fault of either party, and it was fortunate for both that neither misconstrued the situation to the point of no return. At the beginning of regatta week an extensive dock strike was entering its sixth week. It was a dispute between the National Amalgamated Stevedores and Dockers and the larger Transport and General Workers Union, with the former demanding representation on joint negotiating bodies in London, Liverpool, Manchester and Hull. It was a confused and confusing situation, and on the first morning of the regatta *The Times* reported that the striking NASD men had now been urged to return to work by the government, the port employers, the TUC, the TGWU, the Communists, the so-called Trotskyist group who formerly cheered them on in Liverpool, their own general secretary, who had resigned rather than support a continuation of the stoppage, their other national officials, and their executive. The Russian Communists were not being accused of causing the strike: the problem was that the Soviet ship *Strelna* was languishing in Surrey docks, strike-bound with the racing shells on board.

On the Saturday before Henley the National Dock Labour Board regatta was being held at Putney and the dockers' rowing secretary,

Arthur Cratchley, received a telephone call from Hylton Cleaver, the editor of *Rowing Magazine*. Cleaver suggested that Cratchley organize a volunteer gang to go to the *Strelna* there and then and unload the boats. The sportsmen could show the world what they thought of class barriers. Cratchley consulted both the unions and obtained consent, and the men were on Putney Embankment ready to leave when the British shipping agent refused permission to unload unless he got a written guarantee that the ship would not be declared 'black' as a result. This could not be arranged and so the plan fell through.

By the Monday the Soviet oarsmen were in Henley and English clubs were queueing up to lend them boats. Argentinian crews had been withdrawn, and the Swiss, Italians and Poles had not arrived by the start of the weekend. L. D. Williams, the secretary, and Harold Rickett, the chairman, were doing some frantic work on the telephone and by the Tuesday the newspaper reported that the four shells in the *Strelna* would be unloaded by a gang of volunteers from the dockers on strike, provided that a mass meeting that day outside the Surrey and Commercial docks allowed them to do so. A boat transporter waited for four and a half hours. When the chairman, Mr W. Green, said, 'I have a message from the Russian embassy,' there were shouts of 'We don't want to hear it,' and he passed on to other business. Seamen sunned themselves on the deck of the ship near the crated craft, but nothing moved.

The next day was the first of the regatta, and at 10 a.m. the regatta office issued a statement which quoted one they had received from the Soviet coach and interpreter:

> We, the Soviet oarsmen, having discussed the situation which is the result of the fact that the Secretariat of the Henley Royal Regatta has failed in getting our boats off the ships, have decided to withdraw from all events. . . .

The stewards had been influential in getting the ship docked from the queue in the Thames Estuary, but there was not much more they could do. And they suspected that the withdrawal had more to do with the Soviet Embassy than the team manager.

While the Russians packed their things, the stevedores gave permission for the crew of the *Strelna* to unload the boats. Vladimir Kuchmenko, the team manager, was now at the Embassy and he rang the regatta to try and cancel the withdrawal. At 6.05 p.m. the committee issued another statement, which said:

The Soviet crews have requested that they may be allowed to cancel their withdrawal from the regatta. In the exceptional circumstances the committee of management have agreed to the re-admission of crews competing in those events which have not yet begun.

That meant all but the luckless sculler, Tukalov. The eight actually rowed their first heat of the Grand in a borrowed boat to beat Jesus. On the Friday they returned to their own boat, which *The Times* thought was too small for them, and were beaten by Vancouver RC of Canada.

The Vancouver crew, who were made up from the University of British Columbia and Vancouver RC, took Canada by storm in exposing the limitations of the Russians' rocking, windmill style, as the *Daily Express* put it. The *Province* newspaper asked: 'How can you explain this triumph over the hand-picked stars of a vast nation – the defending Henley champions, trained and drilled to'the limit – by a bunch of working kids from that venerable tumbledown shack called the Vancouver Rowing Club? All we can say is – let's roll out the red carpet for Coach Read and his astounding whizzkids.' When the boys scalped the Russians they received a telegram which said:

> Row, row, row your boat,
> Swiftly down the course,
> If the Russians get in front,
> Shoot them in the orse.

The Canadians had stumped up $25,000 to send them to Henley and they, too, had difficulty with their boat because of the strike. It went to Bremen and Cherbourg before getting to Britain. Pennsylvania beat Vancouver in the final in a boat which was flown across the Atlantic by the USAF.

MIT won the Thames cup again, and Russians took the Stewards', Goblets and Double Sculls. The Goblets pair, Zhilin and Emchuck, defeated the Grasshopper Club of Zürich, who drew up almost level with the Soviet oarsmen at the Mile. Thomi Keller, stroking the Swiss, looked across the course and saw a very young man in blazer and boater with his rosy-cheeked teenage English rose sitting in a punt alongside the booms. The pimply youth enunciated in clear Oxford tones: 'Well rowed, Grasshoppers!' and Keller started laughing out loud at the quaintness of it all. There was no way that he and Vollmer could catch the Russians after that. Kettering RC reached the final of the Wyfolds in a sectionalized boat that they built themselves for £50 and 630 man-hours.

In the week before the regatta the Kenton Theatre staged a revue by Gully Nickalls called *Round the Bend*, as well it might, in which Gully impersonated Churchill and several other regatta officials impersonated others. The silverware went abroad again on a fine day after a 'Keep left' sign had been removed from the island, a pedestrian-crossing sign from the Barrier, and a British Railways car-park sign from the roof of Phyllis Court's grandstand.

When the Canadians reached home they were rewarded handsomely for beating the Russians and losing the Grand. They were congratulated by the House of Commons in Ottawa and paraded through the Streets of Vancouver, getting a formal address from the mayor on the Court House steps and being presented with gold medals inscribed: 'In recognition of the fine showing of UBC/VRC eight at Henley, 1955.'

10

Stuart Mackenzie joins the circus
1964: The Diamonds go Down Under and Harvard's chance in ten thousand

Sometime in 1963 Harold Rickett, the chairman of the committee of management, got a letter from Leverett Saltonstall, the Senator for Massachusetts, asking what he thought of the idea of the Harvard junior varsity crew having their reunion at Henley. He meant the crew of 1914 who had won the Grand. They got together for a row every five years and would like to return to the water of their conquest, though they did not know how they would be received in England after they had survived fit and well through two world wars.

As if they needed to take soundings! On Saturday, 4 July 1964, another Independence Day, they paddled well together and neatly into the wind over the last part of the course, exactly fifty years since they won the cup. Sixty-seven of their relatives watched them. So did Her Majesty Queen Elizabeth the Queen Mother, the Princess Margaret and her husband, the Earl of Snowdon, who as Anthony Armstrong-Jones had coxed Jesus crews at Henley and Cambridge in the Boat Race. So did the Harvard crew of 1964 and the Soviet eight who had beaten them in the first round of the Grand. The crew were in the same order and rig as 1914: Leverett Saltonstall (72), US Senator – in the bow; James Talcott (70), President, Talcott Inc. Real Estate; Henry Hixon Meyer (70), lawyer; Henry Stump Middendorf (69) and his twin, John William Middendorf, both in investments; David Percy Morgan (69), Monsanto Chemicals; Louis Curtis (72), Brown Bros. Harriman and Co., bankers; Charles Carroll Lund (69), surgeon; and their coxswain, Henry L. F. Kreger, lawyer. Their average weight without the cox was 174 lbs in 1914 and 9 lbs heavier this year, but the cox had put on 39 lbs in the fifty years. They knew because the official in charge of the weigh-in in 1914 was still there to check up on them. Frederick Wadsworth Busk, the substitute, was there also, surely the longest wait in history of rowing, and so was the manager, Robert Codman Cobb. Only their coach, Robert F. Herrick, was missing, but perhaps he could see a job well done from the Great Enclosure in the Sky.

As a tribute to the regatta the Harvard '14 crew presented a replica of the Grand Challenge Cup so that the one which Warington Smyth and the men of Trinity had first drunk from in 1839 could be put into retirement. It had attended upon more than a hundred victory toasts and travelled to four continents, and was looking a little worser for wear than when the *Black Prince* had borne it to London.

Eliot House, a Harvard 'college' crew, won the Thames Cup, Washington Lee High School beat Groton School in the Princess Elizabeth Cup, and Cromwell of the Nonpareil BC won the Diamonds, so the American influence was well represented in 1964. Phillips Exeter Academy of the USA lost the final of the Prince Phillip Cup to Molesey BC. This was an event for coxed fours introduced in 1963 and presented with its cup by the Duke of Edinburgh. Racing in coxed fours had not been seen at Henley since shortly after 'Danny Boy' Weatherly had proved the potential speed of coxless boats by leaping overboard from Woodgate's Brasenose crew in 1868. Apart from the short-lived Public Schools' Challenge Cup from 1879–84, it took more than ninety years to reintroduce coxed fours, surprising in a country where most of the rowing was done on winding rivers.

Since they first arrived in 1954 the Soviet oarsmen won the Grand three more times before 1964, and were famously beaten by Cornell in 1957. There was no more suspicion about strikes and rules, the Russians having accepted that the Fédération Internationale des Sociétés d'Aviron (FISA – the international rowing federation) was happy to allow Henley to run its own ship. The British public still flocked to see them, no longer as something wild and woolly from Siberia but rather as useful and popular artists seeking fame at the end of an eight-foot spruce.

Some of the background to the Soviet Union's interest in rowing was revealed in a letter to *Rowing Magazine* from Mr M. Knopmuss of Moseley, Birmingham. In 1924, he said, after coaching the Arrow Boat Club in Leningrad for twenty-five years, he smuggled all the club's papers to Britain. Rowing at St Petersburg, as it then was, had been started by the English in 1842 and revived on the Neva after the Crimea in 1864. Several other clubs had grown up and the rowing influences were partly from the Neva ferryman and partly from the likes of T. E. Coulson of London RC. Knopmuss left copies of Lehmann's *Complete Oarsman* and some of Steve Fairbairn's pamphlets for the edification of the new Soviet club. Rowing was one of the sports approved by the new regime because it encouraged competition against the clock or one's self rather than directly against an opponent.

Whether from English how-to-do-it books or Russian translations thereof, whether in creaking old boats by Sims and Salter with whippy old blades by Norris and Ayling, or whether by grit and an embryo boatbuilding industry, the Russians had come, and in 1956 Vjacheslav Ivanov won the Melbourne Olympic title ahead of an Australian and Jack Kelly Jr of the USA. That was the year, incidentally, that the international rowing federation banned Argentina's oarsmen from the Games because they could not be considered as amateurs. Gaston Mullegg, president of FISA, said that a great number of them had received and accepted extremely large sums of money, but a spokesman for the Argentinians said that not to have accepted a car in Peron's day for those who brought honour to their country would have meant gaol.

Ivanov and the Australian, Stuart Alexander Mackenzie, came to Henley the year after the Olympics and, although the Russian was a popular man, it was Mackenzie who carried off the Diamonds. He then did it five more times, with brilliance and a brand of showmanship which bordered on wickedness.

At King's School, Parramatta, Stuart Alexander Mackenzie, the son of a chicken farmer, was a good allround athlete. Tall and handsome, with uncommonly long arms and weighing nearly fourteen stone, he was admirably suited for sculling, and was almost a novice at nineteen when he achieved selection for the Melbourne Games. He worked as a chicken-sexer on his father's New South Wales farm, a specialized talent which he was able to put to good use in the winter months in England. It enabled him to spend a lot of time sculling in the spring and summer, and he made his base Henley-on-Thames. He brought the stands to their feet in his first final, in which he met Ivanov again. Mackenzie got a lead of almost two lengths by the Mile over the Olympic champion, who after the first heat had got a

Top: Russians congratulate Stuart Mackenzie of Mosman RC, Australia, after his fifth successive win in the Diamonds, 1961

Above: From the red to the cerise: Club Krylia hand a souvenir to Leander after beating them in a heat of the Stewards' in 1957

Grand crews
Above: After the race: Club Krasnoe Znamia, USSR, have just been defeated by Cornell in a semifinal in the Grand in 1957. Cornell came from behind, lowered the record by eight seconds and went on to win a close final against Yale
Opposite page
Top: Leander and Thames Tradesmen defeating Harvard by two lengths in the Grand of 1975. Their time of 6.16 equalled that of Ratzeburg of Germany ten years before, but in the semifinals both Harvard and the British crew shared a new record of 6.13. It still stands. Six of the Britons and the cox went on to win silver medals at the Olympic Games in Montreal. From the bow: Len Robertson, Bill Mason, Jim Clark, John Yallop, Richard Ayling, Tim Crooks, Hugh Matheson, Dick Lester, and coxswain Pat Sweeney

Middle: The Olympians who never were: the Charles River Rowing Association, reluctant boycotters of the Moscow Games and winners of the Grand in 1980. From the bow: Sean Colgan, Dick Cashin, Kurt Sommerville, Charles Altekruse, Thomas Woodman, Steve Christensen, John Everett, Bruce Ibbetson, and coxswain John Chatzky
Bottom: Ratzeburg of Germany on their way to winning the Grand of 1965 against Vesper, USA. Karl Adam's crews took the sport by storm in the early 1960s and this one was no exception. Their time of 6.16 took seven seconds off the Soviet record of 1964 and they set records to the Barrier and to Fawley, as the board shows. From the bow: H. Meyer, D. Schreyer, C. Prey, K. Behrens, D. Thomatschek, J. Schröder, H.-J. Wallbrecht, K. Aeffke, and coxswain P. Mainke

Before, during and after.
Preparations on shore,
bringing the boat in, the
finishing 'burn', the end
of the race, and a
coxswain pays the price
of victory

Above: In 1964 London RC collided with a punt before the start of their heat of the Prince Philip with St Neots RC. Here the Thames Conservancy launch brings the crew home while the determined No. 2 man, Peter Coni, pushes the shell back to the pontoon. Coni became Chairman of the Stewards in 1978

Below: The Harvard '14 crew go out for a practice in 1964. From the bow: Leverett Saltonstall, James Talcott, Henry Meyer, the Middendorf twins, David Morgan, Louis Curtis, Charles Lund, and coxswain Henry Kreger

Foreign sparklers and flaws in the Diamonds
Left: Jack Kelly Jr, who travelled with beef and blondes
Below: Vjacheslav Ivanov, USSR, twice the losing finalist to Mackenzie
Bottom: Jim Dietz of New York (left) congratulates Sean Drea of Neptune RC, Eire, on his third successive win in 1975. Drea set the Diamonds record at 7.40 in a heat

Towpath strollers, car-park picnickers, and removal of the swans

bye to the final because the Diamonds holder, Kocerka of Poland, withdrew with a torn back muscle. Then Ivanov came back at him very fast, pushing his rate up very high in the closing stages, and the Australian from Sydney RC won by four feet.

Mackenzie was noticed, and he made sure that he kept on being noticed. He played brinkmanship on the water and psychological warfare off it. Before the regatta started he went on a practice along-side Ivanov and finished looking done in. Ivanov looked jubilant and Mackenzie told inquiring newspaper men that the Russian was too fast and too fit for him. He had sown the seed of false security in the Soviet camp. He met Ivanov again the next year, and the Russian Army sculler set a new record to the Barrier but was several lengths behind at the Mile, and the Australian cruised powerfully home to a verdict of 'Easily' after pausing to raise his cloth cap to the crowd. 'Sorry I couldn't do better, boys, I've got a bad back,' he shouted to the occupants of the press box, and then sculled back down the course for fifty yards, bowing to and acknowledging the spectators, not all of whom were impressed by this un-Henley-like show of brashness. He won a gold medal for Australia in each of those years in the European Championships, at Duisburg and Posnan respec-tively. And also in 1958 he won the Empire Games title on Lake Padarn in North Wales.

The aura of Ivanov brought in the crowds, and so did the unpre-dictability of Mackenzie's performances. People loved to hate him. Would he play cat-and-mouse with a weak or beaten opponent, and would he do it once too often? His physique was beautiful to behold, his sculling looked appalling, ungraceful in the most graceful of events, but he could move a boat in an astonishing way. He could have brought the record down with ease if he had not stopped to talk with friends during a particularly fast race. He got into trouble with regatta officials at Marlow for going on the course in a track suit, and he once wore a bowler hat for a race at an English regatta. Cat-and-mousing was not a new thing in sculling: Mervyn Wood, another Australian, had indulged in it, and so had some of the great professionals of the past like the Canadian, Edward Hanlan, who once performed tricks during a race in Sydney. But showing up one's opponents at Henley was reckoned to be bad form, just as waiting for opponents who had had some misfortune of equipment always used to be good form, almost *de rigueur*. The most embarrassing incident of all had been in 1927 when a powerful Thames eight had dithered between paddling and floating when up against a very weak but plucky crew from Worcester College for the Blind. Thames just couldn't go slowly enough.

Sam Mackenzie from the foothills of the Blue Mountains always wore his Mackenzie tie, and he hated to be called Sam, which was why a lot of people used the nickname derived from his initials. He carried golf clubs in the boot of his car and he denounced the pink-sock brigade at Leander cheerfully, politely and mercilessly while wearing the club's cerise socks himself. The question most often asked of him was, 'How do you sex chickens?' and he always replied, 'You rattle 'em.' He rattled a lot of people at Henley, verbally picking them up and shaking them, pushing them jollily to the limit, and called a viscount a cobber. He applied the rules to himself regarding diet, drink, smoking and everything else rigorously. He was quite fanatical about not drinking and would not go anywhere where someone was smoking. And he carried a vast array of pills and potions as part of his campaign to outdo everybody else. At breakfast at a Continental regatta, for example, he would line up bottles of vitamin pills, Weetabix, lime juice on the table and get all the East Europeans wondering what secret elixir of diet was going to defeat them. Or he would choose the moment when a man with a reputation had put his sculls on the pontoon to rest his own alongside them, showing the greater distance inboard from the button and the short overall length, and therefore Sam's great reach.

For another four years Mackenzie gave it to them in Leander at every opportunity, covering his soft centre with the humour and antics of the showman. He took jam with his Yorkshire pudding, and he drew the crowds in Dunkirk, Amsterdam, Ostend, Prague and Grünau in East Germany, as well as at Henley. Some regattas paid his expenses, he carried his photographic equipment across borders wrapped in smelly old rowing kit, and he traded medicines too in a modest way to East Europeans who, apart from the occasional visit to Henley, were not allowed out to row in the West. He would arrive at the last minute, make a fuss, threaten to scratch maybe, but always came up with the goods and a smile.

In 1959 he completed three Diamonds in a row and did his cat-and-mouse trick with Willis in the semifinal and Harry Parker, the American from Vesper in Philadelphia, in the final. He dawdled with each of them and then killed them with a sudden spurt, and got booed for his trouble. The *Daily Express* blimpishly described him as 'a most infuriating competitor' and the *Daily Mail* hailed him as the regatta's most outstanding personality, a grinning breath of fresh air, a gay entertainer sweeping away Henley's stuffiness. He went to Bled in Yugoslavia to train and had to have an operation for an ulcer, and a month later was beaten by Ivanov in the European championships in Macon. He returned to Henley in 1960 and had an easy passage to the final, in which he beat the Pole Kocerka in a fairly close race. Then while training at Como he had a recurrence of his ulcer and was withdrawn from the Rome Olympic Games two days before racing started. He played practical jokes in the village and watched Ivanov get his second Olympic title.

Ian Tutty of Haberfield RC, Australia, was three stone lighter than Mackenzie when he came up against him in the second round of the 1961 Diamonds. Sam toyed with him and Tutty was furious, saying, 'Mackenzie had me beaten, he just wanted to show off,' and it was hard not to sympathize with Tutty, even if this was the Diamond Sculls. Sam beat the Russian, Tjurin, in the final by nearly three lengths, but could not afford any antics.

In the next year Mackenzie went out in silence. He had an easy time with Tubbs of St Thomas's Hospital and dealt with Kottman of Switzerland without trouble, but he met his match in Eugene Kubiak of Poland. Mackenzie led for a mile, but not by much, and then Kubiak took the lead before the next signal, at a mile and an eighth. Mackenzie was hard on his heels and suddenly there was a clash of blades. There were differences of opinion about who was in whose water. Kubiak was disqualified by the umpire and the official record gives no information at all when it comes to apportioning blame. Some contemporary photographs, however, show the Australian sculling in Leander colours to be firmly in the centre of the course. The crowd was for the most part behind the Pole, Mackenzie was criticized as he paddled up the course, and much wrong information was given out over the public address system, including naming the wrong sculler for disqualification. The Poles in the Goblets scratched from their race later that day in protest, and in Saturday's final Stuart Mackenzie beat Bill Barry, the amateur son of a professional waterman and coach, and was received in near silence along the enclosures for his sixth win in the Diamonds and his sixth pineapple cup.

In six years Mackenzie had cajoled and enchanted and enraged and enlarged the audience at Henley. He had never lost a race there. The next year he did lose one. It was the first round of the Double Sculls with Christopher Davidge, an event they had won together in 1959. They did, however, win the Goblets in 1963. Mackenzie did not compete in the Perth Commonwealth Games in 1962 for Australia because he refused to return home at his own expense to undergo qualification trials. Instead he rowed for Britain in the world championships in Lucerne, where he got the silver medal. He raced for Britain twice by 1964 in European championships, coming fifth with the Barn Cottage eight in 1961, and fifth with Christopher Davidge in the coxless pairs in 1963.

Davidge was a name that could not be put down at this period. The son of a Keble law don who interviewed schoolboys with rowing minds and turned out rowers with legal training, he competed for Eton in their Ladies' Plate crew in 1947 and was in one crew or another until 1963. He had sunk with Oxford and breasted the Tideway waves to return for a Boat Race victory later, and he was one of the small number of people who realized that British oarsmen, not Continentals, were being isolated by fog in the Channel, and did something about it.

What Davidge did was to form a club for oarsmen interested largely in the international affairs of rowing. The founders in 1955 all happened to be Leander men, so the club was a sort of Leander flag of convenience, serious minded without the clutter of club life. It was called Barn Cottage after the old cricket pavilion near the luncheon tent where many of them stayed in the verandahed rear wing during the regatta. At first they rowed in the winter and dispersed to other crews for Henley. They soon found like-minded men among the Molesey crew who won the Wyfolds in 1959. Barn Cottage won the Stewards' in 1958, and in 1960 Molesey won the Grand and Barn Cottage the Stewards'. In 1963 Molesey took the Stewards' and another club with innovative ideas, the Tideway Scullers' School, won it in the next year, while Molesey came to the top of the pile in the Prince Philip for coxed fours. The University of London was the only other British crew to win the Grand in this period, and the American lightweight college boys kept a successful grip on the Thames Cup for six of the nine years from 1955. Apart from his victories in doubles and pairs with Mackenzie, Davidge won the

Goblets twice with Leadley, in spite of their nickname, Deadly and Cabbage. Davidge personified application. Far from showing cabbage-like qualities, he was strong-willed and strong-minded, opinionated and tough.

Barn Cottage and Molesey crews realized that looking stylish did not necessarily make the boat run faster, and they were clearly the most successful British competitors at Henley in the sixties amidst a tremendous challenge from overseas. They believed in fitness and high rating, being inspired by the Germans who won the European championships in 1959. Davidge was quoted by Christopher Brasher, who as a four-minute miler had had reason to question some of the maxims of track athletics in the *Observer*:

> The German crew went over the course at 40 strokes a minute all the way. I'd have no more thought of doing this than flying, but the Germans won and broke the world record. I only wish they would come to Henley. When the Henley record was brought down to 6 mins 30 secs during the American–Russian battle of 1957, many people said that no one's ever going to beat this time. But the Germans would knock up to 10 seconds off the record. . . . They have a lightness of touch and a spring which comes from supreme fitness and athleticism. . . .

There were plenty of ideas around in Britain, vigorously fanned by *Rowing Magazine* under the editorship of Hylton Cleaver. In September 1955 he reprinted a letter by E. R. Thompson from *The Times* which asked whether social, physical, or economic factors were conspiring to prevent the best use of British resources in stemming the tide from abroad. The magazine offered prizes for the best three constructive replies in 300 words, and it got a large mailbag. Dr McEldowney advocated asking Dr Bannister and athletics coaches to help with training, saying that oarsmen were strong on technique but couldn't apply it. Jack Phelps, the Winchester College boatman, said: 'Choose young matured men with strength and sinew, and use the stopwatch, not rule of thumb.' The Scots told the English southerners to travel north to buck up their ideas about potential talent.

All kinds of solutions were offered, and the blame was laid at some curious doors. A. S. Irvine, editor of the *British Rowing Almanack*, said that because of the aftermath of war, the welfare state, or full employment, or something, Britain had become a nation of lookers-on rather than doers, and that every crew should be given a coach. Our rowing is at rock bottom at all levels, said L. Radley, coincidentally with the rise of Fairbairnism. It has lowered the standard of the first-class men. John Edwards wrote from Christ Church, Oxford, to say that it was all the fault of Baron de Coubertin because he said that the important thing was not winning but taking part.

> This, Sir, is completely wrong. Until English crews develop the iron ruthlessness and determination to win which the Continentals have, and which Steve developed in his crews, the chances of them winning against international competition are remote.

If crews adopt the idea of Mendès-France of drinking only milk instead of quantities of beer, the revival of British rowing will be astonishing, said C. H. F. Wilbrenninck. The remedies rolled in. Give . us money for equipment, give us national championships, for we are the only European country without them, learn the fundamental principles, stop expecting top-level crews every year and enjoy your rowing, give us training, give us coaching in the fundamentals, give us organization to give them hell. Make use of what you've got, your strong bases at the ancient universities, your rivers which you can use all the year round, your clubs and men, said Andre Zezelj from Belgrade.

Philip Carpmael won by advocating squad eights to be formed after Henley to train together. Geoffrey Page just missed a prize with his plea for national championships, a chance for all the crews to test each other out, for at Henley they usually never meet. The other prizewinners were for training using other disciplines, tub-pairing for technique, and developing the will to win. The latter, at least, came through with RAF crews, Molesey and Barn Cottage crews, Tideway Scullers' and the University of London. What went unnoticed was the intelligence that back in 1950 Frank Cotton, Professor of Physiology at Sydney, Australia, had designed a rowing machine called an ergonometer which measured performance. Using it, he picked from 200 guinea pigs four men averaging 14 stone 8 pounds who won nine out of ten races in their first season. Foreigners helped the great debate also through the magazine by exploding some myths, notably Zezelj that of the supposed strength and wealth of the socialist states, and Jack Kelly Jr that of the supposedly unified American style, while Stuart Mackenzie fired a salvo or two at the establishment. It was bracing stuff for the club bar. H. S. Crichton Starkey got it in a rhyming nutshell early in the proceedings:

A sacrilegious Tideway coach,
Young, with a name to gain,
Did what no Oar should ever do,
Sat down and racked his brain.
As awful retribution
A nightmare project grew,
To weld into one hybrid whole
All rowing styles he knew!
And thus he came to train an eight
And from the stern, a four,
Which was Eton-Jesus-Conibear –
Sculling – USSR. . . .

Another stage was reached. . . .
When Fairbairn's school acclaimed this style
As gospel Steve had preached,
While those who sported OE ties
In 1884
All swore it was the Classic
As devised by Dr Warre. . . .

The people who went to Henley witnessed some fine racing at this time. The numbers of entries seemed to rise year by year and the list of names now looked considerably different from the interwar years. There was still the struggle between Oxford and Cambridge, with Cambridge generally getting the better of things among the college crews. There was the increasing interest taken by the schools. There were more entries from abroad. The orthodoxy-versus-Steve argument rumbled on, though the battle lines had become more blurred, as the Harvard coach Tom Bolles had observed in 1950. But the main reason for the appearance of such names as Thames Tradesmen and the Metropolitan Police was that the Amateur Rowing Association and the National Amateur Rowing Association had met before the war and agreed that both the ARA and the Henley stewards would remove the 'manual labour' bar from their definition of an amateur by 1 January 1938. The change was brought about because the Australian Olympic eight of 1936 were barred from Henley on the grounds that policemen were manual workers. It took their incredulity to change this outmoded if ever-justifiable Victorian rule which Lehmann and Furnivall had fought against, but, in spite of the efforts of John Cottesloe as honorary secretary of the ARA, it took until

1956 for the ARA and the NARA to amalgamate. After the agreement of 1938, however, the 360 English and Welsh rowing clubs could all be part of one body again, and could all row at Henley, watermen included, unless they had raced for the now defunct money prizes. There was a rare private entry in the Stewards' that year when R. A. F. Macmillan stroked R. A. F. Macmillan's crew to a defeat by Thames.

The appearance of the regatta had changed quite a lot since the Harvard crew of 1914 won the Grand. The stewards' enclosure began after the First World War and engulfed the old club enclosures. The floating grandstand was first used in 1939, the year that Lion Meadow was purchased. Ladies were admitted to membership of the enclosure in 1946, the year when the public address system was introduced. Selwyn's Meadow was bought in 1948 for the luncheon tent, and Butler's field in 1951. By 1962 Bridge Cottage had been bought and had its name changed to Regatta House to serve as the headquarters, replacing Baltic Cottage at the river end of Friday Street, which had been leased in 1945. Green's field had been purchased, along Remenham Lane on the other side of Barn Cottage, and eighteen and a half acres of land on the Bucks bank downstream of Fawley boathouse had been added to the stewards' domain. In 1957 the Berkshire quarter sessions ruled that the right of way on the towpath was conditional on the right of the stewards to close it during regattas. In 1964 foreign crews were allowed in the Princess Elizabeth for the first time. Senator Saltonstall, captain of Harvard '14, presented the replica of the Grand and gave away the prizes, and the crowds celebrated a ten thousand to one chance, a crew surviving fit and well for fifty years.

11

Dick Cashin flies into town
1980: Henley keeps up with the seventies

Richard Marshall Cashin Jr flew into town on the morning of Monday, 30 June 1980. He arrived by British Airways 737 from Amsterdam to Heathrow Airport, London, and was taken to the Five Horseshoes on Remenham Hill, his managers thus avoiding the enervating air which had so bothered Cornell and Yale in the 1890s when they were billeted in the valley in which Henley-on-Thames nestles. He was twenty-seven years old, the second child and eldest son of Richard Marshall Cashin and Mary Catherine Walsh Cashin, born in Washington DC but of good Boston Irish Catholic stock. His father had been in the Foreign Service and thus the family lived in Libya, Ethiopia, Ghana and Indonesia, before moving to Rome where Cashin Sr was head of the World Food Programme's operations. Cashin Jr was six foot four inches tall, weighed 198 pounds, had just graduated from Harvard Business School, and rowed number two in the eight of the Charles River Rowing Association of the USA entered for the Grand Challenge Cup. They were an Olympic crew who had been urged by their government not to take part in the forthcoming Olympic Games in Moscow because of the presence of Soviet forces in the little republic of Afghanistan, the capital of which, Kabul, was being surveyed by British troops when the first Henley was being held in 1839.

The airline had delayed their baggage from Amsterdam, where they had beaten New Zealand, Australia and the second crew of the German Democratic Republic, because the backpacks were of an inconvenient size. The first thing that the crew did in Henley was to leave the Five Horseshoes because they did not like the accommodation there. Beds in caravans in the middle of a farmer's paddock did not appeal to them and so the bow four, Sean Colgan, Cashin, Kurt Sommerville and Charles Altekruse moved to Mrs Wilcox's house off West Street, up past the town hall, and the stern half, Thomas Woodman, Steve Christensen, John Everett, Bruce Ibbetson and cox-swain, John Chatsky, joined the rest of the large Charles River team in the Imperial Hotel, near the station, at £17 per night. The draw had taken place on the Saturday before in traditional fashion, the stewards gathering in the town hall to take pieces of paper out of the Grand Challenge Cup beneath the portraits of George I and the Earl of Macclesfield, and the Charles River eight were to meet Ormsund and Norske Studenters from Norway, another team whose govern-ment and Olympic association were boycotting the Games. The crews in the other half of the draw were also in Henley because of cancelled tickets to Moscow, Waikato RC and Wairau RC of New Zealand meeting Hannover and Hammerdeicher of the Federal Republic of Germany.

The Charles River men's passage started on 12 May at Harvard's Newell boathouse, when candidates for the Olympic team first met under the guiding hand of Harry Parker, the university's chief coach who got a Grand medal himself in 1955 with the University of Penn-sylvania and who lost the final of the Diamonds to Stuart Mackenzie in 1959. It was not until 5 June that the crews were finally sorted out after almost four weeks of gruelling seat trials and tests against Har-vard on the Charles River and at Red Top, Harvard's training base at New London. Colgan's log shows their progress in picture postcards: the USS *Constitution* at Boston, the submarine base at New London, Lake Morey and Camp Lanakila, where they had their first bad experience of accommodation. They were given open cabins with no windows, no screens, open sides, mouldy mattresses, no electricity. The blood-sucking insects were showing no mercy, and the oarsmen occupied the infirmary and dared the camp directors to break them out. By 6 June the crews were in Hannover and three days later they moved to Lucerne to rig their new plastic Empacher boat and take part in the top Swiss regatta, which was regarded as an alternative Olympics since it was to be the largest and grandest meeting of the year, with strong representatives from both Western and Eastern Europe. On both days of the event they finished behind the East Germans and then spent seven hours climbing Pilatus, the pinnacle to the clouds which stands by the town. They slid over the snow fields sitting on their rain slickers, sliding on their butts and steering with their feet, returning to earth via a lake steamer.

The crews then moved to a training camp in Belgium and on to Amsterdam regatta, where the eight celebrated their two wins at Nereus Rowing Club until 3 a.m. of the morning that they left for Heathrow. Colgan and Ibbetson, bow and stroke man respectively, were the two shortest at six feet two inches and lightest at 185 pounds. For both it was their first competition in the royal regatta, while for Cashin it was the third. From Andover School he went to Harvard in 1971 to read economics and Chinese and was impressed as a school football and squash player when he received a letter from Harry Parker about rowing. His image of Parker at the time was as the jutting jaw on the cover of *Sports Illustrated*. It transpired that Parker's policy was to contact every student he spotted at registration who was over six feet tall with an athletic background. Cashin went for a run along the Charles River one morning and followed a sculler back to the boathouse. He introduced himself as an interested party and the sculler rolled his eyes back and said, 'I think you'll do fine.' It was, of course, Parker, and later he called round to the freshman's room and Cashin was thrilled, though nervous because the coach was very quiet. He just sat there and nodded a lot. Cashin thought that he was a strong personality, close to a god, and could not imagine why Parker was interested in him.

A lot had happened since then. Cashin won the Thames Cup with Parker's Harvard crew in 1972. He won a gold medal for his country at the world championships of 1974 on the Rotsee in Lucerne, and in the next year competed in the final of the Grand in another Harvard crew, being beaten by a combined crew from Leander and Thames Tradesmen. In the semifinals Harvard set a record for the Grand of six minutes thirteen seconds in their race with their old boys, Union BC, and as the crew went through the bridge and 'wound down' in quiet water along by the park, Harry Parker cycled along the tow-path uncharacteristically whooping and yelling and ran into two old ladies. Shortly afterwards the combined crew of Leander and Thames Tradesmen equalled Harvard's time when defeating Vesper of Philadelphia, and the British crew went on to beat Harvard in the final.

In 1975 Dick Cashin won the Fishe Fellowship to read economics at Trinity College, Cambridge. His arrival there in the autumn was lonely. He didn't know anybody and had been a kingpin whence he came. His rooms felt sterile and smelt of moth balls from his trunks, and he wandered out to enjoy the spectacular weather. In Neville Court was a boat on slings and Sir Michael Herries told him it was a rowing shell. Cashin told Herries that he knew, so Herries invited him to dinner, which turned out to be First and Third Trinity's 150th anniversary get-together.

Cashin remembers an amazing evening in the great hall, which no longer had the great brazier familiar to Warington Smyth and the crew of 1839. It was dimly lit, the food was mainly potato and lousy, the diners gave him a warm welcome as soon as they realized he was a rower, and he caught hell for passing the port back to his right. The evening ended with people sprinting round Great Court and swimming in the puddles on the lawn, and Herries fixed an appointment for Cashin to see Jardine Matheson and Co., which led eventually to a job in Hong Kong. But during that year he got a Blue in Cambridge's losing Boat Race crew and another for squash, and had a lot of fun coaching a women's college crew. A year later he raced in the Goblets but had to retire with hay fever after winning his first race by a quarter of an inch by his own reckoning.

After Hong Kong he returned to Boston, to the Harvard Business School, and now he was back at Henley as an Olympic oarsman who had had a probable Olympic medal pulled from under him by the US Olympic Committee and a complicated political situation. He was back in the place which first charmed him about rowing, for in 1972 this young student who had travelled the world with his parents felt other-worldly as he sat by the boat tents for four hours a day, surveying the scene. Now he was nursing a pulled neck muscle and contemplating missing a few practice outings to allow it to settle down, with time on his hands to keep warm by the Thames and watch the world go by. It was raining hard and two full days remained before the regatta proper was to begin, time to reflect on what had happened since the Harvard men of 1914 had their reunion in 1964 and since Ratzeburger Ruderclub of Germany knocked seven seconds off the Russians' record for the Grand in 1965, the record whch stood until Cashin's Harvard crew reduced it by a further three seconds in 1975.

John Garton, president of the stewards, said, 'We shall all be chewing gum and talking out of the corners of our mouths in no time at all after this Henley.' There was nobody to defend any of the trophies against the American forces, a situation again caused by the Olympic Games. Most British athletes in most sports were opposed to their government's ever shriller pleas to boycott the Games, and prominent among these were the oarsmen and women. They had organized a petition and encouraged the council of the Amateur Rowing Association to take a strong line in favour of taking part in the Games at meetings of the British Olympic Association. Ironically their resolve had been strengthened by the ignorance of their government's stance and by the somewhat undemocratic and tactless way in which the Prime Minister, Mrs Margaret Thatcher, and her Minister for Sport, Mr Hector Monro, attempted to impose their will, and ironically again the council's argument was presented by its president, Christopher Davidge, once an iron-willed international oarsman who was privately in favour of boycotting the Games.

By July, unlike the Americans and the West Germans and the Norwegians and the New Zealanders, the latter being told that they were not going to Moscow when they assembled to leave for Europe at Auckland airport, the British rowers were preparing for the Games. Their eight was training quietly at Pangbourne and the other crews of an exceptionally strong team were scattered about on lakes in England and Europe. None of them entered Henley. Some rowing correspondents were critical of the team for not showing themselves at Henley. This was soon after they had spent several weeks probing the strength of the Olympic team and criticizing the selectors for not going for the strongest combinations. But Moscow was barely three weeks away and the coaches were taking no chances – unlike the Russians, who were in disgrace because two of their top competitors had been banned by FISA after random dope tests taken at Mannheim regatta showed that they had been taking anabolic steroids, an illegal substance. They were Valentina Semenova and Sergei Posdeev, and they tarnished rowing's reputation which had remained clean until the findings were published on 14 June. As far as Henley was concerned, everybody knew that none of the crews in the Grand would be there if they had been going to the Games.

Garton had become president of the regatta in 1977, retiring from the chairmanship in favour of Peter Coni. He had been in the chair since 1965 when Harold Rickett vacated it, and Garton's years were testing ones for an annual event which by nature unbound itself slowly and cautiously from its traditions. Old stewards never resign, or are not allowed to resign, they just pass on, some of them no doubt lending a hand on the Styx ferry, so that the power of the chairman in such a self-perpetuating oligarchy is often great if not absolute. Garton took the chair of the regatta which he regarded as the showpiece of English rowing at a time when the threat from foreign crews was as great as ever, when the pressures to compete at Henley were greater than ever, when great advances were being made in the sport but when the British at best were treading water. Almost unbelievably, the argument between orthodoxy and Fairbairnism continued although in more muted fashion, while the disagreements about amateur status shifted from abuse of the professional boatmen who were now welcomed, sometimes as members, in the bar of Leander, to blanket suspicion of East Europeans for being fulltimers. The old intellectual exercise of defining the amateur was in danger of transformation into a new parlour game called Spot the Professionals. People in the West thought that people in the East who were paid to be, say, soldiers and given time to row were professionals in all but name. But they were finding it increasingly difficult to reconcile the methods of sponsorship, government finance and squad organization which they themselves were beginning to use with their past ideas of amateurism.

In the years in which he was being groomed for the chair, Garton saw great changes in the regatta. When he rowed for Eton and Magdalen College, Oxford, clubs would bring their own tub pairs and bank tubs to the regatta for practice, would take a fortnight in a house or a hostelry at Henley and bring their own college servants to look after them. Everybody would be in the town or within walking distance of it. Crews would invite their opponents to dinner; Eton at their doctor's house in St Andrew's Road, or Magdalen at the house next to the church, leaning out of the dining-room window to converse with passers-by. They would promenade in the evenings, and one of the principal objects of the exercise was to get to know the coaches of other crews and the dons of colleges and universities. The regatta was the zenith of the Oxford season, and being put up for the stewards' enclosure by his father was the most marvellous thing, Garton thought.

But after the Second World War there was a much more professional approach. The pace of life changed through the years of austerity and the years of reconstruction. The white-flannelled social and athletic enterprise turned to something much more professional. The numbers grew and grew, both on the water and in the enclosures. It became more important to draw financial support to enable the oarsmen to row, and this meant encouraging spectators to dip into their pockets and bring their friends if commercial sponsorship from outside was to be avoided. The difficult part was keeping a balance between the athletic and the social sides of things. There was an important commercial error when the stewards turned down the opportunity of purchasing Phyllis Court, although they did get as far as considering the burrowing of a tunnel under the Thames between the enclosure and the club.

By the time he moved from chairman to president, the man who had introduced gym work to Eton oarsmen when he was captain of boats there in the thirties was, therefore, reigning over a rather different scene. Crews hardly ever met each other, let alone for dinner. Far fewer of them stayed for two weeks. Several commuted from London, and the network of places to stay had spread a good deal further from Henley. There were thousands of cars in acres of car parks, which had provided the regatta with a good reason for moving the fairground off Lion Meadow where its clientele had been the cause of much rowdiness and a certain amount of damage to tentage. Radio-telephones were introduced into umpires' launches in 1965, the last year in which supper was served in the enclosure before the fireworks on Saturday night. The fireworks were still on Saturday but finals moved to Sunday in 1974 on the sound commercial reasoning that more people would have the time to come and watch if two of the weekend days were available instead of one. This move had its critics, though, for most of the crews now pack up and leave after the finals in preparation for work or flights home on Monday morning, missing a rousing final night under the chandeliers of Leander's pink tent or in Remenham's bar or numerous welcoming public houses.

In 1967 new arrangements were introduced at the start which enabled boats in all races to be aligned so that their bows were level on the start line exactly 1 mile and 550 yards from the finish. Thus for the first time all boats covered the same distance regardless of the length of the boat. The practice of firing maroons after crews had cleared the island was discontinued. In 1968 the stewards bought Freddie Brittain's superb library of rowing books. The regatta was held a week later in that year to please the schools, whose examinations clashed with its tradition'al date. The result was that top crews went to Lucerne instead, so in the next year there was a reversion to the old date. In 1969 Nottingham Britannia presented a cup for the Henley Prize, an event for British coxed fours introduced the year before. The cup marked the centenary of the club and the prize was subsequently called the Britannia Cup.

In that year also there came a very important change. There had been growing criticism of the quirkiness of the random draw system because so often an event which promised some epic meetings was spoilt by the cup in the town hall offering up all the best crews in one half of the draw. Henceforth a system was introduced whereby the stewards could select some crews on their track record and then allot them positions in the draw which would keep them apart in the early stages. Thus the draw was still random but the method was designed to ensure that the fastest and strongest were kept apart until semifinal or final rounds. It has had mixed results and provided plenty of entertainment for the press in spotting weak selections and dark horses. In 1970 there was another important change when composite crews were allowed for the first time in first-class events for eights and fours, although they must be entered in the names of not more than two clubs. This did not explain how Jesus and Pembroke colleges of Cambridge entered the Grand in 1948 or St Edmund Hall and Lincoln, Oxford, won the Stewards' in 1959, but it did recognize a fact of life in international rowing. No longer was it worthwhile sending the best club eight to a European, World or Olympic championship. That was now sending lambs for slaughter, and one of Steve's maxims had certainly come home to roost, namely that a crew is only as good as its weakest man. This message got home in Britain in 1968 when a good University of London eight who won the Grand looked like donkeys at the Olympic Games. If Henley was to attract some of the world's best, whether they be from overseas or not and as it unquestionably desired to do, it would have to make it possible for composites, which usually meant national teams, to compete.

In 1971 the composite rule was extended to the Ladies' Plate and the Visitors'. Another proposed development was rejected after great deliberation. The stewards had been investigating the possibility of trimming the banks to widen the course and permit three-

or four-lane racing, and coupled with it the introduction of the international repêchage system. This basically gives every crew at least two chances before they are eliminated from their event. Seventeen foreign associations whose crews had been represented in recent years at the regatta were asked for their opinion, and without exception they replied that they would not like to see Henley changed. They liked the ancient royal show as it was, in spite of its two-horse races and its sudden death for losers. The fact that the stewards contemplated the change, though, showed their concern about the increasing requirements of international competition.

Britain was still without national championships, still without a regatta which would guarantee a meeting between all the best crews in an event, and plans were well advanced for the conversion of some gravel pits into a six-lane still-water course at Holme Pierrepont in Nottinghamshire. By 1973 the course was in use and the stewards were caught in a trap which revealed both the politics of sport and the politics in sport. John Garton as president of the Amateur Rowing Association welcomed the first Nottinghamshire International Regatta as the best thing in Britain since the sliding seat, but as chairman of the Henley management committee he worried about the adverse effect its attractions might have on the entry lists for Henley. Among those attractions at Nottingham was generous sponsorship from the brewers, Guinness, some of which was used to assist the expenses of crews from foreign parts.

The Nottingham regatta was being organized under the rules of FISA, the international rowing federation. In 1972 the International Olympic Committee had expelled South Africa in protest against the policy of apartheid practised there, and it was expected that a similar move would be attempted at the FISA congress to be held in October of 1973. In March that year, then, the Nottinghamshire regatta received a telegram which said: 'Soviet will not participate at Nottingham because of participation of athletes from South African countries, who are not allowed to participate in Olympic Games and excluded by IOC from Olympic movement for carrying out apartheid policy.' Henley was placed conveniently a week after Nottingham in the calendar and the threat was interpreted as applying there also.

The Nottingham officials had already invited the South African Rowing Union to enter a crew from Trident, but they withdrew the invitation when faced with losing a large Soviet team of quality oarsmen and with putting themselves in a provocative position before the international body. Meanwhile, the South African RU had nominated a coxless four from Wemmer Pan to undertake a European tour taking in Nottingham and Henley, and had sent off their Henley entry by registered post. They were, therefore, somewhat miffed to read an agency report in the *Natal Mercury* that their invitation to Nottingham had been withdrawn. That was before they left South Africa. On the Monday morning three weeks before Henley the crew arrived at the Henley regatta office to inquire about boat transport and were handed back the cheque which covered their entry, with no explanation. Much of this was revealed in *The Times* a week later by Jim Railton, the paper's rowing correspondent. A Nottingham official explained the action of his regatta by saying that since it was an invitation event the committee had a right to withdraw invitations. Garton wore his Henley hat in his quotation in *The Times*. South Africa's participation in international rowing would be resolved in due course, he said, but 'Henley is not the place to test the matter'.

Against the wishes of all the parties, therefore, the argument came partially into the open. The South Africans acceded to British requests not to make a fuss; it would be undiplomatic for them to do so in view of their uneasy perch within FISA. Privately, however, they argued strongly that Henley as a private event should abide only by its own rules, which did not exclude South Africans who had sent in their entries correctly. Henley argued that although the regatta ran under its own rules it was an international regatta because FISA recognized it as such. The South Africans argued that whatever special status Henley might claim, the South Africans were still members of FISA. There were resignations from the stewards' enclosure, and several letters to the chairman strongly criticized the stewards for bowing to Soviet pressure.

So in 1973 the Russians rowed at Nottingham and at Henley, the South Africans did not, and the morality of South Africa's participation in international sport was not raised in the argument except by the Soviet telegram. The morality of the Soviet position did not entirely escape examination, but both regattas blushed as they awkwardly sidestepped the issue. FISA did not expel the South Africans. Both Soviet and South African crews have competed at Henley since, though not in the same years. In 1978 the Makoma Club of Zambia withdrew from the Wyfolds because a South African crew was in the event, but in that year the Bulgarians came without objecting to the presence of South African crews.

Also by 1973 the permitted entries for the Ladies' had been advanced to thirty-two, a bank had appeared as part of the facilities, a plan to make some of the erections permanent had been rejected because of vehement opposition from the town, rules preventing the use of dope had been introduced, and crews who committed two false starts were disqualified automatically. It was no longer necessary for every oarsman to finish a race but boats in coxed events must carry their coxswain all the way. In the following year, the year when Sunday finals first came in, a housing plan for Fawley Meadows fell through, a Special Schools race was introduced over a shortened course starting at the Barrier for eights who were involved in examinations, and the chairman of both the regatta and the Amateur Rowing Association, John Garton, got a CBE for services to the sport.

Women were allowed to compete as coxswains from 1975. New qualification rules were introduced for the Wyfolds and the Britannia which immediately had the effect of improving the quality of the competitors, and time trials replaced qualifying races, saving a lot of time and organization. In 1976 the chairman of the Thames Water Authority was made an *ex officio* steward, though he was not elevated to the committee as the town's representative had been in 1973. A boat show was held in September which was a flop but a lottery had been introduced during the regatta which was a success. Queen Elizabeth II celebrated her Jubilee in 1977 and Princess Anne visited the regatta on the Friday, arriving by a barge manned by watermen much as her great-grandfather had done in 1912. In faraway Sydney Rowing Club there was a rueful glance or two at King George's royal standard, hanging there in its case on the wall. The stewards' enclosure had almost four thousand members, and at their December meeting the stewards elected Garton president and Peter Coni chairman.

During Garton's years competitors from overseas kept up their influence in all the open events and foreigners were recognized as a fact of life when Hart Perry of Kent School, USA, was elected a steward in 1975 and Thomi Keller, the Swiss sculler who had broken up with laughter when losing to the Russians in the fifties, joined the exalted ranks in 1977. When not time-keeping at Henley he is president of FISA. Foreigners won the Grand ten times between 1965 and 1979, the Thames and the Ladies' eight times apiece, the Princess Elizabeth eleven times, and the Diamonds eleven out of the possible fifteen. Ernie Arlett, the little mite born on the day George V visited the regatta, brought crews from Northeastern University in Boston, where he had introduced a rowing programme, to the Grand in 1972 and 1973. They were beaten by Russians but their four won the Prince Philip in the second of those years.

There were many highlights and much of interest. The Egyptian Police came and went, drawing spectators like the Japanese did in the thirties. Tall and lean crews from Ridley College, Canada, won the Princess Elizabeth five times in the seventies. Ratzeburg came with their coach, Karl Adam, in 1965 and broke the record in the Grand final when Vesper pushed them hard all the way. Both crews maintained a very high rate of striking throughout and the Germans came in half a length in front and sliced seven seconds from the record. They were the crew that people came to watch that year. The power which they displayed gave an inkling of what was happening elsewhere. Adam had never rowed himself, and when he began coaching on the Küchensee for his village club near Lübeck, he was not blessed with isms of orthodoxy or Fairbairn's disciples. He evolved a stroke which was more or less continuous movement, not allowing for poise before the blade hits the water or a sudden heave at the beginning of the stroke or waiting till the cows came home while the boat ran. Coupled with a fitness acquired by weight-lifting, sculling, running and skiing, his crews acquired the stamina to keep a high rating for 2000 metres or for the longer Henley course. They were cutting a searing path in international events. They used big 'spade' blades and were soon to have their boats fitted with a new style of clog, a running shoe attached to the stretcher with a quick-release clip for emergencies.

The endeavour and spirit behind Adam would have been recognized by Colin Porter, who had trained in the fifties by running from RAF Benson to Henley bridge and back with all the oarsmen at the airfield. He wrote a book of which the title, *Rowing to Win*, tells most of his story. It was published in 1959 with an introduction by Christopher Davidge, who reported a remark in the enclosure concerning a Molesey or a Barn Cottage crew with which Porter and himself were involved: 'Oh well, they think of nothing else but winning races.' Lou Barry's Tideway Scullers' School thought a lot about winning races also, and came to the fore in English rowing at this time with the

University of London hot on their heels, but there was still something lacking. Porter attacked the obsession with style which was still prevalent even after some of his crews had pointed the way. The University of British Columbia men who had won two medals at the 1956 Olympic Games had covered 4000 miles on the water in the six months beforehand. That made Jesus College's thousand-mile crews of the forties look somewhat tame. In the year before Porter's plea Peter Haig-Thomas and M. A. Nicholson published a book called *The English Style of Rowing*, significantly omitting the word orthodox, which roundly attacked Fairbairnism and most of its gospels for reducing rowing to its lowest common denominator.

Meanwhile John McKeown, graduate of Jesus, was spreading the gospel, in his case along the Bristol Avon in the hours after teaching O-level Latin and English to boys who could look out of their cold classroom windows onto that very Close where Sir Henry Newbolt bade them play up and play the game. Down by the sewage works at St Anne's he did not, could not, follow the master explicitly because Clifton College possessed appalling fixed-seat boats in which to start people off. He did not produce fast crews but a lot of trouble was taken with boys of all shapes and sizes, and there was much enjoyment and spirit in the club. If the influence of Steve was more successful in Latin O-Level passes than winning pots at Saltford regatta, this was not McKeown's fault.

No doubt similar things were happening on the Thames, the Wear and the New Zealand Avon, and they pointed up the dilemma. Steve was right; so were Haig-Thomas and Nicholson and the ghosts of Warre, Kindersley and Bourne. Desmond Hill wrote a little book in 1963 pleading for truce, for concentration on a foundation stroke, and showed that there could be one in his *Instructions in Rowing*. Four years later John Williams introduced a symposium of various branches of science applied to rowing with another appeal to the supporters of the art. He asked them at least to look at what science has to offer, to consider the hydrodynamic, mechanical, biomechanical, physiological and psychological aspects of their sport. Does it matter? Yes, Karl Adam would say, and Porter and Davidge and Garton, and an increasing number of others. Adam was showing the results already. For a sport which is largely about the effective and repetitive use of one stroke, or two if sculling is regarded as a difference of kind, then how the stroke was done mattered.

From Ratzeburg's visit in 1965 to the European championships of 1973, where Christopher Baillieu and Michael Hart won bronze medals in the Double Sculls, no British oarsman got a medal at European, World or Olympic championships. Henley saw a succession of East German and Soviet crews take the Grand, only broken by the University of London in 1968 when there were no overseas competitors. A young Thames Tradesmen four lost the Wyfolds in 1970 when they were disqualified for bad steering in the dying moments of the final. It was a controversial decision and in gratitude the stroke attributed a part of the anatomy to the umpire which it is very doubtful he possessed. It made Vivian Nickalls's drunken and shocking remark in the thirties that 'The Norwegians are all virgins, y'know' sound very tame. Trident of South Africa paddled across the line and offered a re-row, so unhappy were they with the decision, but the stewards stood by their umpire, and there were tears for the Tradesmen in the boat tent. The next year they met the same crew in the first round of the Stewards' and beat them soundly, going on to take the cup.

These lads were coached by Jim Railton, a sprinter who had been employed as a trainer by the Amateur Rowing Association before he became *The Times*'s rowing correspondent. They went on to become part of a team, a small team, that revived Britain's international fortunes in the seventies. Baillieu and Hart were the first to strike metal in 1973, but they were followed by a steady stream of medal winners including world and Olympic silver medals by eights coached by Bob Janousek. The revival had a number of contributory causes which included small units like the Thames Tradesmen crew who set their sights beyond the horizon, the determination by Garton and Coni and others who were in executive positions in the ARA to appoint a national professional coach to get things moving, ambitious oarsmen at the universities and in such clubs as Leander and Tideway Scullers', and a chance contact with the Czechoslovakian coach Bohumil Janousek at the European championships in Austria, who made it known that he was thinking of a move. He arrived in the winter of 1969 and got the job. He came endowed with medals for his country and a degree in physical education from Charles University, Prague, but with no knowledge of English. He was christened Bob because nobody could pronounce Bohumil, and between then and the Olympic Games of 1976, when his eight almost won the gold, he inspired men and coaches, gave them new goals and made full use of the 2000-metre course at Holme Pierrepont, which was the scene of the 1975 world championships.

Talented, popular and hard-working as he was, Janousek could not do this on his own. He was a highly qualified common denominator, a catalyst who could claim attention from the disparate corners of English rowing. At the very least they would give him the freedom to hang. Public schools and artisans clubs, the Tideway and the provinces, universities ancient and modern, the traditionalists in the stewards' enclosure and the traditionalists of a different hue in their favourite corners of Henley's boat tents, all would at least listen and some would help him try. When he left coaching to build boats in 1976 he left a different world to the one he found in the cold winter of 1969. Coaches and oarsmen were talking the same language, the financial and administrative organization was stronger, a proper coaching award scheme had been started and the base of the pyramid was at least sound. Two important new fixtures, Nottinghamshire International Regatta and the annual national championships, joined the rowing calendar.

In its early years the new regatta in Nottingham brought more and stronger foreign crews to Henley, not fewer as had been feared. Lou Barry's Tideway Scullers' won the Grand in 1971 and Janousek's men in 1975, with three Soviet victories splitting them. The Irishman Sean Drea took the Diamonds three times in succession from 1973–75, a popular and colourful winner, although not quite in Mackenzie's class of *enfant terrible*. It was a decade when Irish crews had great success at Henley, which they had not had for a hundred years. University College, Dublin, took the Ladies' in 1974, Garda Siochana – the Dublin police – took the Thames in 1975 and the Prince Philip in 1977 and 1979, and Trinity College, Dublin, the Ladies' in 1977.

This last win prompted a letter from Maurice Horan of County Dublin to the captain of Leander.

Dear Captain [it said], I am returning in a separate parcel a club flag which adorned the garden flag pole during the regatta in 1950 when Trinity College Dublin were beaten in the final of the Ladies' Plate. Having been the coach of the crew at that time and in fact lost the Ladies' in 1934 to Jesus by three feet I recovered the flag from one John Leather who had walked up the pole just as daylight appeared. Since when I have kept the flag with the object of returning same to the club when TCD won the Ladies'. Now this has at last happened after so many years of effort I have the greatest pleasure in sending to you the old flag which I hope will appear again flowing gently to a Bushes Wind. I may add that the flag has not seen the light of day since 1950, but is in good condition.

The correspondence was framed and added to the many pictorial records on the walls of Leander Club.

Another aspect of the British determination not to be left as impotent spectators on the world rowing scene also showed itself at Henley. After a run of six consecutive foreign victories, lightweight crews from London RC won the Thames Cup in 1977 and 1978. Wearing their true colours they were part of a national training team, but they achieved what the Americans had been achieving for years.

So John Garton's years were busier than ever before. The regatta was bigger, more noisy, faster, for better or for worse. Among its bereavements were Harold Rickett, the former chairman, and Lieutenant Colonel C. D. Burnell, DSO, OBE, once the strongest sweep in England, senior steward and 'father' of the regatta. They died in 1968 and 1969 respectively, and in 1973 Gully Nickalls passed away. In terms of changing the rules, little happened in the first two years of Peter Coni's chairmanship, save tinkering with the age limits permitted for competitors in the Princess Elizabeth and bringing the coxes' weight rule into line with the international rules. But his first year was eventful before the regatta started. Kingston RC, a club with a long history, which once caused the stewards to change their rules because the captain was seen shortly before the regatta recruiting likely college men for his crews, and which once had the legally minded and mischievous Woodgate as its president, sent in an entry for the Double Sculls in 1978 in the names of A. Hohl and P. Bird, correctly signed by the captain, Gus Gait. The crew turned out to be the leading British women's crew of the day, Mrs Astrid Ayling and Mrs Pauline Hart, who had made the entry under their maiden names. Coni unmasked the false entry to the press and rapped Kingston's knuckles in a statement which said that it was sad that a long-established club should think it reasonable behaviour to make a deliberately false declaration signed by the captain. He added that the stewards had no fear of the Sex Discrimination Act.

At the same time there was the embarrassment of the missing entry of Christiania Roklub of Oslo. Christiania planned to celebrate their centenary by winning the Thames Cup, which they had taken in 1922 and for which they had set the record in a heat in 1976. They booked accommodation for three crews and thirty supporters but forgot to send their entry forms. A special envoy flew in to address the stewards but arrived after the meeting he was trying to catch. Representations were made by Prince Harald of Norway to the British ambassador in Oslo and by the Norwegian ambassador in London, but to no avail. The stewards sadly stood by their rules because they had done so in the past.

Now it was 1980. The weather was fickle. The British eight was at Pangbourne rehearsing for the Moscow Games. They drove up to Henley to hang about the boat tents and sneak a look at the course, half wishing they could get at the Americans, West Germans and New Zealanders, some of whom they had beaten on the Continent in recent weeks. Dick Cashin was telling himself that his neck would be all right for the race, and his crew were cheerfully confident, almost arrogant.

There would be no mistake about this one. They were going to win it, and the Russians and East Germans were going to hear about it, and with luck their ambassador, Kingman Brewster, would be here to see them do it, as well as the superb women's team from their country who were also deprived of competition in the Soviet Union. They wore their US Olympic team singlets and shorts with proud defiance and although expressing sympathy for the political stance which their government had taken over the Afghanistan crisis and the incarceration of American hostages in Teheran which was hazily linked to it, they were not thinking warm thoughts about President Jimmy Carter in his election year.

On the evening of Wednesday, 2 July, two hundred crews retired to roost early, for there were a hundred races next day and only half of them would survive.

12

Peter Coni's early rise and Sean Colgan's late dip
1980: Four days in the life of a regatta

On the dewy morning of 3 July 1980 nothing stirs in Henley at 4.45 a.m., not even the crow of a cockerel, as an open Bentley, 1938, makes its way down New Street and along Riverside, turns onto the bridge and into Remenham Lane and is driven to the main gate of the stewards' enclosure. Peter Coni QC, in his third year of office as chairman of the management committee, steps out carrying a shirt, a pair of white flannels and a London RC tie, and makes his way to the regatta office. It is locked. Coni's voice rings out over the empty enclosure. 'Is anybody about?' There is no response from the night security guard or from his Alsatian. The chairman does not have his own key. After a quarter of an hour there is still no sign of the guard and Coni has worked up a fine mood for his morning tour of inspection. He finds the manager of Edgingtons, the tentage contractor, hard at work in one of the grandstands and borrows a screwdriver from him with which he prises open the window of his office. With the aid of a chair he goes head-first through the window. Thus begins the regatta of 1980.

Coni collects his clipboard and sets off towards the boat tents, noting down shoddy tentage walls near the stewards' entrance, muddy puddles to be filled in after yesterday's heavy rain, stray barriers left where they shouldn't be, waste bins to be emptied. He checks that the competitors' showers are working, inspects vehicles in the competitors' park behind Leander Club. He slaps parking stickers on those which do not have correct passes, including Leander Club's minibus, and he curses himself for not having any wellies as the dew on the long grass soaks his shoes and creeps up his trouser legs. He wakes two

huddles in sleeping bags and tells them that even if they are competitors they must get the right sticker for their car, and says, 'All right,
go back to sleep.' He sets off for the luncheon tents, on the way noting
four boat trailers that are out of place in their park, and spies two little
tents under the hedge at the far side of the field. The car next to them
has Irish number plates. Coni twangs a couple of guy ropes, says
'Anyone at home?' very loudly, and in response to grunts from inside
makes his set speech.

'Good morning, gentlemen. When you wake up please remove
yourselves to the far side of the river where there is an excellent camp
site which even has loos and showers, and where you'll be a lot more
comfortable. Camping is not allowed in the trailer park. Please stir
yourselves at eight o'clock.'

Entrance to the lunch tent is easy since the back is not secured. He
walks through the kitchen, sees that there are no fire extinguishers in
the eating area and that the barrier between the chairman's table and
the expected throng is not in place. His list grows and his handwriting
gets larger.

Returning to the enclosure he finds that there is a gap at the back of
the champagne bar, a door missing from the back of another bar, that
there are not enough chairs in the bandsmen's rest tent nor any for the
cloakroom attendants in the Gents. He stands legs straight and apart,
blue blazer unbuttoned, holding the clipboard with his right hand and
his fast-moving pen with the other, looking just like a Spy cartoon of a
well-barked tyro. The inspection is completed with the visit to the
Ladies to ensure gilt mirrors and toilet rolls are in place, his legal mind
working over well-worn points. Are the mirrors installed? Yes, they
are. Good. Are the toilet-roll holders fitted? No, they are not. He walks
swiftly to the general enclosure and back to check the seating and the
stands, leaving a trail of footprints on the dew-fresh velvety lawns. A
heron stands motionless on a prime spectating spot under the soft blue
sky, surveying the fresh morning on Henley reach.

Coni finishes his inspection in the stewards' private bar and cloakroom and the Royal Loo, complete with washstand and delicate
marble-toned formica, for on Sunday HRH Prince Michael of Kent is
coming to give away the prizes. At 5.50 he returns to the committee
room, ladles six spoonfuls of coffee into the percolator, and takes off
his sodden shoes and socks. He hunts for a towel on which to dry his
feet. At six o'clock the secretary, Richard Goddard, arrives and pours

out coffee while Coni changes his trousers, puts on a clean shirt, his London RC tie and the cerise socks of Leander, and lights a Balkan Sobranie Turkish, in a short holder. They sit down and Coni swiftly works through his list for Goddard.

'The fencing and walls behind the bars are not secure. . . . There are four trailers in the middle of the car park which shouldn't be there, and several cars without stickers. . . . There are no coat hooks in the scouts room. . . . I want the TUC Day of Action sticker removed from the door to the store, and the no smoking one off the stewards' cloakroom. . . . There should be more chairs and tables in the Bridge Bar, there are never enough there. . . . The loose linoleum at the entrance to the disabled loo should be taped over. . . . Check the seat numbers, though it's too late to change them. . . . The light over the Cundall painting in the prize tent isn't working, I've tried both switches all ways. . . . There's an unpainted door in the secretary's tent, though that's fiddling while Rome burns. But three things in particular. There are no fire extinguishers, someone must do a round with loo rolls, and someone must check all the notices. I didn't have time, and if there's nothing there you don't notice it isn't there.'

The next official to arrive is Mark Jabale, Dominican monk and headmaster of Belmont Abbey School in Herefordshire, who is in charge of boat tents.

'Morning, Chairman,' he says.

'Morning, Mark. There are four trailers in the middle of the competitors' park. Have 'em removed quickly, please.'

Jabale sets off on his first task. Ron Sharp, the regatta's groundsman and odd-job organizer, puts his head in the room and is sent on several ways, and the minutely detailed inventory of faults develops into a discussion of specific tentage items and the distribution of chairs between the bars. Coni finishes where he began, with the canvas outside the main entrance. 'Anyway, that piece out there is hanging like a private pissed on parade,' his brown eyes and mouth giving hint of the first smile of the day, and he throws down his pen. Goddard settles his huge frame back in his chair for a few moments and surveys his list.

'It was worse last year,' he says. 'Some years we haven't been able to put the piles in because there was too much water coming down the river, and once we couldn't empty the staff loos because there was too much water around.'

Praise God and plumbing, the sun is beginning to dry the grass and the canvas, and outside thirteen men are hard at work putting out the deckchairs. There are sounds of oars as early practice starts for some of the crews. The big Norwegian eight glides smoothly down the course, watched by their coach and their manager from the bank. Coni is in his tiny office off the committee room rummaging among two telephones, Tippex, ashtray and stack of in-trays on his desk, talking to someone in the outer office. Several pairs of training shoes and a fine pair of hand-made buckskin lace-ups, £95 in Jermyn Street, lie behind the door, several shirts, blazers and pairs of creams hang roughly on the pegs. The desk has an electric typewriter, and there is a card table in the corner with a mirror, a hair brush, a clothes brush, and leather books of the chairman's records for 1976 and 1979. He finds what he is looking for, a toilet roll which serves as tissue – possibly the only one extant at that hour of the morning – and blows his nose before setting off for breakfast in Leander at 6.45 a.m.

Angus Robertson arrives. He is the voice of Henley, the man who makes most of the announcements at the regatta and prides himself on getting his tongue correctly round the consonants and vowels of whatever language is necessary from Poplar, Blackwall and District Rowing Club to Amsterdamsche Studenten Roeivereeniging Nereus of Holland. This year he will have Waikato and Wairau of New Zealand, Hannoverscher and Hammerdeicher of the Federal Republic of Germany, and the Club Nautico Mar del Plata of Argentina to deal with, and he goes off to his pitch on the floating grandstand to make final tests on the public address system. For the first time it has been decided to give the spectators in the enclosures information about the track record of some of the crews.

Goddard clears the desks which together make a large table, in preparation for the 7.15 committee meeting. Morning coffee cups, newspapers, and the chairman's screwdriver, stationery and the large chart which shows how many seats are available on the launches and to whom they are allotted for each race are removed. Coni returns after his coffee and toast and bacon and eggs and the committee file in on time, while various supplicants, including Harry Parker, coach of the Charles River Rowing Association of the USA, wait around in the outer office. Meanwhile other stewards move swiftly and quietly about, collecting flags and stopwatches, clipboards and two-way radios, badges and passes and messages, all wearing their blazers and whites, most of them in cerise Leander ties and with a variety of allegiances revealed in their large peaked caps and blazers – Oxford and Cambridge Blues, London and Thames and Leander clubs. Very few others are represented. They go off on foot or in launches to their allotted tasks, and outside a boatman wipes down *Amaryllis*, the umpire's sleek launch to be used for the first race at 8 a.m.

What Coni dreads most of all on this day is a launch to break down, for the regatta has a record number of entries, with a hundred races to get through, most of them at five-minute intervals, which means two races on the course at once. He sets off at 7.45 to umpire the first race himself and the president, John Garton, is there also. By this means they can inspect the installations of the course from the water, checking on the booms, the starting arrangements, the progress board opposite the enclosure, the timekeeping arrangements, and the existence of the finishing post, a popular souvenir. Queen's University, Belfast, for example, have acquired at least two of them over the years.

The launch glides down the course, passing between two crews who are pacing one another hell for leather past the enclosure. Then it slips between the booms on to the Buckinghamshire side of the river, closer to moored motor cruisers and a line of tents which are little private hospitality enclosures for clients of the regatta and their guests. It passes the camping ground and the fields of Remenham, where Brakspears are setting up a bar in a barn on the Berkshire bank, and turns a little to port to take the old course and keep the island to starboard. From this angle the cupola from which W. W. Smyth and his friends watched Henley regatta's first ever Grand is almost hidden by the weeping beech, which has grown enormous, cascading into the water. It slips past the nest of a great crested grebe, the female sitting while the male darts about under the island trees which everywhere obscure the banks, and swings round the north end, behind the twin floating platforms which John Garton designed. A boy lies on each platform awaiting the crews, while on the bank David Chipp, editor-in-chief of the Press Association and aligneur, stands in his canvas box. About fifty people wait in silence on the bank in the cool sunlight.

On the launch Coni and Garton chat quietly to the passengers. Fourteen people are allowed in all. Besides the chairman and president are two boatmen, three timekeepers equipped with stopwatches, a radio link to the finish, and a clipboard on which to write a report of the race with records of ratings, wind direction and strength, and the distance between the crews at certain points relayed to them as they go past by judges in boxes by the booms. There is also a newspaper reporter, and relatives and friends of the crews, including the lady who is putting up Clare College, Cambridge. Shortly before eight o'clock Clare take up position on the Berkshire station, sliding between the piles and backing down until their stern makes contact with the stakeboat boy and Emmanuel College, Cambridge, do likewise on the Bucks side.

At precisely eight o'clock Coni stands up in the bows of the launch, erect, feet apart. He has two furled flags in front of him, one red for starting, one white for warning crews whose steering goes haywire. He says, very clearly, 'Clare and Emmanuel: when I see that you are straight and ready I shall start you like this.' He holds the red flag vertically above his head while saying, 'Are you ready?' and sweeps it downwards smartly to his right at the moment he says, 'Go!' The crews get straight, coxes keeping their arms raised until they are satisfied that they are pointing straight towards the finish, their men going through nervous gestures, shuddering, grimacing, pushing hair back or dipping a hand in the water. They don't look at the other crew. 'Are you ready?' Coni barks. 'Go.' Several fingers press the buttons of stopwatches, sixteen blades dip into the water together and swirl it towards the stern of the boats, and Clare and Emmanuel streak off to open the Ladies' Plate for 1980, the umpire's launch in breezy pursuit.

It is rather early for regatta-goers, even if the sun is up, but soon the car parks begin to fill and the traffic gets heavier down Remenham Hill and down the Fairmile on the other side of town. Some walk from the station, and the buses stop opposite the Catherine Wheel on their way to Oxford or outside the Kenton Theatre in New Street on their way to London. Boatmen gather in their traditional area of the tents to gossip and exchange anecdotes of the past year, to fly kites and sound out rumours of cheats and intrigue, to set the gearing of the outriggers and tinker with the fittings of their craft. In the old days they always had the same bell tent and used to sleep there, and the Thames Conservancy men used to sleep under canvas next to the wall of Leander's garden. They were once trapped in there, unable to come out for fear of public opinion outside the Little White Hart on the other bank of the river, after some enterprising revellers had stolen all their trousers in the dead of night and strung them on a line down river.

Since the old bell tents gave way to one large hangar the watermen have gathered in their original groups, and they are the unofficial eyes and ears of the regatta. If there were ever a suggestion of drug-taking, for example, they would be the first to find out, says the president, and good relations between them and the stewards are essential.

The crews' amenities tent has opened rather late for breakfast, an hour and a quarter after racing started on this exceptionally early day. Soon there are a few dozen oarsmen and some coaches tucking into bacon and eggs and debating the rather inflationary price of tea, and reporters gather at the tables outside while scanning their programme for the likeliest races for a story. A mother pushes her pram in, just out for a walk to see what is happening. And every five minutes Mr Robertson's voice tells them all reassuringly who is leading who at the Barrier and what their strike rate is, and the launches carry their flannelled, capped and button-holed and blazered umpires and timekeepers and guests up and down the course. Five students from Imperial College turn up with a banner to protest British sporting links with South Africa and are allowed to hand out leaflets outside the boat tent, but they missed their train at Paddington and so arrived too late to see Witwatersrand Unversity beat Nereus of Holland in a heat of the Ladies' Plate.

During the luncheon interval the press are entertained at Leander by British Petroleum, the sponsors of the club's crews, and there is a little drama being played out at Wimbledon. An oarsman from Dartmouth College's crew in the Visitors' has been taken seriously ill in the night and their coach, Dick Grosman, has secured a postponement of their race against St Paul's School, Concord, until the afternoon in the hope that he can find a substitute. This is hard as the crew are from New York State, but he has found that a member of the club is touring Europe with his mother and sister and is believed to be in London. After trans-Atlantic telephone calls he finds the hotel where the Badgers are staying near Hyde Park, and the clerk says she thinks they have gone to watch the tennis at Wimbledon. Grosman and his wife drive down there and the All England Club refuse to put out a loudspeaker message for the innocent Badger. Grosman returns to a meeting with the stewards at 3 p.m. and gets another deferment. Eventually Badger's sister is contacted at the hotel and she finds her brother sunbathing in Hyde Park late in the afternoon. He rushes to Paddington, catches a British Rail high-speed train to Reading, is taken by car to Henley, and is in the boat, somewhat surprised, by the closing stages of the day's racing. He helps Dartmouth to beat the school from his home town, Concord, and earns himself a large steak this evening.

During the afternoon there are signs of life in some of the tents in Fawley Meadows which are rented out by the stewards to companies as private enclosures. They are a safe distance from the rowing men but are a faint ghost of Henley's past when the Oxford barges and the Vanderbilts' houseboat and the private enclosures of London clubs and Cambridge colleges afforded pockets of exclusiveness to the chosen few. An eight from Njord in Holland has a nasty accident with a double sculler and lose the bows of their boat. The stern four men row it back to base, its jagged bow skimming above the water, to the delight of photographers and the dismay of Henley Rowing Club, who have lent it to the Dutchmen. The young security guards at the enclosure gate are looking uncomfortable in their ill-fitting uniforms, but theirs is a long and thankless task, and they do not have experience of the Oxford college servants or scouts who have always done the job until now. The scouts are fewer in number and are confined to tasks inside the enclosure. The new men are there to guard the silverware and the old rules: badges must be shown, jackets must be worn by men, trousers are not allowed for women, nor denim suits, nor transistor radios, nor children under ten, the last a new rule which has caused some indignant letters to the press.

As the band of the Grenadier Guards plays near the champagne bar Coni has a little time to think about tomorrow's programme and the royal visit on the finals day. He also umpires a couple of races and has personal guests to entertain, though in this he has the assistance of Mrs Sue Cavendish as his hostess. John Garton and his wife Elizabeth look after the official guests. Royal visits must be planned to the last detail and there have been some near misses in recent times. Coni once entered the boat tent on a last minute check before showing a princess round and found a naked girl there, changing before a swim. On another occasion a cigarette set light to the canvas just as Princess Alexandra's tea was being poured so the party discreetly moved to the other end of the stewards' own little lawn. No sooner had this occurred than a security man told them there was an unidentified Aer Lingus bag in the floating grandstand. There was nothing for it but to speed to the inspection of the silverware on display in another part of the enclosure. 'Is tea always as exciting as this at Henley?' asked the princess. The bag belonged to an official of the Irish Amateur Rowing Union.

The impeccable timing of the programme was threatened by geese on one royal occasion. John Garton was preparing to start the final of the Grand with a royal party aboard the umpire's launch when the course was blocked by a flotilla of geese by the island. He showed them the chairman's red flag, which is supposed to make all lesser species take avoiding action, but this had no effect; nor did shouting, waving and hissing by those on the bank. When matters were in danger of becoming undignified the situation was saved by the driver of the launch, who produced a packet of half-eaten sandwiches from under his seat. These were passed to spectators, who cast bread upon the waters near the bank, and when the geese went a-scavenging the race was started before they could so much as swallow.

In the afternoon the chairman keeps his fingers crossed that all the launches will keep going, for there will be chaos if anything breaks down. He turns his attention to the second day's programme which is the hardest to arrange because of oarsmen doubling-up in events. It reaches the noticeboard outside the secretary's office immediately after the National Anthem at the close of racing at 7.45 p.m., and the chairman is smoking a Sobranie beside it. For the first time in this very long day Coni and secretary Goddard manage smiles which are more than false bonhomie. Tension dissolves as the stewards and officials return their stopwatches, flags and radios for safe keeping. Coni takes a break as they wander in and out of the committee room, sipping a pint of lime juice and a large gin and tonic. Launch tickets for tomorrow are discussed and laid out on their chart, and somebody is told to make sure there are enough programmes as they had run out at two o'clock. A presentation is to be made to Ivy Batty who has kept the ladies' loo for twenty-five years. And further instruction is needed for the security men to teach them the difference between firm politeness and firm crassness.

By this time the Grand eights are creeping home from their evening outings, watched by anyone lucky enough to spot one. The bars are closing, the crews have gone for dinner, some visitors are still picnicking in the car park, and the pubs are doing a steady trade. This is the first year that anyone can remember when public houses have not had all-day licences in Henley. Their applications were refused by the magistrates because it was alleged that drinkers were coming to town by the busload in 1979. But the regatta bars and the clubs got their extensions under the English licensing laws, and the publicans are a little put out for the bonanza week of the year.

Over a pint in the Two Brewers a coach from Seattle asks a reporter where he can find a copy of Fairbairn, and one of Bourne. The fair is under way discreetly up the road to Wargrave, no longer visible from the regatta but still playing its part, even if its vehicles no longer come in procession down Remenham Hill to be led to their pitch by the regatta secretary, and even if the proprietor no longer keeps his takings in a tin box, a sort of miniature panthermanticon, buried in a hole under his bed. In those days the fair paid the regatta £1000 rent in untraceables, half at the beginning and half at the end, though the secretary had to attend early on the morning after to get his money. After closing time the town streets are still busy, there is a queue at the fish and chip shop and men in boaters are eating cheeseburgers and drinking Coke in the Wimpy bar. Badger and the Dartmouth crew have just left the Catherine Wheel. Anybody walking past Leander shortly before 11 p.m. would have heard a fine rendering of 'The Road to Mandalay', and anyone peeking through the door of the portrait-clad private dining room would have seen the Lady Victoria Boat Club of Belfast at their annual Henley reunion, dressed in their best and well into the cigars and champagne. In fine voice, too.

A light still burns in the darkness of the enclosure, and it is in the committee room. At eleven o'clock Coni, Goddard, David Cazes, who once played a nigger minstrel in a Gully Nickalls farce and who does not look the part, being ruddy and short, and Richard Crowden, the chairman's personal assistant, await the arrival of the programme proofs. They looked tired and a little ragged at the edges. There are thin curling sandwiches on a tray, mingled with tomato slices and dry bits of parsley, and black coffee. They have not had any dinner, having already spent several hours in checking the programme, which is newly prepared for each day of the regatta. It begins to rain, drubbing on the roof of the tent. A telephone call announces that Messrs Higgs have completed the book proofs, and a few minutes later John Luker brings them in. Eager hands distribute them and Cazes starts reading like a litany while others check for times, names, discrepancies in results or in spacing. They have to go through it a second time because nobody checked the race times in the front against the race times page by page. Luker has a list of half a dozen blemishes and everything is finished by 11.55 p.m. 'And it's still Thursday,' Crowden says, and Coni says his favourite catchphrase which he has not reached for very much on the busiest day in the history of Henley regatta. 'I like it, I like it a lot.' A relieved and tired man, he drives his Bentley off through the damp streets of the town to his rented house to get a few hours' sleep before black coffee prefaces another, though not quite so early, start.

And so the kaleidoscope with delirium tremens that Jingle Junior on the Jaunt had reported back to *Punch* a hundred years before swings into its second day of 1980. There are more pretty girls in unsuitable shoes tottering about on the lawns where never a plastic cup, let alone a sponsor's name, is seen. Champagne and Pimms and beer flow, it gets harder to get a seat for which members now pay an annual subscription of £25, and it is clear that the problems of inflation, the minimum lending rate and unemployment encompass concepts unknown in these parts. Punts and skiffs are a rare commodity these days, but there are a few out, with a few old gramophones playing seventy-eights and many old blazers that have seen better days. The Thames Water Authority launch leads convoys of hired motor cruisers up and down stream from time to time, and the umpires' launches slip along on business, including the *Amaryllis* built in 1911 and said to have been used by an admiral or a general on the Tigris or the Euphrates during the First World War.

There are lavish picnics and strawberry teas, reunions and chance meetings. Clonmel RC has a good sing-song in the Little Angel, answered by Kingston supporters in the other half of the dining room. Guests take their landladies to luncheon in the marquee, fourteen-year-olds hike to Henley to see the school crew and slip off to the fair. Dick Cashin nurses his neck and then gets back into his boat, watched by day trippers, holiday-makers off the hire boats, guests on steamers sponsored as newts, and the occasional man of the road, au pair, or resting hiker. Gypsy women sell good-luck sprays of heather, and the official souvenir stall sells discreet ties and jerseys, elegant ashtrays and tablemats. A hundred heads narrowly avoid being severed by sleek shells and jutting riggers on their way to and from the stream; a thousand shutters click, a dozen movie cameras purr. And a coxswain from New Zealand describes the regatta to the world's press as a Mickey Mouse affair.

He has good reason to be angry, even if his charges are responsible for putting themselves out of the regatta before they have dipped a blade in the water in combat. Messrs Mabbott, Trask, Stanley and Rodger of North Shore and Hawkes Bay rowing clubs got together to go to the Moscow Games. When their rowing association withdrew them at the last minute after being threatened with financial penalties by their government, they were sent out to the Prince Philip Cup instead. On the start they were penalized by disqualification for doing two false starts in their first-round tie with Ridley Graduates BC of Canada. They argued that the umpire, Dr David Jennens, had not conducted himself consistently in his two attempts to get the race off, one man claiming that Jennens had time to drink a cup of tea between asking whether they were ready and dropping the red flag. But they know the rules, and the umpire's decision is final. It is a long way to travel for an ignominious end to their season.

On the Saturday the enormous crowd is treated to a demonstration by three Venetian gondolas which have been brought to the Thames by the Generali Nautical Club of Venice to publicize their traditional rowing and their city. They are graceful and magnificent, their crews tossing their oars at the end of the rowing course. By this stage of the regatta five selected crews have been eliminated, and so the 'pink ayatollahs', as *The Times* calls them, are blushing with embarrassment about the let-down in their intelligence when it comes to picking scullers. Their forecasts for the eight-oared events are, however, much better. Among the day's races, which are by now taking place with a decent interval between them so that there is plenty of time to recharge a glass or fetch a coffee and brandy to fend off a chill breeze which forewarns a shower, are two promising semifinals in the Grand. In the first one the Charles River crew beat the Norwegians by two-thirds of a length, and everyone is surprised by the power of the Norwegians. They do not have a reputation for eight-oared rowing, although all the men in the boat have been around at important international regattas for a few years, the best known of them being Alf Hansen, who with his brother Frank is the holder of the world and Olympic titles for double sculls. They may have earned their trip to Henley as compensation for not going to Moscow in fours and pairs, but they have set out to beat the Americans and maintain their ambition with each and every stroke. It is a fast race and is as exciting for the hundreds lolling in the fields at Remenham as it is for the thousands in the stewards' enclosure and in Phyllis Court.

Then comes the second semifinal three hours later, and the odds in favour of the Americans winning the cup falter a little. Waikato and Wairau rowing clubs of New Zealand are on the Berks station, wearing dark green strip which makes them look a little less menacing than their usual national colour of black, and on the Bucks side are Hannover and Hammerdeicher of West Germany. They are also a well-seasoned crew in international affairs and include Peter-Michael Kolbe, a former world champion in sculls who has failed to win the Diamonds in two attempts. Their average weight is fifteen stone, the heaviest crew in the event and half a stone per man heavier than the New Zealanders. Several of the latter have won silver medals in the 1979 world championships. The German boat is called *Oldies but Goldies* and their coxswain lies in the bows, unusual for an eight. The Germans are nervous and they show it by jumping the start. They are given a warning by umpire Coni and get away at the second attempt. It is almost a repeat of the other race, the Germans pressing hard all the way. The times to the Barrier and Fawley are the same and the determined New Zealanders in the best race of their turbulent season get home by a length in six minutes twenty-five seconds, a second slower than the Americans' time. Harry Parker is leaning on an old bicycle, anonymous amongst the crowd, at the start of this race, and what he sees gives him something to think about in preparing Cashin and the rest of his crew for the following day's finale. At Wimbledon Bjorn Borg is well on the way to his fifth consecutive singles title.

That evening is the evening of the fireworks. A performance of *A Midsummer Night's Dream* is drawing to an end in Mill Meadow on the town side of the bridge. There is a traffic jam for miles around on the country roads as those who are in try and get out, those who are out try and get in, and the wise and the inebriated stay put. The Thames is like a motorway as cruisers and launches jostle for the best positions down by the regatta enclosure. Skiffs and punts shoot through the bridge and canoes dart between them. There is delirium tremens inside Leander and a pink ayatollah sky outside, and as dusk falls the hearties gather in the crews' room to watch the pyrotechnics while hundreds of townies and oarsmen and girlfriends and American tourists and children crush into the regatta enclosure and gaze towards the sky. The kaleidoscope of flashing colours picks out the shadowy outline of boats and plays on the people's faces as they dutifully, naturally, emit their Ooooohs! and Aaaaaahs! Someone has done a lot of preparation to produce such wonders from the darkened fields of Fawley, and it is rumoured that it is a vicar with a liking for explosives.

By this stage of the regatta there are a lot of competitors with the freedom to celebrate elimination and a decreasing number who have come to realize that they are not dreaming of rowing at Henley, but are doing it. And there are some who just expect to anyway. Peter Coni drives his Bentley carefully this night to his reserved parking space behind Leander as soon as the tented camp is locked up. He goes into the bar to have a drink with some of the lads. 'Hello, Peter, what'll you have?' say several voices as he enters.

Finals day starts fine, the parish church filling to the portals for the traditional regatta service. In the morning there is superlative racing in the semifinals of the Ladies' Plate and the Thames Cup. Yale beat Trinity College, Dublin, by three feet and Witwatersrand beat Harvard by half a length. The selected crews in the Thames get through, the London RC lightweights beating Neptune of Eire and the University of London beating Thames Tradesmen's RC. The first final is the Prince Philip, in which Charles River beat another American combination, Yale University and Potomac BC. Then the Borchelt brothers of Potomac have a ludicrously easy win over Palmer and Laurie of Eton Vikings. Then it is lunch time, and after a decent interval of an hour and a half is ended by rain and the rapid packing-up of picnics, St Paul's School of Concord beat St Joseph's Academy of the USA in the Princess Elizabeth. Who said something about too many foreign crews from the direction of those deckchairs? The vociferous demonstration on behalf of people out of work goes almost unheeded when chanting starts outside the Little White Hart, although the trouble which might occur between well-oiled rowing buffs and demonstrators gives Coni and the policeman in charge, Peter Winship, cause for concern. 'My bowels turn to water at the thought of it,' says the chairman.

At three o'clock precisely Colgan, Cashin, Sommerville, Altekruse, Woodman, Christensen, Everett, Ibbetson and Chatzky are sitting in their sleek plastic nameless shell on the Berks station off Miss Mackenzie's Island, the same island which Smyth and his friends had landed on so long ago when it belonged to Miss Mackenzie's ancestor, Squire Freeman. On the Bucks station are the New Zealanders Robinson, Robertson, Sutherland, Wilson, Hansen, Logan, Johnston, McAuley and coxswain Cotter.

The gentleman from *The Times*, Jim Railton, has won the news-paper men's ballot for their one seat in the umpire's launch for the race, and Prince Michael of Kent is there too, for he is to give away the prizes. Dick Cashin has long since thrown away the white and blue wrist bands which accompanied his winning streak for two years until the Grand of 1975. He is wearing the same racing shirt that he wore for the semifinal, unwashed, as are those of the rest of the crew. He is confident of winning, and he is confident for his coach, Harry Parker, that retiring man whom Cashin sees as an absolute, as the only man in rowing that he trusts entirely. 'If Parker says it's going to rain on a bright sunny day,' Cashin says, 'then bring a slicker.'

It is quite something to be the focus of critical attention, listen to the starter, watch for his dropping of the red flag, and get the sudden spring of the first few strokes right. Both crews get away but the Americans have a very rough ride for the first ten, and Colgan in the bow hits a duck with his blade. The Americans weigh over fourteen stone a man in their slightly wiffy Olympic shirts and the New Zealanders are four pounds a man heavier. Their plastic and fibreglass boat and their long big-bladed oars by Dick Dreissigacker of Vermont bear little resemblance to the *Black Prince* or the sticks used by Trinity in 1839, and they cover the course in almost two minutes less than Smyth did. It is a good race, the crews putting the pressure on one another constantly until the Americans get a respectable lead by Fawley and come home with a bit of clear water between them and McAuley's crew. They cheer their opponents and paddle off smartly through the bridge to wind down, and they take so long that the waiting crowds by the pontoons almost give them up for drowned.

Eventually, however, they slip quietly into a landing stage as Morris dancers perform on a neighbouring pontoon. They throw cox Chatzky in the river, which doesn't surprise him. There is no sign of Parker, but he must have permitted himself a grin and there must be a sparkle in his eye even if he doesn't ride off and run down an old lady. There is a lot of applause and the Kiwis come up in the boat tent to shake the Americans by the hand. 'We got a terrible start, we thought they'd be closer. It's a pity the English couldn't be here, but it's not their fault,' they tell the cluster of reporters. What are you going to do tonight? 'Break our balls off,' says Dick Cashin.

Before the prize-giving the Grenadier Guards play 'Land of Hope and Glory' and bedraggled but smiling couples lurch in dance in the quagmire that was a close-cropped lawn a few hours earlier. The waitresses, rotund matrons or fresh-faced girls waiting for the art schools to take them in the autumn, are still making a brave face of it in their austere black after four days of dispensing champagne and Pimms as if the world is about to end. The guardsmen launch into a popular tune of the day, 'Didn't we have a wonderful time the day we went to Bangor?' and a forest of colourful umbrellas parts as the chairman leads Prince Michael to the stand. The prince recalls his own days in a Sandhurst crew at Bedford regatta, sympathizes with the Olympic impasse which faced so many here, but hopes that Henley had made up for their disappointment, and hands out the cups and medals.

The Charles River crew link hands and stretch skyward before the crowd to take the applause, and then they file out of the arena and away through the sodden deckchairs, Colgan balancing the base of the Grand on his head. They gather under a large waterside tree some way away, round the smiling Harry Parker, and show him the medals and the cup from which they will all sup this night. Meanwhile the royal prince's distribution of silverware to mainly foreign fields tells the story of the rest of the day: the Double Sculls to Walter and Ford of Victoria City RC, Canada; the Stewards' to the Charles River Rowing Association, USA; the Britannia to Leander Club; the Diamonds to Ricardo Ibarra of Argentina; the Visitors' and the Thames to the University of London; the Wyfolds to Nottingham Boat Club; the Ladies' Plate to Yale; and the Special Race for Schools to Shrewsbury.

At the Catherine Wheel the Americans have dinner with a ton of champagne. It is a little quieter under the chandeliers in the pink and white striped tents on Leander's lawn, but pretty steamy in the bar there, where at one stage a lightweight oarsman pins a very large heavyweight over the counter after some injudicious remark. One gentleman is caught trying to make off with another's umbrella. Irishmen are everywhere and Witwatersrand students are celebrating their defeat in the garden. Peter Coni can afford more than one gin this night before he needs to return to his home on the unfashionable side of Pimlico and think about some work at the other kind of bar. Much later, when most of the boat trailers that were leaving have left and when most of the Americans are at last tucked up in bed, Sean Colgan and Jim Dietz, the sculler, jump off the bridge in the buff, and are flushed out of the bushes by a long-suffering Bobby with a baton. So ends the last all-male Henley.

13

The Great Enclosure in Elysium
1981: The Gentlemen's Cup and the view
beyond the Styx

After Henley in 1980 the rowing season rolled on. There were at least twenty more regattas in England in July alone, including the three days of the national championships at Holme Pierrepont. In the Olympic Games regatta fifteen men won medals: silvers for the eight behind the East Germans after they rowed through the Soviet crew in the closing stages, bronzes for the coxless four and coxless pair, and the best result in modern times – and that meant ever. In August the lightweight crew that lost the final of the Thames Cup won gold medals in the international lightweight championships in Belgium, and there were medals for juniors too. The men who had put in months of work piling and booming the course at Henley and erecting stands and boat racks began weeks of work to take them down again, storing the booms in the old regatta boathouse adjacent to the defunct Carpenters Arms and the deckchairs in the black hut in the trees of Lion Meadow. They would have time, too, to do some more work on the mural they were painting on the inside of the hut doors depicting the car park and the tents and the church tower outside, with the chairman's Bentley in the middle and a dog cocking its leg at it. 'I like it,' Peter Coni QC was saying, 'I like it a lot.'

Coni has much to think about for the event of 1981. The stewards have announced already that a quadruple sculling event will be introduced, the only international class of boat besides coxed pairs which Henley did not accommodate, and there will be invitation races for women's fours and double sculls. The regatta has gone through many changes and two enforced stoppages because of world wars since its foundation in 1839, but 1980 has been a real watershed. Women have had almost no role in its history except as guests and decoration and something to be seen, but henceforward their advancing place in the sport will be recognized, if only on a small scale. The boat tent will have to be extended once more and the showers segregated. Some of the booms need replacing as well. Coni wants to expand the enclosure also, because on some days the crush is claustrophobic. Early returns from the regatta office, from the ladies who look after the receipts and the membership lists and entries and inquiries and accommodation requests and a hundred and one items, suggest that he will have enough money to do it, and to replace the year's quota of booms. Apart from landladies who cater for the creature comfort of the men, and the corps of long-suffering waitresses, and Ivy Batty who attends the ladies' loo, and a handful of female coxswains, the office workers are the only representatives of their sex who have played an active part in the circus.

The committee of management may also have to look at ways of rationalizing some of the events, because the number of people wanting to row at Henley causes them headaches with the timetable. Do they need a fifth day, and wouldn't that be too much? Are not the Thames Cup and the Ladies' Plate too similar in attraction and spread of ability? Should there be more stringent qualifications for the Diamonds? Will there be a Gentlemen's Cup for the ladies? And won't that cause havoc in Fleet Street, where this year some know-all on *The Times* had followed style so religiously that he changed Ladies' to Women's? An Irish newspaper once headlined a Trinity victory in the Ladies' with: 'Trinity girls win Henley prize'. It could yet come true.

Coni's rise to prominence among the stewards was through St Catharine's College, Cambridge, the London Rowing Club, of which he was captain and stroke of crews who didn't win any of Henley's cups, then the Amateur Rowing Association. His success is attributable to administrative ability and a mind which can see signs for the future, even if other stewards' wives have to organize a rota to get his shirts washed and ironed for his duties in the tents. We will leave him in his house, the walls lined with the David Hockney prints which he collects and adores, with the collection of stamps from Bosnia-Herzegovina awaiting insertion in the album on the sort of rainy day which never comes, and visit the Great Enclosure in the Sky some years hence, when the quick and the dead are all in it together.

Thousand upon thousand of oarsmen and scullers have reached the

Elysian waters through the records kept by H. T. Steward, T. A. Cook, C. T. Steward, H. Playford and J. L. Garton, and R. D. Burnell. Now they slide past, Smyth in the *Black Prince* with the three crowns of Trinity on her bow, Woodgate's Brasenose four with little Weatherley swimming for his life from a gaggle of water lilies, endless light blues of Eton, Oxford's seven-man crew, the Columbia students and the Shoe-wae-cae-mettes. There goes the skeleton of Shinkel with Cornell, the cerise of Leander, the Belgians, the Harvard crimsons and the men from Jesus. There goes Casamajor and Nickalls after Nickalls after Nickalls, and Kelly the fiddler, Kelly the bricky, and Kelly the son. . . . There goes the deaf and dumb Gollan, and the Beresfords, and Sam Mackenzie, doffing his cap and calling a viscount a Pom. . . . There goes Ivanov and a plethora of Russians, Germans democratic and federal, Japanese and Egyptians. . . . There goes Sean Drea and the boys upholding the honour of Old Trinity, chased by the Dublin police. There go the toffs and the Tradesmen, the college boys and dockers, the schoolboys and the lightweights. Dynasties of various hue. There go the Corinthians and the Olympians, boated or banished. There follow brilliant flotillas from England's rivers and corners of the globe, the Armada of Losers.

The enclosures seem endless, stretching from the comfort of the chandeliered pink palace to the pleasant and wild informality by Temple Island. Beech woods stretch into the hills and there is a golden cornfield marking a hazy horizon beyond the start. Among the company, which exhibits every fad of the tailor's, the hatter's, the haberdasher's art, are a crew staying at Badger's, which Kenneth Grahame turned into Toad Hall, and one staying at Blandy House where, in 1752, Mary Blandy had poisoned her father over an affair of the heart and had a celebrated trial. A Harvard man is lamenting the decline in his *alma mater*'s power of starting wars, for their last Grand win in 1959 produced only a Chinese invasion of Tibet. Someone is denouncing the atomic idiot who named a Nevada nuclear site the Diamond Sculls. The bridge is lined with carriages and the launch is full of kings, and over there is Steve, skipping delicately at the age of fifty-seven, knowing that his portrait hangs by Cranmer's in Jesus College. His friend Hutch looks on as he chats endlessly to the throng who mill about.

> The best coach for any crew is the bows of a faster boat coming behind
> them. . . . Fixed seats are an abomination and should be done away with.

One wants to make rowing pleasant; one does not want to have men eating their breakfast off the mantelpiece. . . . If you can't do it easily you can't do it at all. . . . Sit back until the cows come home. . . . Loose and easy, lazy and long. . . .

Half his listeners understand, half do not.

Don't get into controversies on style as language is far too imperfect a medium to express ideas. . . . She is a hard mistress; for all the sweat and labour, she grants, perhaps, the finest immediate rewards in proportion to her pains – to the tyro a few moments now and then, when the boat runs, and eight oars are one, and he is in heaven.

Here and there along the banks where red-faced coaches in boaters and blazers ride horses and bicycles, hold megaphones and electronic stopwatches and stroke timers, is a sunbather with a copy of Steve's big red book, *Three Hundred Tips on Rowing.* . . .

Further upstream is a daunting man on a soapbox. It is the Rev. Dr Warre, austere and a modern incarnation of the ship-swift king of the Phaeacians and son of Poseidon and Periboea, as Sir Theodore Cook would say when he got carried away. Great changes in boats and their fittings have taken place in the last half century, Warre is saying. 'But the art of rowing is still the same, full of manly endeavour, full of self-sacrifice, full of delight,' and he begins to give readings from his *Grammar of Rowing.*

Over there, near the champagne bar, is the headquarters of the Nickalls family. Jimmy Rice, the Columbia coach, says as he walks past, 'Only those with strong backs and weak minds ever rowed.' Old Tom Nickalls, father of the dynasty, once advised his sons to play cricket because that way they could see the world instead of someone else's neck, or something to that effect. Guy retaliates to the American that a coach is 'the man who has forgotten more about rowing than anybody else ever knew. He is usually a perfectly sane man with a vile temper and yet he often acts in a perfectly insane manner,' he says. His own experience has borne him out at Yale, where his efforts were scorned in the *First H Book* by George S. Mumford – admittedly a Harvard writer in a Harvard book:

Mr Guy Nickalls, the well-known English amateur, had coached the Yale crews for several years. As a teacher of rowing on this side of the water he did not seem to improve with practice.

Ah, well. His brother Vivian is quoting the poem against himself from some Eights Week rag: 'You're skilled at sculling, yet your skill is rather skill of hand than skill at skull.' Gully is there too, telling a group of Russians in English that he is not trying to do them down, drowning in his anecdotage.

There are houseboats great and small on the river, steam launches and punts at the booms and pretty girls galore, and gipsy touts and minstrel bands, and handsome Yanks and Belgians wearing their sock-suspenders and smoking cigars. And a fairground in full swing.

There are prophets of doom. Piggy Eyre thinks that undoubtedly the Tideway clubs have an uphill and ceaseless struggle against the forces of ease and enjoyment which have so insidiously encroached on the battleground of British manliness. T. G. Bowles MP puts it all down to the substitution of tea for beer at breakfast. Muttlebury is wandering about in his shortest pair of shorts, and Peter Coni is chain-smoking Balkan Sobranies, and John Garton is saying to someone with a cheerful grin, 'Jumbo Edwards, bless his stupid old heart. I'm convinced that all his stuff on training was wrong. . . . ' Old Archibald Maclaren is discoursing on the virtues of muscular and respiratory power and denouncing the use of egg in sherry. 'Exercise,' he says, 'diet, sleep, air, bathing and clothing . . . .' An American author, Samuel Crowther, is telling somebody about the sliding seat:

> With the play of the legs in the stroke the oarsman is apt to be larger below the waist than above in distinction to the oarsman of the previous age, and the wiry man is generally preferred to the stouter build.

His honour Justice Maughan is jotting down his thoughts on Trinity Hall:

> Those who row do not row for themselves, for they have personified that composite entity, the Boat, as deity whose immediate interests they are bound to serve regardless of their own personal comfort. In frost and in heat, in sunshine and in rain, the servants of this strange goddess must go to the river at the appointed time. . . . They must submit on dreary, sunless afternoons, while moisture drops from the willows, and when aches and pains afflict their unhappy limbs, to hear sometimes, with bitterness in their hearts but without thought of reply, the continuous criticism and sometimes objurgations of a coaching friend or fiend upon the bank. . . . The boat seems to be becoming more sluggish and comfortless, the time more ragged, the rolling more evident, and the water more and more like molten lead.

Many are those who Maughan, but most have also found common ground with Lord Cottesloe, who says that rowing in an eight-oared boat when it really goes perfectly together and goes well is probably about as near heaven as one can get on earth. People who have never tried it cast doubts, setting other available pleasures against it, and Cottesloe tempers his view a jot by admitting that being a galley slave is a bit of a savoury, but he maintains that there is great joy to be had from it. And he is toasted by oarsmen from Salford to Shanghai, from Vancouver to Waikato, from the worst crews imaginable, because they once had that heavenly feeling, even if only for a few strokes.

There is Porter and Davidge and Mackenzie again, thinking up some plot of one-upmanship, there is Lou Barry chastizing his men with a knowing twinkle in his eye, there is Bob Janousek saying little but doing a lot, there is Harry Parker saying nothing. There is Chris Baillieu, the voice of British rowers in the 1970s:

> I enjoy rowing in a macabre, masochistic sort of way, but we are not here for any ethereal good British sporting feeling. We are here to win.

Regatta (Italian), to wrangle, to cope or fight for mastery.

Jingle Junior, Mr Punch's man on the jaunt, has gatecrashed another party. While Lord Desborough is punting along and worrying about the definition of an amateur and the presence of foreigners in such numbers, Theodore Cook, born by his own admission a crusty Tory, is extolling the virtues of Sims the boatbuilder.

> As George Sims did it, the thing savoured of Turner's notion of perspective, a realization of what should be, without any knowledge of what must be. There was that strange sympathy in the boat builder which was in Matt Taylor, and the Claspers too, and which is outside all calculation. He possessed the accuracy of the eye to see and of the hand to fashion exactly what he had in his mind. . . . I have always felt that in building a boat which slipped through the water like a trout George Sims must have succeeded because he was nearer nature than the theoretical mathematician, because in spite of methods which may fairly be described as ignorant and empirical, he possessed an intuitive skill which was worth more than any scientific hypothesis.

What tribute from a craftsman to a craftsman!

In this company too is Rudie Lehmann with his charming wife Alice, born liberal and Liberal by inclination, enjoying a Havana and issuing invitations to row in house crews at Fieldhead, and writing verses about coaching on the Cam and Muttlebury's shorts. And Robert Forster, writer and coach, watching the seekers of fame at the end of eight-foot spruces and wondering at the seriousness of it all. Their company is good and their table is plentiful, there is a strawberry mountain and a dozen magnums of best bubbly and, bless us, here come the whole staff of *Punch* on their summer outing, and some from the *Field* too. Before things get out of hand in this meeting of tories and liberals, the last word will be left to Theodore Cook. His politics will not necessarily find favour but his view of his sport will yet. He has tried many sports and he thinks rowing has found an element which others lack. When we gather for the happiest week in all the year, he says, it is the brotherhood of rowing, the comradeship of the oar that we recall, when eight men who have trained until they have become a single drive, a single thrust of forward-flashing wrists, face suddenly the crisis towards which that selfless toil has led them, and know that every link in all that pulsing chain of flesh and blood rings true. For us, he says, there are no centuries or duck's eggs, no goals or gallery kicks, no individual distinctions where the crew are all in all.

> The rattle of the riggers at the finish, the music of the tide beneath her body as she shot between the strokes, the grim yet heartening sound of splendid and unbroken strength when all eight blades crashed in together – these are the things that no one who has heard and felt them will ever forget.

Some delirium. Some tremens. Some kaleidoscope.

Winners at Henley

Grand Challenge Cup

1839	First Trinity BC, Cam.	8.30	
1840	Leander Club	9.15	
1841	Cambridge Subscription Rooms	—	
1842	Cambridge Subscription Rooms	8.30	
1843	Oxford University BC	9.0	
1844	Etonian Club, Oxf.	8.25	
1845	Cambridge University BC	8.30	
1846	Thames Club, London	8.15	
1847	Oxford University BC	8.0	
1848	Oxford University BC	9.11	
1849	Wadham College Oxf.	—	
1850	Oxford University BC	RO*	
1851	Oxford University BC	7.45	
1852	Oxford University BC	—	
1853	Oxford University BC	8.3	
1854	First Trinity BC, Cam.	8.15	
1855	Cambridge University BC	8.32	
1856	Royal Chester RC	—	
1857	London RC	7.55	
1858	Cambridge University BC	7.26	
1859	London RC	7.45	
1860	First Trinity BC, Cam.	8.45	
1861	First Trinity BC, Cam.	8.10	
1862	London RC	8.5	
1863	University College, Oxf.	7.42	
1864	Kingston RC	7.43	
1865	Kingston RC	7.25	
1866	Etonian Club, Oxf.	8.29	
1867	Etonian Club, Oxf.	7.54	
1868	London RC	7.20	
1869	Etonian Club, Oxf.	7.28	
1870	Etonian Club, Oxf.	7.18	
1871	Etonian Club, Oxf.	8.5	
1872	London RC	8.27	
1873	London RC	7.52	
1874	London RC	7.41	
1875	Leander Club	7.19	
1876	Thames RC	7.26	
1877	London RC	8.2½	
1878	Thames RC	7.42	
1879	Jesus College, Cam.	8.39	
1880	Leander Club	7.3	
1881	London RC	7.23	
1882	Exeter College, Oxf.	8.11	
1883	London RC	7.51	
1884	London RC	7.27	
1885	Jesus College, Cam.	7.22	
1886	Trinity Hall, Cam.	6.53½	
1887	Trinity Hall, Cam.	6.56	
1888	Thames RC	7.1	
1889	Thames RC	7.4	
1890	London RC	7.4½	
1891	Leander Club	6.51	
1892	Leander Club	7.48½	

* RO: rowed over.

1893	Leander Club	7.12
1894	Leander Club	7.22
1895	Trinity Hall, Cam.	7.30
1896	Leander Club	7.43
1897	New College, Oxf.	6.51
1898	Leander Club	7.13
1899	Leander Club	7.12
1900	Leander Club	7.6
1901	Leander Club	7.4²/₅
1902	Third Trinity BC, Cam.	7.17
1903	Leander Club	7.9
1904	Leander Club	7.20
1905	Leander Club	6.58
1906	Club Nautique de Gand, Belgium	7.9
1907	Sport Nautique de Gand, Belgium	7.31
1908	Christ Church, Oxf.	7.10
1909	Royal Club Nautique de Gand, Belgium	7.8
1910	Magdalen College, Oxf.	7.19
1911	Magdalen College, Oxf.	7.2
1912	Sydney RC, Australia	7.6
1913	Leander Club	7.11
1914	Harvard Athletic Assoc. BC, USA	7.20
1920	Magdalen College, Oxf.	7.24
1921	Magdalen College, Oxf.	6.54
1922	Leander Club	7.36
1923	Thames RC	6.45
1924	Leander Club	8.3
1925	Leander Club	6.53
1926	Leander Club	6.56
1927	Thames RC	7.16
1928	Thames RC	6.56
1929	Leander Club	7.0
1930	London RC	6.59
1931	London RC	7.33
1932	Leander Club	7.19
1933	London RC	7.36
1934	Leander Club	6.45
1935	Pembroke College, Cam.	6.52
1936	FC Zürich Ruder Club, Switzerland	7.25
1937	R. Wiking, Germany	7.33
1938	London RC	6.58
1939	Harvard University, USA	7.40
1946	Leander Club	7.1
1947	Jesus College, Cam.	7.14
1948	Thames RC	7.2
1949	Leander Club	6.54
1950	Harvard University, USA	7.23
1951	Lady Margaret BC, Cam.	7.16
1952	Leander Club	6.38
1953	Leander Club	6.49
1954	Club Krylia Sovetov, USSR	7.16
1955	University of Pennsylvania, USA	6.56
1956	Centre Sportif des Forces de l'Armée Française	7.6
1957	Cornell University, USA	6.53
1958	Trud Club, USSR	6.40
1959	Harvard University, USA	6.57
1960	Molesey BC	6.35
1961	Central Sport Club of the USSR Navy	6.43
1962	Central Sport Club of the USSR Navy	6.40
1963	University of London	6.38
1964	Zjalghiris Viljnjus, USSR	6.25
1965	Ratzeburger RC, Germany	6.16
1966	TSC Berlin, Germany	6.35
1967	SC Wissenschaft DHfK, Germany	6.46
1968	University of London	7.56
1969	SC Einheit, Dresden	6.28
1970	ASK Vorwärts, GDR	6.34
1971	Tideway Scullers' School	6.46
1972	WMF Moscow, USSR	6.33
1973	Trud Kolomna, USSR	6.23
1974	Trud Club, USSR	6.34
1975	Leander Club and Thames Tradesmen's RC	6.16
1976	Thames Tradesmen's RC	6.25
1977	University of Washington, USA	6.27
1978	Trakia Club, Bulgaria	6.51
1979	Thames Tradesmen's RC and London RC	6.35
1980	Charles River Rowing Association, USA	6.35

Ladies' Challenge Plate

1845	St George's Club, London	8.25	
1846	First Trinity BC, Cam.	—	
1847	Brasenose College, Oxf.	9.0	
1848	Christ Church, Oxf.	—	
1849	Wadham College, Oxf.	—	
1850	Lincoln College, Oxf.	RO	
1851	Brasenose College, Oxf.	8.10	
1852	Pembroke College, Oxf.	RO	
1853	First Trinity BC, Cam.	8.15	
1854	First Trinity BC, Cam.	7.55	
1855	Balliol College, Oxf.	7.58	
1856	Royal Chester RC	—	
1857	Exeter College, Oxf.	7.57	
1858	Balliol College, Oxf.	7.51	
1859	First Trinity BC, Cam.	7.55	
1860	First Trinity BC, Cam.	RO	
1861	First Trinity BC, Cam.	8.10	
1862	University College, Oxf.	8.17	
1863	University College, Oxf.	7.23	
1864	Eton College	RO	
1865	Third Trinity BC, Cam.	—	
1866	Eton College	8.16	
1867	Eton College	7.55	
1868	Eton College	7.25	
1869	Eton College	7.58	
1870	Eton College	7.46	
1871	Pembroke College, Oxf.	7.59	
1872	Jesus College, Cam.	8.35	
1873	Jesus College, Cam.	7.53	
1874	First Trinity BC, Cam.	8.6	
1875	Trinity College, Dublin	7.30	
1876	Jesus College, Cam.	7.31	
1877	Jesus College, Cam.	8.23	
1878	Jesus College, Cam.	8.52	
1879	Lady Margaret BC, Cam.	8.52	
1880	Trinity Hall, Cam.	7.26	
1881	First Trinity BC, Cam.	7.51	
1882	Eton College	8.37	
1883	Christ Church, Oxf.	7.51	
1884	Eton College	7.37	
1885	Eton College	7.21	
1886	Pembroke College, Cam.	7.17	
1887	Trinity Hall, Cam.	7.10	
1888	Lady Margaret BC, Cam.	7.18	
1889	Christ Church, Oxf.	7.22	
1890	Balliol College, Oxf.	7.16	
1891	Balliol College, Oxf.	7.20	
1892	First Trinity BC, Cam.	7.43½	
1893	Eton College	7.32	
1894	Eton College	7.36	
1895	Eton College	7.25	
1896	Eton College	8.6	
1897	Eton College	7.1	
1898	Eton College	7.3	
1899	Eton College	7.20	
1900	New College, Oxf.	7.18	
1901	University College, Oxf.	7.28	
1902	University College, Oxf.	7.16	
1903	Magdalen College, Oxf.	7.33	
1904	Eton College	7.20	
1905	Eton College	7.12	
1906	First Trinity BC, Cam.	7.23	
1907	Trinity Hall, Cam.	7.44	
1908	Jesus College, Cam.	7.5	
1909	St John's College, Oxf.	7.9	
1910	Eton College	7.16	
1911	Eton College	6.56	
1912	Eton College	7.4	
1913	First Trinity BC, Cam.	7.24	
1914	Pembroke College, Cam.	7.24	
1920	Christ Church, Oxf.	7.30	
1921	Eton College	7.9	
1922	Brasenose College, Oxf.	7.47	
1923	Trinity College, Oxf.	6.55	
1924	Shrewsbury School	8.4	
1925	Lady Margaret BC, Cam.	7.7	
1926	Jesus College, Cam.	7.5	
1927	First Trinity BC, Cam.	7.29	
1928	Jesus College, Cam.	7.6	
1929	First Trinity BC, Cam.	7.16	
1930	Lady Margaret BC, Cam.	7.10	
1931	Jesus College, Cam.	8.7	
1932	Shrewsbury School	7.40	
1933	Lady Margaret BC, Cam.	7.38	
1934	Jesus College, Cam.	6.48	
1935	Trinity Hall, Cam.	7.7	
1936	First Trinity BC, Cam.	7.48	
1937	Clare College, Cam.	7.38	

1938	Radley College	6.56	1963	Royal Military Academy,	
1939	Clare College, Cam.	8.13		Sandhurst	6.55
1946	Jesus College, Cam.	7.8`	1964	Pembroke College, Cam.	6.47
1947	First and Third Trinity		1965	St Edmund Hall, Oxf.	6.49
	BC, Cam.	7.21	1966	Lady Margaret, Cam.	7.4
1948	Eton College	7.15	1967	First and Third Trinity	
1949	Lady Margaret BC, Cam.	6.50		BC, Cam.	7.3
1950	New College, Oxf.	7.25	1968	Cherwell BC	8.23
1951	Pembroke College, Cam.	7.25	1969	ASR Nereus, Holland	6.55
1952	Lady Margaret BC, Cam.	6.50	1970	GSR Aegir, Holland	7.0
1953	Jesus College, Cam.	7.0	1971	University of London	7.0
1954	First and Third Trinity		1972	DSR Laga, Holland	6.59
	BC, Cam.	7.33	1973	Harvard University, USA	6.35
1955	Queens' College, Cam.	7.26	1974	University College, Dublin	6.58
1956	Peterhouse, Cam.	7.41	1975	University of London	6.31
1957	Pembroke College, Cam.	7.11	1976	Trinity College,	
1958	Jesus College, Cam.	6.51		Hartford, USA	6.49
1959	Lady Margaret BC, Cam.	7.13	1977	Trinity College, Dublin	6.53
1960	Eton College	6.50	1978	Imperial College, London	6.59
1961	Lady Margaret BC, Cam.	7.4	1979	Yale University, USA	7.14
1962	Queens' College, Cam.	6.54	1980	Yale University, USA	6.37

Thames Challenge Cup

1868	Pembroke College, Oxf.	7.46	1890	Thames RC	7.21½
1869	Oscillators Club, Surbiton	RO	1891	Molesey BC	7.18
1870	Oscillators Club, Surbiton	7.53	1892	Jesus College, Cam.	8.10
1871	Ino RC	8.36	1893	Thames RC	7.49
1872	Thames RC	8.42	1894	Trinity College, Oxf.	7.58
1873	Thames RC	8.2	1895	Nereus BC, Amsterdam,	
1874	Thames RC	8.19		Holland	7.29
1875	London RC	7.33	1896	Emmanuel College, Cam.	8.7
1876	West London RC	7.36	1897	Kingston RC	7.9
1877	London RC	8.29	1898	Trinity College, Oxf.	7.19
1878	London RC	7.55	1899	First Trinity BC, Cam.	7.25
1879	Twickenham RC	8.55	1900	Trinity College, Cam.	7.24
1880	London RC	7.24	1901	Trinity Hall, Cam.	7.23
1881	Twickenham RC	7.50	1902	Trinity Hall, Cam.	7.34
1882	Royal Chester RC	—	1903	Trinity College, Dublin	7.37
1883	London RC	8.5	1904	Caius College, Cam.	7.30
1884	Twickenham RC	7.48	1905	Thames RC	7.28
1885	London RC	7.36	1906	Christ's College, Cam.	7.23
1886	London RC	7.8½	1907	Christ's College, Cam.	7.45
1887	Trinity Hall, Cam.	7.20	1908	Wadham College, Oxf.	7.15
1888	Lady Margaret BC, Cam.	7.19	1909	Wadham College, Oxf.	7.21
1889	Christ Church, Oxf.	7.16	1910	Anglian BC	7.36

1911	First Trinity BC, Cam.	7.13
1912	RC de Paris, France	7.33
1913	Oriel College, Oxf.	7.30
1914	Caius College, Cam.	7.27
1920	Thames RC	7.43
1921	Christiania Roklub, Norway	7.12
1922	Worcester College, Oxf.	7.56
1923	First Trinity BC, Cam.	7.12
1924	Maidenhead RC	8.29
1925	First Trinity BC, Cam.	7.16
1926	Selwyn College, Cam.	7.9
1927	Thames RC	7.34
1928	Thames RC	7.23
1929	Browne and Nichols School, USA	7.28
1930	Vesta RC	7.23
1931	London RC	7.43
1932	London RC	7.41
1933	Kent School, USA	7.30
1934	Thames RC	7.4
1935	London RC	7.5
1936	Tabor Academy, USA	7.44
1937	Tabor Academy, USA	7.31
1938	Kent School, USA	7.3
1939	Tabor Academy, USA	7.53
1946	Imperial College BC	7.11
1947	Kent School, USA	7.22
1948	Princeton University, USA	7.20
1949	Princeton University, USA	6.58
1950	Kent School, USA	7.34
1951	University of Pennsylvania, USA	7.19

1952	University of Pennsylvania, USA	7.3
1953	Royal Air Force	6.59
1954	Massachusetts Institute of Technology, USA	7.24
1955	Massachusetts Institute of Technology, USA	7.21
1956	Princeton University, USA	7.10
1957	Princeton University, USA	7.8
1958	Harvard University, USA	6.57
1959	Harvard University, USA	7.15
1960	Harvard University, USA	6.47
1961	University of London	6.59
1962	National Provincial Bank	6.46
1963	Queens' College, Cam.	6.53
1964	Eliot House, USA	6.55
1965	Isis BC	6.37
1966	Harvard University, USA	6.57
1967	Cornell University, USA	7.6
1968	Leander Club	8.8
1969	Leander Club	6.43
1970	Leander Club	7.01
1971	Harvard University, USA	6.48
1972	Harvard University, USA	6.55
1973	Princeton University, USA	6.45
1974	Antwerpse Roeivereniging, Belgium	6.52
1975	Garda Siochana BC, Eire	6.37
1976	Harvard University, USA	6.39
1977	London RC	6.37
1978	London RC	6.54
1979	Leander Club	6.49
1980	University of London	6.26

Princess Elizabeth Challenge Cup

1946	Bedford School	4.54*
1947	Bedford School	7.25
1948	Bedford School	7.20
1949	Winchester College	7.11
1950	St Paul's School	7.44
1951	Bedford School	7.27
1952	Radley College	7.0
1953	St Paul's School	7.6

1954	Winchester College	7.59
1955	Shrewsbury School	7.24
1956	Eton College	7.25
1957	St Paul's School	7.19
1958	St Edward's School	6.59
1959	St Edward's School	7.15
1960	Shrewsbury School	6.53
1961	Shrewsbury School	7.7

*Shortened course from Remenham Barrier.

1962	Radley College	6.58	1971	Pangbourne College	7.4
1963	Nautical College,		1972	Kent School, USA	7.2
	Pangbourne	7.2	1973	Ridley College, Canada	6.56
1964	Washington–Lee High		1974	Holy Spirit High	
	School, USA	6.52		School, USA	7.10
1965	Tabor Academy, USA	6.44	1975	Ridley College, Canada	6.32
1966	Emanuel School	6.55	1976	Holy Spirit High	
1967	Eton College	7.3		School, USA	6.37
1968	J.E.B. Stuart High		1977	Ridley College, Canada	6.53
	School, USA	8.17	1978	Eton College	7.10
1969	Washington–Lee High		1979	Ridley College, Canada	6.59
	School, USA	7.0	1980	St Paul's School,	
1970	Ridley College, Canada	7.6		Concord, USA	7.19

Stewards' Challenge Cup

1841	Oxford Club, London		1868	London RC	8.22
	(The Midge)	—	1869	London RC	8.36
1842	Oxford Club, London		1870	Etonian Club, Oxf.	8.5
	(The Midge)	9.16	1871	London RC	9.9
1843	St George's Club,		1872	London RC	9.21
	London	10.15	1873	London RC	8.23
1844	Oxford University BC	9.16	1874	London RC	9.0
1845	Oxford University BC	8.25	1875	London RC	7.56
1846	Oxford University BC	—	1876	London RC	8.27
1847	Christ Church, Oxf.	RO	1877	London RC	9.7
1848	Christ Church, Oxf.	RO	1878	London RC	8.37
1849	Leander Club	—	1879	Jesus College, Cam.	9.37
1850	Oxford University BC	RO	1880	Thames RC	7.58
1851	Cambridge University BC	—	1881	Hertford College, Oxf.	8.15
1852	Oxford University BC	—	1882	Hertford College, Oxf.	—
1853	Oxford University BC	8.57	1883	Thames RC	—
1854	Pembroke College, Oxf.	9.38	1884	Kingston RC	—
1855	Royal Chester RC	—	1885	Trinity Hall, Cam.	7.53
1856	Argonaut Club, London	—	1886	Thames RC	7.39
1857	London RC	8.25	1887	Trinity Hall, Cam.	7.53
1858	London RC	RO	1888	Trinity Hall, Cam.	8.25
1859	Third Trinity BC, Cam.	8.25	1889	Thames RC	7.53
1860	First Trinity BC, Cam.	9.26	1890	Brasenose College, Oxf.	7.37
1861	First Trinity BC, Cam.	9.35	1891	Thames RC	7.45
1862	Brasenose College, Oxf.	9.40	1892	Royal Chester RC	8.38
1863	University College, Oxf.	8.24	1893	Magdalen College, Oxf.	7.45
1864	London RC	8.45	1894	Thames RC	8.20
1865	Third Trinity BC, Cam.	8.13	1895	London RC	7.43
1866	University College, Oxf.	9.28	1896	London RC	8.42
1867	University College, Oxf.	8.45	1897	Leander Club	7.30

1898	Leander Club	7.42
1899	Magdalen College, Oxf.	7.51
1900	Leander Club	7.55
1901	Third Trinity BC, Cam.	7.54
1902	Third Trinity BC, Cam.	7.45
1903	Third Trinity BC, Cam.	8.5
1904	Third Trinity BC, Cam.	7.30
1905	Leander Club	RO
1906	Leander Club	7.36
1907	Magdalen College, Oxf.	8.42
1908	Magdalen College, Oxf.	7.40
1909	Thames RC	7.38
1910	Winnipeg RC, Canada	7.52
1911	Thames RC	7.35
1912	New College, Oxf.	7.36
1913	New College, Oxf.	—
1914	Leander Club	7.52
1920	Magdalen College, Oxf.	8.3
1921	Magdalen College, Oxf.	7.32
1922	Eton Vikings Club	8.25
1923	Third Trinity BC, Cam.	7.30
1924	Third Trinity BC, Cam.	8.37
1925	Third Trinity BC, Cam.	7.27
1926	Thames RC	7.34
1927	Thames RC	8.1
1928	Thames RC	7.43
1929	First Trinity BC, Cam.	7.32
1930	London RC	7.34
1931	London RC	8.45
1932	Thames RC	8.9
1933	Pembroke College, Cam.	8.16
1934	Pembroke College, Cam.	7.24
1935	FC Zürich Ruder Club, Switzerland	7.14
1936	FC Zürich Ruder Club, Switzerland	7.50
1937	Leander Club	8.32
1938	Leander Club	7.33
1939	RC Zürich, Switzerland	8.9
1946	Leander Club	7.48
1947	Thames RC	8.4
1948	Thames RC	7.48
1949	Trinity College, Oxf.	7.13

1950	Hellerup Roklub, Denmark	8.3
1951	Thames RC	7.53
1952	Thames RC	7.24
1953	Leander Club	7.25
1954	Club Krylia Sovetov, USSR	8.26
1955	Club Krylia Sovetov, USSR	7.40
1956	Thames RC	8.6
1957	Club Krylia Sovetov, USSR	7.35
1958	Barn Cottage BC	7.16
1959	St Edmund Hall and Lincoln College, Oxf.	7.39
1960	Barn Cottage BC	7.10
1961	Trud Club, USSR	7.23
1962	Trud Club, USSR	7.23
1963	Molesey BC	7.16
1964	Tideway Scullers' School	7.11
1965	Quintin BC	6.55
1966	Roforeningen Kvik, Denmark	7.17
1967	SGD Potsdam, Germany	7.31
1968	Nautilus (Midlands) Club	8.53
1969	ASR Nereus, Holland	7.6
1970	SGD Potsdam, GDR	7.22
1971	Thames Tradesmen's RC	7.12
1972	Spartak Moscow, USSR	NTT*
1973	University of London	7.3
1974	Dynamo Club, USSR	7.12
1975	Potomac BC, USA	6.50
1976	Univ. of British Columbia and Vancouver RC, Canada	7.10
1977	London RC	RO
1978	Trakia Club, Bulgaria	RO
1979	London RC	7.19
1980	Charles River Rowing Association and Dartmouth College, USA	7.4

*NTT: no time taken.

Prince Philip Challenge Cup

1963	Auckland RC, New Zealand	7.32
1964	Molesey BC	7.25
1965	Leander Club	7.3
1966	SGD Potsdam, Germany	7.19
1967	ASK Vorwärts, Germany	7.39
1968	Tideway Scullers' School	9.8
1969	DSR Laga, Holland	7.19
1970	Konstanz/Wetzlar, GFR	7.24
1971	London RC and University of London	7.39
1972	St Catharine's RC, Canada	7.22
1973	Northeastern University RA, USA	7.13
1974	Lady Margaret BC and First and Third Trinity BC, Cam.	7.32
1975	University of London	7.2
1976	Thames Tradesmen's RC	RO
1977	Garda Siochana BC, Eire	7.35
1978	Trakia Club, Bulgaria	7.35
1979	Garda Siochana BC, Eire	7.37
1980	Charles River Rowing Association, USA	7.11

Visitors' Challenge Cup

1847	Christ Church, Oxf.	9.0
1848	Christ Church, Oxf.	RO
1849	Second Trinity BC, Cam.	RO
1850	Christ Church, Oxf.	—
1851	Christ Church, Oxf.	9.0
1852	Argonaut Club, London	—
1853	Argonaut Club, London	9.2
1854	Lady Margaret BC, Cam.	8.48
1855	Lady Margaret BC, Cam.	—
1856	Lady Margaret BC, Cam.	—
1857	Pembroke College, Oxf.	8.40
1858	First Trinity BC, Cam.	—
1859	Third Trinity BC, Cam.	RO
1860	First Trinity BC, Cam.	RO
1861	First Trinity BC, Cam.	8.57
1862	Brasenose College, Oxf.	9.40
1863	Brasenose College, Oxf.	RO
1864	University College, Oxf.	RO
1865	Third Trinity BC, Cam.	RO
1866	University College, Oxf.	8.49
1867	University College, Oxf.	RO
1868	University College, Oxf.	8.15
1869	University College, Oxf.	9.5
1870	Trinity College, Dublin	8.36
1871	First Trinity BC, Cam.	9.8
1872	Pembroke College, Oxf.	9.28
1873	Trinity College, Dublin	RO
1874	Trinity College, Dublin	8.47
1875	University College, Oxf.	8.20
1876	University College, Oxf.	8.5
1877	Jesus College, Cam.	9.7
1878	Columbia College, New York, USA	8.42
1879	Lady Margaret BC, Cam.	9.22
1880	Third Trinity BC, Cam.	8.16
1881	First Trinity BC, Cam.	8.22
1882	Brasenose College, Oxf.	9.23
1883	Christ Church, Oxf.	—
1884	Third Trinity BC, Cam.	8.39
1885	Trinity Hall, Cam.	7.41
1886	First Trinity BC, Cam.	8.20½
1887	Trinity Hall, Cam.	8.8
1888	Brasenose College, Oxf.	7.59
1889	Third Trinity BC, Cam.	8.6
1890	Brasenose College, Oxf.	7.42
1891	Trinity Hall, Cam.	7.45
1892	Third Trinity BC, Cam.	8.23
1893	Third Trinity BC, Cam.	8.21
1894	New College, Oxf.	RO
1895	Trinity College, Oxf.	8.17
1896	Caius College, Cam.	8.29
1897	Trinity College, Oxf.	7.53
1898	New College, Oxf.	7.37
1899	Balliol College, Oxf.	8.1
1900	Trinity College, Cam.	7.53
1901	Balliol College, Oxf.	8.27
1902	Jesus College, Cam.	7.59
1903	University College, Oxf.	8.25

1904	Third Trinity BC, Cam.	7.46
1905	Trinity Hall, Cam.	7.53
1906	Third Trinity BC, Cam.	7.49
1907	Magdalen College, Oxf.	8.7
1908	Magdalen College, Oxf.	7.30
1909	Christ Church, Oxf.	7.53
1910	Trinity Hall, Cam.	7.56
1911	Third Trinity BC, Cam.	7.37
1912	Christ Church, Oxf.	8.19
1913	Pembroke College, Cam.	8.13
1914	Lady Margaret BC, Cam.	8.26
1920	Merton College, Oxf.	8.26
1921	Lincoln College, Oxf.	7.44
1922	Third Trinity BC, Cam.	8.28
1923	Magdalen College, Oxf.	7.44
1924	Third Trinity BC, Cam.	9.14
1925	Third Trinity BC, Cam.	7.45
1926	Christ Church, Oxf.	8.15
1927	Christ's College, Cam.	8.16
1928	First Trinity BC, Cam.	7.54
1929	Third Trinity BC, Cam.	7.46
1930	Brasenose College, Oxf.	8.6
1931	Pembroke College, Cam.	8.45
1932	Jesus College, Cam.	8.21
1933	Christ's College, Cam.	8.16
1934	First Trinity BC, Cam.	7.38
1935	Jesus College, Cam.	7.40
1936	Jesus College, Cam.	8.34
1937	Trinity Hall, Cam.	8.16
1938	Oriel College, Oxf.	7.18
1939	Trinity Hall, Cam.	8.9
1946	First and Third Trinity BC, Cam.	7.59
1947	Trinity Hall, Cam.	8.0
1948	Magdalen College, Oxf.	7.51
1949	Clare College, Cam.	7.31
1950	Lady Margaret BC, Cam.	8.8
1951	Trinity Hall, Cam.	8.9
1952	Pembroke College, Cam.	7.15
1953	Magdalen College, Oxf.	7.29
1954	First and Third Trinity BC, Cam.	7.57
1955	Trinity Hall, Cam.	7.58
1956	Merton College, Oxf.	7.47
1957	Pembroke College, Cam.	7.33
1958	Keble College, Oxf.	7.32
1959	Pembroke College, Cam.	7.50
1960	First and Third Trinity BC, Cam.	7.31
1961	St Edmund Hall, Oxf.	7.27
1962	Keble College, Oxf.	7.53
1963	Christ's College, Cam.	7.32
1964	Pembroke College, Cam.	7.27
1965	St Edmund Hall, Oxf.	7.13
1966	Lady Margaret BC, Cam.	7.31
1967	Magdalene College, Cam.	7.45
1968	Imperial College BC	9.25
1969	Eton College	7.22
1970	Fitzwilliam College, Cam.	7.40
1971	University of London	7.34
1972	University of London	7.26
1973	First and Third Trinity BC, Cam.	7.15
1974	Pembroke College, Cam.	7.25
1975	Ealing High Schools	7.12
1976	University of London	7.21
1977	University of Washington, USA	NTT
1978	Durham University	7.29
1979	Strode's College and Wallingford School	7.26
1980	University of London	7.26

Wyfold Challenge Cup

1855	Royal Chester RC	—
1856	Argonaut Club, London	—
1857	Pembroke College, Oxf.	8.30
1858	First Trinity BC, Cam.	RO
1859	First Trinity BC, Cam.	8.21
1860	London RC	10.8
1861	Brasenose College, Oxf.	9.43
1862	London RC	9.20
1863	Kingston RC	8.50
1864	Kingston RC	RO
1865	Kingston RC	8.23
1866	Kingston RC	—
1867	Kingston RC	—
1868	Kingston RC	8.32

1869	Oscillators Club, Surbiton	—
1870	Thames RC	8.34
1871	Thames RC	9.6
1872	Thames RC	8.42
1873	Kingstown Harbour BC	8.37
1874	Newcastle RC	9.0
1875	Thames RC	8.10
1876	West London RC	8.24
1877	Kingston RC	RO
1878	Kingston RC	8.44
1879	London RC	9.56
1880	London RC	8.4
1881	Dublin University BC	8.8
1882	Jesus College, Cam.	8.58
1883	Kingston RC	8.51
1884	Thames RC	8.58
1885	Kingston RC	—
1886	Thames RC	8.4
1887	Pembroke College, Cam.	7.50
1888	Thames RC	7.59
1889	London RC	7.58
1890	Kingston RC	7.46
1891	Royal Chester RC	7.50
1892	Molesey BC	8.42
1893	Molesey BC	8.28
1894	Thames RC	8.16
1895	London RC	8.16
1896	Trinity College, Oxf.	8.41
1897	Kingston RC	8.0
1898	Kingston RC	8.28
1899	Trinity Hall, Cam.	7.57
1900	Trinity Hall, Cam.	8.14
1901	Trinity Hall, Cam.	8.9
1902	Burton-on-Trent RC	7.43
1903	Kingston RC	8.23
1904	Birmingham RC	8.1
1905	London RC	7.59
1906	London RC	7.58
1907	Magdalen College, Oxf.	8.49
1908	Thames RC	7.55
1909	Balliol College, Oxf.	7.44
1910	Trinity Hall, Cam.	8.9
1911	Pembroke College, Cam.	7.40
1912	Queens' College, Cam.	8.3
1913	Lady Margaret BC, Cam.	8.1
1914	London RC	8.35
1920	Thames RC	8.10
1921	Jesus College, Cam.	7.46
1922	Thames RC	9.6
1923	Imperial College BC	7.50
1924	Royal Chester RC	9.16
1925	Thames RC	7.35
1926	London RC	7.59
1927	Thames RC	8.23
1928	Trinity Hall, Cam.	7.47
1929	Thames RC	7.44
1930	London RC	7.52
1931	Thames RC	9.13
1932	London RC	8.29
1933	London RC	8.28
1934	Reading RC	7.36
1935	Reading RC	7.39
1936	London RC	8.26
1937	London RC	8.20
1938	London RC	7.41
1939	Maidenhead RC	9.10
1946	King's College, London	7.57
1947	Quintin BC	8.19
1948	Victoria Lake RC, South Africa	7.55
1949	Lensbury RC	7.41
1950	Royal Engineers	8.13
1951	Caius College, Cam.	7.55
1952	Corpus Christi College, Cam.	7.28
1953	Royal Air Force	7.38
1954	Royal Engineers	8.6
1955	Thames RC	7.51
1956	Royal Engineers	7.56
1957	National Provincial Bank	7.49
1958	Burton Leander RC	7.35
1959	Molesey BC	7.45
1960	St Thomas's Hospital	7.24
1961	National Provincial Bank	7.28
1962	Force Navale Belge, Belgium	7.30
1963	Nottingham and Union RC	7.24
1964	Sons of the Thames RC	7.19
1965	Derby RC	7.6
1966	Norwich Union	7.28
1967	Tideway Scullers' School	7.29

1968 Severn Scullers RC	9.6	1974 Porcellian Club, USA	7.37
1969 London RC	7.16	1975 Thames Tradesmen's RC	6.57
1970 Trident RC, South		1976 London RC	6.56
Africa	NTT	1977 City Orient RC	7.15
1971 Harvard University, USA	7.37	1978 Molesey BC	7.38
1972 Leander Club	7.25	1979 Wallingford RC	7.35
1973 Thames Tradesmen's RC	7.12	1980 Nottingham BC	7.13

Britannia Challenge Cup

1968 Crowland RC	9.32	1975 Leander Club	7.18
1969 Kingston RC	7.32	1976 Tideway Scullers' School	7.22
1970 London RC	7.32	1977 Tideway Scullers' School	7.28
1971 Hereford RC	7.45	1978 Kingston RC	7.44
1972 Wallingford RC	7.39	1979 City Orient RC	7.50
1973 Isis BC	7.19	1980 Leander Club	7.24
1974 Wallingford Schools	7.51		

Silver Goblets and Nickalls' Challenge Cup

1845 G. Mann and F. M. Arnold (Caius College, Cam.)	—
1846 M. Haggard and W. H. Milman (Christ Church, Oxf.)	—
1847 W. S. Falls and W. Coulthard (St George's Club, London)	—
1848 M. Haggard and W. H. Milman (Christ Church, Oxf.)	—
1849 E. G. Peacock and F. Playford (Thames Club, London)	—
1850 J. J. Hornby (Brasenose College, Oxf.)	
and J. W. Chitty (Balliol College, Oxf.)	—
1851 J. Aitken (Exeter College, Oxf.)	
and J. W. Chitty (Balliol College, Oxf.)	—
1852 H. R. Barker and P. H. Nind (Christ Church, Oxf.)	RO
1853 R. Gordon and J. B. Barlee (Christ's College, Cam.)	10.0
1854 W. F. Short (New College, Oxf.)	
and E. Cadogan (Christ Church, Oxf.)	9.36
1855 A. A. Casamajor and J. Nottidge (Wandle Club)	—
1856 A. A. Casamajor and J. Nottidge (Argonaut Club, London)	—
1857 E. Warre and A. P. Lonsdale (Balliol College, Oxf.)	9.22
1858 H. H. Playford and A. A. Casamajor (London RC)	—
1859 E. Warre (Balliol College, Oxf.)	
and J. Arkell (Pembroke College, Oxf.)	9.0
1860 A. A. Casamajor and W. Woodbridge (London RC)	11.50
1861 W. Champneys and W. B. Woodgate (Brasenose College, Oxf.)	—
1862 W. Champneys and W. B. Woodgate (Brasenose College, Oxf.)	9.45
1863 R. Shepherd and W. B. Woodgate (Brasenose College Oxf.)	RO
1864 J. R. Selwyn and R. A. Kinglake (Third Trinity BC, Cam.)	9.29
1865 J. C. F. May and F. Fenner (London RC)	9.7
1866 E. L. Corrie and W. B. Woodgate (Kingston RC)	9.23

1867	E. L. Corrie and M. M. Brown (Kingston RC)	9.49
1868	W. C. Crofts and W. B. Woodgate (Brasenose College, Oxf.)	—
1869	A. de L. Long and W. Stout (London RC)	9.20
1870	E. L. Corrie and E. Hall (Kingston RC)	—
1871	A. de L. Long and F. S. Gulston (London RC)	10.17
1872	A. de L. Long and F. S. Gulston (London RC)	—
1873	C. C. Knollys and A. Trower (Kingston RC)	9.22
1874	A. de L. Long and F. S. Gulston (London RC)	10.3
1875	W. Chillingworth and C. Herbert (Ino RC)	—
1876	S. Le B. Smith and F. S. Gulston (London RC)	8.55
1877	W. H. Eyre and J. Hastie (Thames RC)	—
1878	T. C. Edwards-Moss and W. A. Ellison (Etonian Club, Oxf.)	9.14
1879	R. H. Labat and F. S. Gulston (London RC)	11.16
1880	W. H. Eyre and J. Hastie (Thames RC)	8.45
1881	W. H. Eyre and J. Hastie (Thames RC)	9.4
1882	D. E. Brown and J. Lowndes (Hertford College, Oxf.)	—
1883	G. Q. Roberts and D. E. Brown (Twickenham RC)	9.22
1884	J. Lowndes and D. E. Brown (Twickenham RC)	9.1
1885	H. McLean and D. H. McLean (Etonian Club, Oxf.)	—
1886	F. E. Churchill and S. D. Muttlebury (Third Trinity BC, Cam.)	8.40
1887	C. T. Barclay and S. D. Muttlebury (Third Trinity BC, Cam.)	8.15
1888	N. P. Symonds (Cambridge University BC) and E. Buck (Oxford University BC)	—
1889	J. C. Gardner and S. D. Muttlebury (Cambridge University BC)	8.25
1890	Lord Ampthill and G. Nickalls (Oxford University BC)	8.38
1891	Lord Ampthill and G. Nickalls (Leander Club)	8.36
1892	V. Nickalls and W. A. L. Fletcher (Oxford University BC)	9.7
1893	V. Nickalls and W. A. L. Fletcher (Oxford University BC)	8.44
1894	V. Nickalls and G. Nickalls (Formosa BC)	9.35
1895	V. Nickalls and G. Nickalls (London RC)	9.11
1896	V. Nickalls and G. Nickalls (London RC)	9.10
1897	E. R. Balfour and G. Nickalls (Leander Club)	8.59
1898	A. Bogle and W. J. Fernie (Thames RC)	8.41
1899	C. K. Philips and H. W. M. Willis (Leander Club)	8.49
1900	C. J. D. Goldie and G. M. Maitland (Trinity College, Cam.)	8.33
1901	H. J. Hale and F. W. Warre (Balliol College, Oxf.)	8.50
1902	W. Dudley Ward and C. W. H. Taylor (Third Trinity BC, Cam.)	8.36
1903	L. Klaus and A. Ehrenberg (Victoria RC, Berlin, Germany)	8.45
1904	C. J. D. Goldie and C. W. H. Taylor (Third Trinity BC, Cam.)	8.33
1905	R. H. Nelson and P. H. Thomas (Third Trinity BC, Cam.)	8.40
1906	B. C. Johnstone and R. V. Powell (Third Trinity BC, Cam.)	9.15
1907	B. C. Johnstone and R. V. Powell (Leander Club)	8.52
1908	H. R. Barker and A. C. Gladstone (Christ Church, Oxf.)	8.26
1909	B. C. Johnstone and E. G. Williams (Leander Club)	8.30
1910	J. S. Burn and G. L. Thomson (Leander Club)	8.45
1911	J. Beresford and A. H. Cloutte (Thames RC)	8.15

1912	B. Logan and C. G. Rought (Thames RC)	8.36
1913	A. A. Swann and S. E. Swann (Trinity Hall, Cam.)	8.39
1914	A. A. Swann and S. E. Swann (Trinity Hall, Cam.)	9.2
1920	G. O. Nickalls and R. S. C. Lucas (Magdalen College, Oxf.)	8.53
1921	J. A. Campbell and H. B. Playford (Jesus College, Cam.)	8.52
1922	G. O. Nickalls and R. S. C. Lucas (Magdalen College, Oxf.)	9.19
1923	W. F. Godden and R. E. Eason (Trinity College, Oxf.)	8.12
1924	C. R. M. Ely and J. A. Macnabb (Third Trinity BC, Cam.)	10.6
1925	R. E. Morrison and E. C. Hamilton-Russell (Third Trinity BC, Cam.)	8.17
1926	H. R. Carver and E. C. Hamilton-Russell (Third Trinity BC, Cam.)	8.36
1927	R. A. Nisbet and T. N. O'Brien (London RC)	9.23
1928	G. C. Killick and J. Beresford Jr (Thames RC)	9.57
1929	G. C. Killick and J. Beresford Jr (Thames RC)	8.32
1930	W. A. Prideaux and H. R. N. Rickett (Third Trinity BC, Cam.)	8.42
1931	H. R. A. Edwards and L. Clive (Christ Church, Oxf.)	9.57
1932	H. R. A. Edwards and L. Clive (Christ Church, Oxf.)	9.5
1933	J. H. C. Powell and J. E. Gilmour (Eton Vikings Club)	9.17
1934	H. Braun and H. G. Moller (R. Wiking, Germany)	8.9
1935	T. S. Cree and D. W. Burnford (Jesus College, Cam.)	8.20
1936	R. F. Offer and J. S. Offer (Kingston RC)	9.17
1937	E. W. Wingate and W. D. Baddeley (Vesta RC)	9.43
1938	W. G. R. M. Laurie and J. H. T. Wilson (Leander Club)	8.8
1939	C. B. Sanford and H. Parker (Trinity Hall, Cam.)	9.5
1946	J. F. Burgess and C. G. Burgess (Leander Club)	8.47
1947	J. H. Pinches and E. M. Sturges (London RC)	8.46
1948	W. G. R. M. Laurie and J. H. T. Wilson (Leander Club)	8.30
1949	A. S. F. Butcher and T. H. Christie (Thames RC)	8.20
1950	J. Rosa and C. van Antwerpen (Société Royale Nautique Anversoise, Belgium)	9.10
1951	J. G. P. Crowden (Pembroke College, Cam.) and C. B. M. Lloyd (Lady Margaret BC, Cam.)	8.52
1952	H. C. I. Bywater and T. H. Christie (Westminster Hospital BC)	8.6
1953	R. Baetens and M. Knuysen (Antwerp SC, Belgium)	8.10
1954	I. Buldakov and V. Ivanov (Club Khimik, USSR)	8.44
1955	I. Buldakov and V. Ivanov (Club Khimik, USSR)	8.30
1956	R. J. M. Thompson and G. M. Wolfson (Pembroke College, Cam.)	8.45
1957	D. A. T. Leadley and C. G. V. Davidge (Leander Club)	8.17
1958	D. A. T. Leadley and C. G. V. Davidge (Leander Club)	8.4
1959	R. B. Norton and H. H. Scurfield (Hertford College, Oxf.)	8.20
1960	I. L. Elliott and D. C. Rutherford (Keble College and Magdalen College, Oxf.)	7.58
1961	V. Lehtelä and T. Pitkänen (Vlakeakosken Vesiveikot, Finland)	8.9
1962	W. Neuss and K.-G. Jordan (RC Nassovia Hochst, Germany)	8.2
1963	C. G. V. Davidge and S. A. Mackenzie (Leander Club)	7.55
1964	J. R. Kiely and J. M. S. Lecky (Leander Club)	7.53
1965	P. Gorny and G. Bergau (ASK Vorwaerts, Rostock, Germany)	7.42

1966	J. Lucke and H.-J. Bothe (TSC Berlin, Germany)	8.31
1967	M. Gelpke and K. Jacob (SC Einheit, Dresden, Germany)	8.18
1968	A. J. Sutton and P. J. W. Sharp (Sons of the Thames RC)	NTT
1969	U. Bitterli and U. Fankhauser (See-Club, Luzern, Switzerland)	7.56
1970	H. Schreiber and M. Schmorde (SC Dynamo, Berlin, GDR)	8.17
1971	G. A. S. Locke and T. J. Crooks (Leander Club)	8.7
1972	J. Broniec and A. Slusarski (KKW Bydgoszcz, Poland)	7.59
1973	M. Borchelt and R. T. Adams (Potomac BC, USA)	7.42
1974	N. Ivanov and V. Eshinov (Dynamo Club, USSR)	7.59
1975	H. A. Droog and R. J. Luynenburg (ASR Nereus, Holland)	7.36
1976	I. F. Luxford and C. D. Shinners (Sydney University, Australia)	7.30
1977	J. Clark and J. Roberts (Thames Tradesmen's RC)	7.54
1978	J. Clark and J. Roberts (Thames Tradesmen's RC)	8.12
1979	A. C. D. Wiggin and M. D. A. Carmichael (Leander Club)	8.10
1980	M. Borchelt and F. Borchelt (Potomac BC, USA)	8.2

Double Sculls Challenge Cup

1939	J. Beresford Jr and L. F. Southwood (Thames RC) and G. Scherli and E. Broschi (Societa Canottieri Nettuno di Trieste, Italy), dead heat	8.35
1946R.	E. Panelo and E. D. Chafuen (Buenos Aires RC, Argentina)	8.8
1947	W. E. C. Horwood and D. C. H. Garrod (Quintin BC)	8.23
1948	B. Piessens (Antwerp SC) and W. A. Collet (Société Royale Sport Nautique de Bruxelles, Belgium)	8.2
1949	E. W. Parsner and A. E. Larsen (DFDS Roklub, Denmark)	7.39
1950	E. W. Parsner and A. E. Larsen (DFDS Roklub, Denmark)	8.21
1951	P. P. Bradley and R. D. Burnell (Leander Club)	8.41
1952	R. George (Union Nautique de Liège) and J. van Stichel (Antwerp SC Belgium)	7.37
1953	E. Schriever and P. Stebler (Seeclub, Zürich, Switzerland)	7.37
1954	E. Schriever and P. Stebler (Seeclub, Zürich, Switzerland)	8.46
1955	G. Zhilin and I. Emchuk (Club Burevestnik, USSR)	7.55
1956	S. C. Rand and W. H. Rand (Royal Air Force RC)	7.47
1957	A. Berkutov and Y. Tukalov (Club Krasnoe Znamia, USSR)	7.41
1958	A. Berkutov and Y. Tukalov (Trud Club, Leningrad, USSR)	7.21
1959	C. G. V. Davidge and S. A. Mackenzie (Leander Club)	7.55
1960	G. C. Justicz and N. J. Birkmyre (Birmingham RC and Ariel RC)	7.17
1961	G. C. Justicz and N. J. Birkmyre (Birmingham RC and Ariel RC)	7.38
1962	G. C. Justicz and N. J. Birkmyre (Leander Club)	7.39
1963	M. B. Alwin and W. van der Togt (Willem III and Rotterdamsche SRS, Holland)	7.30
1964	G. C. Justicz and N. J. Birkmyre (Leander Club)	7.32
1965	M. Studach and M. Bürgin (Grasshopper Club, Zürich, Switzerland)	7.1
1966	M. Haake and J. Brückhandler (TSC Berlin, Germany)	7.20
1967	M. Studach and M. Bürgin (Grasshopper Club, Zürich, Switzerland)	7.47

1968 P. A. Barry and R. M. Findlay
(Tideway Scullers' School and National Provincial Bank) 9.18
1969 D. Oswald and M. Bürgin
(SN de Neuchâtel and Grasshopper Club, Zürich, Switzerland) 7.35
1970 T. McKibbon and J. van Blom (Long Beach RA, USA) 7.43
1971 M. A. Brigden and C. A. Brigden (Walton RC) 8.21
1972 P. G. R. Delafield and T. J. Crooks (Leander Club) 7.24
1973 M. J. Hart and C. L. Baillieu (Leander Club) 7.11
1974 G. Korshikov and A. Timoshinin (Dynamo Club, USSR) 7.23
1975 M. J. Hart and C. L. Baillieu (Leander Club) 7.23
1976 R. Prentice and M. S. Spencer (London RC) 7.22
1977 M. J. Hart and C. L. Baillieu (Leander Club) 7.20
1978 M. J. Hart and C. L. Baillieu (Leander Club) 7.44
1979 J. Clark and C. L. Baillieu
(Thames Tradesmen's RC and Leander Club) 7.32
1980 P. Walter and B. Ford (Victoria City RC, Canada) 7.27

Diamond Challenge Sculls

1844 T. B. Bumpsted (London Amateur Scullers Club) 10.32
1845 S. Wallace (Leander Club) 11.30
1846 E. G. Moon (Magdalen College, Oxf.) —
1847 W. Maule (First Trinity BC, Cam.) 10.45
1848 W. L. Bagshawe (Third Trinity BC, Cam.) —
1849 T. R. Bone (London) —
1850 T. R. Bone (Meteor Club) —
1851 E. G. Peacock (Thames Club) —
1852 E. Macnaghten (First Trinity BC, Cam.) —
1853 S. R. Rippingall (Peterhouse, Cam.) 10.2
1854 H. H. Playford (Wandle Club) —
1855 A. A. Casamajor (Argonaut Club, London) 9.27
1856 A. A. Casamajor (Argonaut Club, London) —
1857 A. A. Casamajor (London RC) —
1858 A. A. Casamajor (London RC) RO
1859 E. D. Brickwood (Richmond) 10.0
1860 H. H. Playford (London RC) 12.8
1861 A. A. Casamajor (London RC) 10.4
1862 E. D. Brickwood (London RC) 10.40
1863 C. B. Lawes (Third Trinity BC, Cam.) 9.43
1864 W. B. Woodgate (Brasenose College, Oxf.) 10.10
1865 E. B. Michell (Magdalen College, Oxf.) 9.11
1866 E. B. Michell (Magdalen College, Oxf.) 9.55
1867 W. C. Crofts (Brasenose College, Oxf.) 10.2
1868 W. Stout (London BC) 9.6
1869 W. C. Crofts (Brasenose College, Oxf.) 9.56
1870 John B. Close (First Trinity BC, Cam.) 9.43

1871	W. Fawcus (Tynemouth RC)	10.9
1872	C. C. Knollys (Magdalen College, Oxf.)	10.48
1873	A. C. Dicker (Lady Margaret BC, Cam.)	9.50
1874	A. C. Dicker (Lady Margaret BC, Cam.)	10.50
1875	A. C. Dicker (Lady Margaret BC, Cam.)	9.15
1876	F. L. Playford (London RC)	9.28
1877	T. C. Edwards-Moss (Brasenose College, Oxf.)	10.20
1878	T. C. Edwards-Moss (Brasenose College, Oxf.)	9.37
1879	J. Lowndes (Hertford College, Oxf.)	12.30
1880	J. Lowndes (Derby)	9.10
1881	J. Lowndes (Derby)	9.28
1882	J. Lowndes (Derby)	11.43
1883	J. Lowndes (Twickenham RC)	10.2
1884	W. S. Unwin (Magdalen College, Oxf.)	9.44
1885	W. S. Unwin (Magdalen College, Oxf.)	9.22
1886	F. I. Pitman (Third Trinity BC, Cam.)	9.5
1887	J. C. Gardner (Emmanuel College, Cam.)	8.51
1888	G. Nickalls (Magdalen College, Oxf.)	8.36
1889	G. Nickalls (Magdalen College, Oxf.)	8.56
1890	G. Nickalls (Magdalen College, Oxf.)	8.57½
1891	V. Nickalls (Magdalen College, Oxf.)	RO
1892	J. J. K. Ooms (Neptunus RC, Amsterdam, Holland)	10.9
1893	G. Nickalls (Magdalen College, Oxf.)	9.12
1894	G. Nickalls (Formosa BC)	9.32
1895	Hon. R. Guinness (Leander Club)	9.11
1896	Hon. R. Guinness (Leander Club)	9.35
1897	E. H. Ten Eyck (Wachusett BC, Worcester, USA)	8.35
1898	B. H. Howell (Trinity Hall, Cam.)	8.29
1899	B. H. Howell (Thames RC)	8.38
1900	E. G. Hemmerde (University College, Oxf.)	8.42
1901	C. V. Fox (Guards Brigade RC)	8.52
1902	F. S. Kelly (Balliol College, Oxf.)	8.59
1903	F. S. Kelly (Leander Club)	8.41
1904	L. F. Scholes (Toronto RC, Canada)	8.23
1905	F. S. Kelly (Leander Club)	8.10
1906	H. T. Blackstaffe (Vesta RC)	8.35
1907	Captain W. H. Darell (Household Brigade BC)	9.24
1908	A. McCulloch (Leander Club)	8.25
1909	A. A. Stuart (Kingston RC)	8.30
1910	W. D. Kinnear (Kensington RC)	8.51
1911	W. D. Kinnear (Kensington RC)	8.14
1912	E. W. Powell (Eton Vikings Club)	8.49
1913	C. McVilly (Derwent RC, Tasmania)	8.49
1914	G. Sinigaglia (Lario Club, Como, Italy)	9.0
1920	J. Beresford Jr (Thames RC)	8.57
1921	F. E. Eyken (Delft University BC, Laga, Holland)	8.26

1922 W. M. Hoover (Duluth BC, Minnesota, USA)   9.32
1923 M. K. Morris (London RC)   8.23
1924 J. Beresford Jr (Thames RC)   10.32
1925 J. Beresford Jr (Thames RC)   8.28
1926 J. Beresford Jr (Thames RC)   8.45
1927 R. T. Lee (Worcester College, Oxf.)   9.6
1928 J. Wright (Argonaut RC, Canada)   8.24
1929 L. H. F. Gunther (Roei-Zeilvereening de Amstel, Holland) 8.42
1930 J. S. Guest (Don RC, Canada)   8.29
1931 R. Pearce (Leander BC, Hamilton, Canada)   10.3
1932 H. Buhtz (Berliner RC, Germany)   9.15
1933 T. G. Askwith (Peterhouse, Cam.)   9.7
1934 H. Buhtz (Berliner RC, Germany)   8.10
1935 E. Rufli (FC Zürich Ruder Club, Switzerland)   8.15
1936 E. Rufli (FC Zürich Ruder Club, Switzerland)   9.22
1937 J. Hasenohrl (Ruderverein Ellida, Austria)   9.12
1938 J. W. Burk (Penn Athletic Club, USA)   8.2
1939 J. W. Burk (Penn Athletic Club, USA)   9.13
1946 J. Séphériadés (Société Nautique de la Basse Seine, France) 8.21
1947 J. B. Kelly Jr (University of Pennsylvania, USA)   8.49
1948 M. T. Wood (New South Wales Police RC, Australia)   8.24
1949 J. B. Kelly Jr (University of Pennsylvania, USA)   8.12
1950 A. D. Rowe (Leander Club)   9.11
1951 T. A. Fox (Pembroke College, Cam.)   8.59
1952 M. T. Wood (Sydney RC, Australia)   8.12
1953 T. A. Fox (London RC)   8.12
1954 P. Vlaşic (Mornar Club, Yugoslavia)   8.42
1955 T. Kocerka (AZS Bydgoszcz, Poland)   8.33
1956 T. Kocerka (AZS Bydgoszcz, Poland)   8.37
1957 S. A. Mackenzie (Sydney RC, Australia)   8.25
1958 S. A. Mackenzie (Sydney RC, Australia)   8.6
1959 S. A. Mackenzie (Sydney RC, Australia)   8.39
1960 S. A. Mackenzie (Leander Club)   8.3
1961 S. A. Mackenzie (Mosman RC, Australia)   8.34
1962 S. A. Mackenzie (Leander Club)   8.38
1963 G. Kottmann (Belvoir RC, Switzerland)   8.9
1964 S. Cromwell (Nonpareil RC, USA)   8.6
1965 D. M. Spero (New York Athletic Club, USA)   7.42
1966 A. Hill (BSG Motor Baumschulenenweg, Germany)   8.15
1967 M. Studach (Grasshopper Club, Zürich, Switzerland)   8.27
1968 H. A. Wardell-Yerburgh (Eton Vikings Club)   10.25
1969 H.-J. Böhmer (SC Dynamo, Berlin, Germany)   8.6
1970 J. Meissner (Mannheimer Ruderverein Amicita, GFR)   8.18
1971 A. Demiddi (Club de Regatas Rosario, Argentina)   8.8
1972 A. Timoshinin (WMF Moscow, USSR)   8.10
1973 S. Drea (Neptune RC, Eire)   7.53

1974 S. Drea (Neptune RC, Eire)	8.20
1975 S. Drea (Neptune RC, Eire)	7.56
1976 E. O. Hale (Sydney RC, Australia)	7.47
1977 T. J. Crooks (Leander Club)	8.11
1978 T. J. Crooks (Leander Club)	8.25
1979 H. P. Matheson (Nottingham BC)	8.36
1980 R. D. Ibarra (Club Nautico Mar del Plata, Argentina)	8.14

Special Race for Schools (shortened course)

1974	Radley College	4.47	1978	Bedford School	4.57
1975	Shrewsbury School	4.33	1979	St Paul's School	4.47
1976	Shrewsbury School	4.44	1980	Shrewsbury School	4.34
1977	St Edward's School	4.38			

Events which are no longer included in the Henley programme:

Presentation Cup for Fours without Coxswains

1869	Oxford Radleian Club	8.40	1872	London RC	RO

Public Schools' Challenge Cup for Fours

1879	Cheltenham College	11.6	1882	Magdalen College School	—
1880	Bedford Grammar School	8.42	1883	Hereford School	—
1881	Bedford Grammar School	9.22	1884	Derby School	—

Town Challenge Cup for Fours

1839	'The Wave', Henley	—	1851	No entry	
1840	'The Dreadnought', Henley	10.15	1852	No entry	
			1853	No entry	
1841	The Dreadnought Club, Henley	RO	1854	Defiance BC, Wargrave	9.5
1842	The Dreadnought Club, Henley	RO	1855	Henley BC	—
			1856	Henley BC	—
1843	The Albion Club, Henley	10.45	1857	Henley BC	RO
1844	Henley Aquatic Club	10.5	1858	Henley BC	RO
1845	Henley Aquatic Club	RO	1859	Henley BC	RO
1846	The Dreadnought Club, Henley	RO	1860	The Dreadnought Club, Henley	11.0
1847	The Dreadnought Club, Henley	RO	1861	Henley BC	RO
			1862	Oxford Staff RC	9.56
1848	The Dreadnought Club, Henley	—	1863	Henley BC	9.15
			1864	Henley BC	10.32
1849	The Albion Club, Henley	RO	1865	Henley BC	9.7
1850	First Albion, Henley	—	1866	Eton Excelsior RC	9.28
			1867	Eton Excelsior RC	—

1868	Henley RC	RO		1877	Marlow RC	10.16
1869	Eton Excelsior RC	—		1878	Henley RC	—
1870	Eton Excelsior RC	—		1879	Greenwood Lodge BC,	
1871	Reading RC	—			Wargrave	—
1872	Marlow RC	—		1880	Reading RC	8.32
1873	Henley RC	—		1881	Reading RC	8.45
1874	Marlow RC	9.34		1882	Reading RC	—
1875	Marlow RC	RO		1883	Marlow RC	—
1876	Marlow RC	—				

District Challenge Cup for Fours

1840	The Dreadnought Club, Henley	11.11		1843	The Albion Club, Henley	RO
				1844	Windsor and Eton Club	—
1841	The Dreadnought Club, Henley	RO		1845	Henley Aquatic Club	10.12
				1846	No entry	
1842	Windsor and Eton Club	—		1847	No entry	

District Goblets for Pair Oars

1858	L. F. Chapman and W. Pyle (Staines)	—
1859	E. J. Giles and H. Sergeant (Henley)	—
1860	J. Dolley and T. Dolley (Oxford)	—
1861	J. O. Hopkins and G. Norsworthy	11.0
1862 and 1863	No entry	
1864	H. Hunt and F. W. Pescud (Henley)	10.30
1865	L. W. Carter and H. L. Cripps (Eton and Parmoor)	—
1866	G. H. Morrell and F. Willan (Oxford)	10.11
1867	F. Prickett and J. Plowman (Oxford City Club)	RO

Local Amateur Scullers' Race

1846	H. Sergeant	—		1852	T. Piper	—
1847	H. Sergeant	—		1853	W. Popjoy	—
1848	H. Sergeant	—		1854	T. Piper	—
1849	E. J. Giles	—		1855	E. J. Giles	—
1850	F. Williams	—		1856	E. J. Giles	—
1851	A. Ive	—		1857	E. J. Giles	—

Notes: From 1847–54 the Wyfold Challenge Cup was given to the winners of the challenge heat for the Grand. The Double Sculls started in 1939 as a centenary event for presentation prizes, becoming a challenge event in 1946.

The Britannia was known as the Henley Prize in 1968, before Nottingham Britannia presented the challenge cup. The experimental short course was used in 1923.

How Henley Records Have Fallen

The tables show record times to Fawley and the Finish from 1924, the year in which the new straight course was adopted. The fastest record time before 1924 is also included, but real comparisons are fruitless because although the course has always been nominally the same length of 1 mile 550 yards – except when the shortened straight version was tried in 1923 – the actual distance travelled by boats has varied, particularly when the course was wider and included bends and bays.

There remain several factors which make comparisons unreliable. Water conditions vary considerably even though the Thames Water Authority endeavours to control the stream by manipulating the weirs up river and at Marsh and Hambledon. Wind conditions often change by the hour and can vary on different parts of the course. Then there is the nature of the two-horse race: evenly matched crews or brilliant tacticians will produce different results from that of a contest of the mighty versus the weak. The psychological effect of chasing a record can also affect a crew's performance. There are certainly some very fast crews who have never approached records as well as some who have surprised themselves by their performance on the day. The most that can be read from the figures is a general trend, explained only by a complex formula which includes the above factors as well as developments in physique, training and fitness, and the design and weight of equipment. Equal fastest times are not shown.

Times marked * were recorded in heats.

Grand Challenge Cup

Year	Crew	Fawley	Finish
1891	Leander Club		6.51
1913	Leander Club	3.19*	
1925	Leander Club	3.17	
1934	London RC	3.15*	
1934	Leander Club		6.44*
1952	Leander Club	3.11*	6.38
1957	Cornell, USA		6.30*
1957	CK Znamia, USSR	3.8*	
1964	CZ Viljnjus, USSR	3.7*	6.23*
1964	CZ Viljnjus, USSR	3.5	
1965	Ratzeburg, Germany	3.0	6.16
1975	Harvard, USA		6.13*

Ladies' Challenge Plate

Year	Crew	Fawley	Finish
1911	Eton College	3.19	
1921	Pembroke College, Cam.		6.55
1934	Trinity College, Dublin	3.18	
1934	Jesus College, Cam.		6.48
1949	Lady Margaret BC, Cam.	3.13*	6.43*
1970	GSR Aegir, Holland		6.42*
1973	Harvard, USA	3.10*	
1973	University College, Dublin		6.37*
1973	DSR Laga, Holland	3.10*	6.36*
1973	Harvard, USA	3.9*	6.34*
1973	University of Wisconsin, USA		6.32*
1975	University of London	3.8*	6.30*
1975	University of London	3.6	
1976	Trinity College, Hartford, USA		6.24*

Thames Challenge Cup

Year	Crew	Fawley	Finish
1921	Corpus Christi College, Cam.	3.25*	7.6*
1926	Kingston RC	3.24*	
1934	Westminster Bank	3.22*	6.59*
1934	London RC		6.58*
1949	Lady Margaret BC, Cam.	3.19*	6.51*
1953	Princeton University, USA	3.18*	6.45*
1960	Harvard USA	3.13*	6.39*
1962	National Provincial Bank	3.11*	6.37*

Year	Crew	Fawley	Finish
1965	Isis		6.35*
1965	Derby	3.9	
1973	Princeton, USA	3.8*	6.33*
1975	Quintin	3.7*	
1975	Quintin	3.6*	
1975	Quintin	3.5*	
1976	Henley		6.32*
1976	Christiania, Norway	3.4*	6.25*

Princess Elizabeth Challenge Cup

Year	Crew	Fawley	Finish
1952	Radley	3.21*	6.57*
1965	Emanuel	3.14*	6.44*
1973	Ridley, Canada	3.11*	6.38*
1975	St Paul's, Concord, USA		6.36*
1975	Ridley, Canada	3.10*	6.35*
1975	Ridley, Canada		6.32

Stewards' Challenge Cup

Year	Crew	Fawley	Finish
1908	Magdalen College, Oxf.	3.36*	7.28*
1925	Third Trinity, Cam.		7.27
1930	London RC	3.35	
1934	Pembroke College, Cam.	3.33	7.24
1935	FC Zürich, Switzerland	3.28	7.14
1949	Trinity College, Oxf.		7.13
1960	Barn Cottage		7.10
1960	St Edmund Hall/Lincoln College, Oxf.	3.28*	
1962	Molesey	3.27*	7.1*
1965	Quintin	3.22	6.55
1973	TC Leningrad, USSR	3.18*	
1975	Potomac, USA		6.50

Prince Philip Challenge Cup

Year	Crew	Fawley	Finish
1963	Auckland, NZ		7.27*
1963	Nereus, Holland	3.36*	
1964	Molesey BC		7.25
1965	Leander	3.25	7.3
1973	Northeastern Univ., USA	3.21*	7.0*

Visitors' Challenge Cup

Year	Crew	Fawley	Finish
1908	Magdalen College, Oxf.	3.41	7.30
1911	Third Trinity, Cam.	3.39	
1925	Third Trinity, Cam.	3.37	
1938	Oriel College, Oxf.	3.31	7.18
1952	Pembroke College, Cam.	3.30	7.15
1965	St Edmund Hall, Oxf.		7.13
1973	University of London	3.26*	7.9*
1975	Ealing High Schools	3.24*	
1975	Hampton GS		7.8*
1976	Salisbury School, USA	3.23*	
1976	University of London		7.4*

Wyfold Challenge Cup

Year	Crew	Fawley	Finish
1921	Jesus College, Cam.	3.39*	7.35*
1934	Reading RC	3.38	
1949	Lensbury RC		7.24*
1952	Corpus Christi College, Cam.	3.36*	
1953	RAF	3.31*	7.20*
1960	Crowland	3.30*	7.16*
1962	University of London		7.13*
1962	Nottingham and Union	3.28*	
1965	Derby	3.25	7.6
1973	Thames Tradesmen's RC		7.2
1975	Nottingham and Union	3.20*	
1975	Leander		7.0*
1975	Thames Tradesmen's RC		6.57*
1976	University College and Hospital	3.18*	
1976	Potomac, USA		6.54*

Britannia Challenge Cup

Year	Crew	Fawley	Finish
1968	Thames	3.36*	7.34*
1969	Kingston		7.32
1973	University of London	3.33*	
1973	University of London	3.29*	7.22*
1973	Isis	3.28*	7.15*
1975	Leander	3.25*	
1976	Tideway Scullers' School		7.11*

Silver Goblets and Nickalls' Challenge Cup

Year	Crew	Fawley	Finish
1906	B. C. Johnstone and R. V. Powell	3.51*	
1911	J. Beresford and A. H. Cloutte and		
	B. Logan and C. G. Rought (dead heat)		8.8
1952	H. C. I. Bywater and T. H. Christie		8.5*
1953	R. Baetens and M. Knuysen, Belgium	3.46*	7.51*
1957	M. Plaksin and S. Soldatov, USSR	3.42*	
1962	J. M. S. Lecky and H. B. Budd		7.49*
1964	J. R. Kiely and J. M. S. Lecky		7.48*
1965	P. Gorny and G. Bergau, Germany	3.41*	7.35*
1973	M. Borchelt and R. T. Adams, USA	3.40*	
1976	I. F. Luxford and C. D. Shinners, Australia	3.39	7.30

Double Sculls Challenge Cup

Year	Crew	Fawley	Finish
1939	J. Beresford and L. F. Southwood	3.58	8.27
1946	R. E. Panelo and E. D. Chafuen, Argentina	3.52	8.8
1948	B. Piessens and W. Collet, Belgium	3.47*	7.54*
1949	E. W. Parnser and A. Larsen, Denmark	3.39*	7.27*
1953	E. Schriever and P. Stebler, Switzerland	3.32*	7.21*
1960	G. C. Justicz and N. H. Birkmyre		7.17
1965	M. Studach and M. Bürgin	3.27*	7.1*
1973	M. J. Hart and C. L. Baillieu	3.23*	6.59*

Diamond Challenge Sculls

Year	Crew	Fawley	Finish
1905	F. S. Kelly	3.55	8.10
1934	H. Buhtz, Germany	3.50	
1938	J. W. Burk, USA		8.2
1953	R. George, Belgium		8.0*
1960	S. A. Mackenzie	3.48*	
1962	S. A. Mackenzie	3.47*	
1964	S. Cromwell, USA		7.54*
1965	D. M. Spero, USA		7.42
1965	A. Hill, Germany	3.43*	
1973	S. Drea, Eire	3.42*	
1975	S. Drea, Eire	3.41*	7.40*

Fastest recorded times

Official times to Fawley were instituted in 1906, and to Remenham Barrier in 1929. Times marked * were set up in a heat.

Eight-oared events

Grand	Barrier	Fawley	Finish
Ratzeburger RC, Germany, 1965	1.46	3.0	
Harvard University, USA, 1975			6.13*
Leander Club/Thames Tradesmen's RC, 1975			6.13*

Ladies' Plate			
Isis BC, 1975	1.48*		
University of London, 1975		3.6	
Trinity College, Hartford, USA, 1976			6.24*

Thames			
Quintin BC, 1975	1.49*		
Christiania Roklub, Norway, 1976	1.49*	3.4*	6.25*

Princess Elizabeth			
St Paul's School, Concord, USA, 1975	1.52*		
Ridley College, Canada, 1975	1.52*	3.10*	6.32

Four-oared events

Stewards' (coxless)	Barrier	Fawley	Finish
Trud Leningrad, USSR, 1973		3.18*	
Lady Margaret BC, Cambridge, 1975	1.57*		
Potomac BC, USA, 1975			6.50

Prince Philip (coxed)			
Northeastern University RA, USA, 1973	1.58*	3.21*	7.0*

Visitors' (coxless)			
Salisbury School, USA, 1976	2.0*	3.23*	
University of London, 1976			7.4*

Wyfold (coxless)			
Thames Tradesmen's RC, 1973	1.53*		
University College and Hospital, 1976		3.18*	
Potomac BC, USA, 1976			6.54*

Britannia (coxed)			
Leander Club, 1975	2.0*	3.25*	
Tideway Scullers' School, 1976			7.11*

Pairs, doubles and sculls

Silver Goblets	Barrier	Fawley	Finish
D. Ebner and D. Losert, Austria, 1966	2.8*		
I. F. Luxford and C. D. Shinners, Australia, 1976		3.39	7.30

Double Sculls			
M. J. Hart and C. L. Baillieu, 1973	2.1	3.23*	6.59*
U. Isler and H. Ruckstuhl, Switzerland, 1973	2.1		

Diamond Sculls			
S. Drea, Eire, 1975	2.9*	3.41*	7.40*

Selected Bibliography

Henley records

H. T. Steward, *Henley Royal Regatta (1839–1902)*, Grant Richards, 1903.
Sir Theodore A. Cook, *Henley Races (1903–1914)*, OUP, 1919.
C. T. Steward, *Henley Records (1919–1938)*, Hamish Hamilton, 1939.
Henley Royal Regatta (1939–1968), 2 vols., The Stewards of Henley Royal Regatta, 1969.
Henley Royal Regatta Records (1969–1974), The Stewards of Henley Royal Regatta, 1976.
Henley Royal Regatta Records (1975–1979), The Stewards of Henley Royal Regatta, 1980.

Biography

Gilbert C. Bourne, *Memories of an Eton Wet Bob*, OUP, 1933.
T. A. Cook, *The Sunlit Hours*, Nisbet, 1925.
H. R. A. (Jumbo) Edwards, *The Way of a Man with a Blade*, Routledge & Kegan Paul, 1963.
Steve Fairbairn, *Fairbairn of Jesus*, Bodley Head, 1931.
C. R. L. Fletcher, *Edmond Warre*, John Murray, 1922.
John Lehmann, *Whispering Gallery* (contains memories of his father, R. C. Lehmann), Longman Green, 1955.
G. O. (Gully) Nickalls, *A Rainbow in the Sky*, Chatto & Windus, 1974.
Guy Nickalls, *Life's a Pudding*, Faber and Faber, 1939.
Major Vivian Nickalls, *Oars, Wars and Horses*, Hurst & Blackett, 1932.
W. B. Woodgate, *Reminiscences of an Old Sportsman*, Eveleigh Nash, 1909.

Thames and Henley

J. R. L. Anderson, *The Upper Thames*, Eyre Methuen, 1970.
A Guide to Henley-upon-Thames and its Vicinity, Hickman & Kinch; Simpkin & Marshall, London, first published 1838.
The Oarsman's Guide to the Thames and Other Rivers, Searle & Sons, 1857.
John Southerdon Burn, *A History of Henley on Thames*, Longman, 1861.

Rowing, history and technique

G. C. Bourne, *A Textbook of Oarsmanship*, OUP, 1909.
E. D. Brickwood, *Boat Racing*, Horace Cox, 1876.
R. D. Burnell, *Henley Regatta*, OUP, 1957.
R. D. Burnell, *Swing Together*, OUP, 1952.
Hylton Cleaver, *A History of Rowing*, Herbert Jenkins, 1957.
Samuel Crowther and A. Ruhl, *Rowing and Track Athletics*, Macmillan, New York, 1905.
Steve Fairbairn on Rowing, Nicholas Kaye, 1951.
P. Haig-Thomas and M. A. Nicholson, *The English Style of Rowing*, Faber & Faber, 1958.
Robert F. Herrick, *Red Top, Reminiscences of Harvard Rowing*, Harvard University Press, 1948.
Desmond Hill, *Instructions in Rowing*, Museum Press, 1963.
Robert F. Kelley, *American Rowing*, G. P. Putnam's Sons, 1932.
Peter King, *Art and a Century of Canadian Rowing*, Amberley House, Toronto, 1980.
R. C. Lehmann, *The Complete Oarsman*, Methuen, 1908.
R. C. Lehmann and others, *Rowing*, Isthmian Library, A. D. Innes & Co., 1898.
Archibald Maclaren, *Training in Theory and Practice*, Macmillan, 1866.
Thomas C. Mendenhall, *A Short History of American Rowing*, Charles River Books, Boston, 1980.
Colin Porter, *Rowing to Win*, Stanley Paul, 1959.
A. C. Scott and J. G. P. Williams (eds.), *Rowing, A Scientific Approach: A Symposium*, Kaye & Ward, 1967.
Edmond Warre, *On the Grammar of Rowing*, OUP, 1909.
W. B. Woodgate, *Boating*, Badminton Library, Longman Green & Co., 1888.

Club histories

Henry Bond, *A History of the Trinity Hall BC*, W. Heffer & Sons, 1930.
F. Brittain and H. B. Playford, *The Jesus College BC*, W. Heffer & Sons, 1928.

R. D. Burnell and H. R. N. Rickett, *A Short History of Leander Club, (1818–1968)*, Leander Club.

John Arthur Carver, *The Vancouver Rowing Club, a History: 1888–1980*, Aubrey Roberts, Vancouver, 1980.

J. V. S. Glass and J. Max Patrick, *The Royal Chester R C Centenary History, 1838–1938*, James Laver, Liverpool, 1939.

T. F. Hall, *History of Boat Racing in Ireland*, IARU, 1937.

The History of the Lady Margaret BC, 1825–1926, The Johnian Society; vol. 2: *1926–1956*, The Johnian Society.

Magdalene BC, 1828–1928, Magdalene College Association, 1930.

W. W. Rouse Ball, *A History of First Trinity BC*, Bowes & Bowes, 1908.

Rev. W. E. Sherwood, *Oxford Rowing*, Henry Frowde, 1900.

Reports of the London Rowing Club, 1856–1868, LRC.

L. C. Smith, *Annals of Public School Rowing*, Blackwell, 1919.

J. T. Swann, *Trinity Hall BC, 1928–1949*.

W. C. Wace, *Brasenose Rowing*, Brasenose College Monographs, Blackwell, 1909.

Index